Globalization and the Politics of Development in the Middle East

At the beginning of the twenty-first century countries in the Middle East and North Africa contend with the threats and opportunities of economic globalization, the driving force of change in the contemporary world. As Clement Henry and Robert Springborg confirm in their straightforward and, at times, irreverent analysis of the region's response to these challenges, it is globalization which is the key to an understanding of economic reform.

Through an investigation of the structures of state and civil society, including financial systems, they also demonstrate that there is a correlation between economic performance and democratization. In other words, the more open and liberal a polity, the more effective is its economy in responding to globalization. By dividing countries in the region into particular categories – military dictatorships, as exemplified by the "bullies" and the "bunker states," and monarchies and conditional democracies – the authors signal their conclusions: that democracies and monarchies have a better chance of benefiting from economic globalization than the bullies and bunkers, but politics stands in the way of necessary reforms, even in the most promising prospects, such as Israel and Turkey.

With its up-to-date, original, and incisive approach to the politics and economics of the Middle East and North Africa, this will be an essential purchase for students and policy-makers, and for anyone trying to come to grips with economic globalization generally.

CLEMENT M. HENRY is Professor of Government at the University of Texas at Austin. His publications include *The Mediterranean Debt Crescent: A Comparative Study of Money and Power in Algeria, Egypt, Morocco, Tunisia and Turkey* (1996) and (with co-editor Kate Gillespie) *Oil in the New World Order* (1995).

ROBERT SPRINGBORG is Director of the American Research Center in Egypt. Until 1999 he was Professor of Middle East politics at Macquarie University. His most recent publication (with Abdo Baaklini and Guilain Denoeux) is *Legislative Politics in the Arab World* (1999), while his book *Politics in the Middle East* (1993), which he co-authored with James A. Bill, is now in its fifth edition.

The Contemporary Middle East 1

Series editor: Eugene L. Rogan

Books published in **The Contemporary Middle East** series address the major political, economic and social debates facing the region today. Each title comprises a survey of the available literature against the background of the author's own critical interpretation which is designed to challenge and encourage independent analysis. While the focus of the series is the Middle East and North Africa, books are presented as aspects of a rounded treatment, which cut across disciplinary and geographic boundaries. They are intended to initiate debate in the classroom, and to foster understanding amongst professionals and policy-makers.

Globalization and the Politics of Development in the Middle East

Clement M. Henry

University of Texas at Austin

and

Robert Springborg

American Research Center in Egypt

CAMBRIDGE UNIVERSITY PRESS
Cambridge, New York, Melbourne, Madrid, Cape Town, Singapore, São Paulo

Cambridge University Press
The Edinburgh Building, Cambridge CB2 8RU, UK

Published in the United States of America by Cambridge University Press, New York

www.cambridge.org
Information on this title: www.cambridge.org/9780521623124

First published 2001
Fifth printing 2005

A catalogue record for this publication is available from the British Library

Library of Congress Cataloguing in Publication data
Henry, Clement M., 1937–
Globalization and the politics of development in the Middle East /
Clement M. Henry and Robert Springborg.
    p.   cm. – (Contemporary Middle East: 1)
Includes bibliographical references.
ISBN 0 521 62312 X (hardback) – ISBN 0 521 62631 5 (paperback)
1. Middle East – Economic conditions – 1979–   .
2. Middle East – Politics and government – 1979–   .
3. Globalization. I. Springborg, Robert. II. Title. III. Series.
HC415.15.H463 2001
338.956–dc21   00-067452

ISBN 978-0-521-62312-4 hardback
ISBN 978-0-521-62631-6 paperback

Transferred to digital printing 2007

To George and Mildred Springborg
and to our spouses,
Elizabeth N. Bouri and Anne-Marie Drosso

Contents

List of figures	*page*	x
List of tables		xi
Preface and acknowledgments		xiii
Glossary		xvii
Map. The Middle East and North Africa		xx

1	Overview	1
2	The challenges of globalization	30
3	Political capacities and capitalist legacies	62
4	Bunker states	99
5	Bully praetorian states	134
6	Globalizing monarchies	168
7	Fragmented democracies	194
8	Conclusion	223

References	230
Index	241

Figures

1.1 Per capita GNP growth rates by region, 1961–1998   *page* 4
1.2 Per capita GNP average growth rates by country,
     1965–1998   5
1.3 The Ten Commandments of the Washington Consensus   13
2.1 Oil rents and foreign aid, 1990–1998   32
2.2 Conventional arms imports, 1989–1998   34
2.3 Workers' remittances, 1975–1998   37
2.4 Capital resources for developing countries, 1990–1998   45
2.5 Cumulative capital flows by region, 1990–1998   47
2.6 Cumulative capital flows by country, 1993–1998   50
2.7 Central government debt as a percentage of GDP, 1985–1998   55
2.8 External debt as a percentage of GNP, 1998   57
3.1 Freedom House ratings, 1999–2000   65
3.2 Contract-intensive money ratios (CIM), 1997   80
3.3 Newspapers per 1,000 people, 1996   82
3.4 Relative political capacities   84
4.1 Credit to private sector by contract – intensive money   101
4.2 Military spending as percentage of central government
     expenditure, 1993 and 1997   104
4.3 Algeria's cash economy, 1964–1998   110
7.1 Composite indicator of economic openness, 1998–1999   197

Tables

1.1	Human Development Index, 1997	*page* 3
1.2	Human Poverty Index, 1997	7
2.1	Oil revenues 1972–1998 and as percentages of export earnings and government revenues, 1997	40
2.2	Intra-industry trade index	43
2.3	Debt service as a percentage of exports	53
3.1	Evolution of manufacture exports, 1987–1998, and effective duty rates on imports, 1997	68
3.2	Macroeconomic indicators	70
3.3	State-owned enterprises	73
3.4	Structure of government revenues, *c.* 1998	77
3.5	Commercial bank credit and stock market activity, 1998	86
3.6	Ownership and degree of concentration of commercial banking systems	88

Preface and acknowledgments

We were commissioned by the editors of the series in which this volume appears to produce a manuscript on the politics of economic development in the Middle East and North Africa (MENA). In fact we have written a book that seeks to describe and explain the responses of that region to the threats and opportunities posed by economic globalization, the driving force of change not only for these, but for virtually all economies in the developing, not to say developed, world. We have sought to avoid the normative debate over the phenomenon. We have also not speculated on the possible consequences for the MENA of increasing criticism of and resistance to globalization and its standard bearers. We have assumed that at least for the foreseeable future this criticism and resistance are unlikely to fundamentally alter the course or momentum of economic globalization, whatever its consequences for the rhetoric and actions of such standard bearers as the IMF and World Bank.

We are convinced that globalization should be the starting point for understanding economic change in the region. It is the primary thesis against which all countries of the region are struggling to form responses. The widely perceived analogy, at least in the MENA, between today's globalization and yesterday's colonialism provides an analytical framework with which to understand not only the region's response as a whole to 'awlaama (the newly coined Arabic term for globalization), but also the strategies employed by individual countries and particular social forces within them. Similar to the colonial dialectic which pitted the region's traditional, radical, and revolutionary nationalists against imperialism, the "globalization dialectic" is now generating three distinct stances contending with what is simultaneously a threat and an opportunity, both politically and economically. Aspiring globalizers contend with reactive moralizers in search of new syntheses that might promote the needed reforms in the name of the authentic Islam.

We have examined the structures of state and civil society that channel the reactions to globalization of different social forces. Particularly vital for civil society is the role of financial systems, the private components of which generate the material resources that sustain civil society. We have, therefore, paid particular attention to those financial systems and the constraints they impose upon political elites while providing them with opportunities to benefit from globalization.

Our investigations suggest a direct correlation between economic performance and the degree of democracy that obtains in any given national political economy in this region. The more open and liberal a polity, the more effective has been its economy in responding to globalization. Additionally encouraging from the perspective of democratization is that the capacity to formulate and execute effective national responses clearly depends not just on the states of the region, but on their respective civil societies as well. Those states that have waged literal or metaphorical wars against their civil societies and the autonomous capital that is both the cause and product of civil society can and sometimes do formulate economic textbook responses to globalization. Those responses, however, are dead letters in the absence of implementation capacity, which only a dynamic civil society appears to be able to provide. On the other hand, those states with comparatively robust civil societies appear to have less autonomy in formulating economic policies, but the greater implementation capacity their civil societies provide more than makes up for policy deficiencies.

Our findings may be read to imply that liberalization and democratization, were they to proceed, would benefit MENA economies. Indeed, they suggest that in the absence of more open, liberal polities, MENA economies are likely to stagnate in comparison to their global competitors. They further suggest that while many responses to globalization are possible, the phenomenon itself will generally support the opening of political economies, even if within a framework of Islamicization. This in turn implies a "win–win" situation, whereby globalization induces political changes that are in turn beneficial for national economic growth. But it may also inspire craftier and more intrusive forms of authoritarianism.

It is worth remembering that, as the eminent MENA economist Charles Issawi once noted, Murphy's Law applies with a vengeance in this region of the world. Bearing that in mind, we will shy away from predicting that globalization will work wonders for the political economies of the region and observe only that the potential for it to do so is there. As we hope the book demonstrates, moreover, there are obstacles aplenty to the realization of the rosy scenario in all the countries of the region, whether they are praetorian republics, monarchies, or democracies.

Finally, our observations reflect a cumulative total of about seven decades of intermittent teaching and field work in the MENA, and we wish to thank our many friends and acquaintances in the region for generously sharing their insights with us over the years. They are too numerous to name and of course bear no responsibility for the conclusions we have drawn in this book. However, Hasan Ersel, Chief Economist of Yapi Kredit Bankasi, deserves special mention for his timely responses to email that gave us a better understanding of the Istanbul Stock Exchange. Clement Henry also wishes to thank Abdelmounaim Dilami and Nadia Salah, the publisher and editor-in-chief, respectively, of *L'Economiste*, for their extraordinary hospitality during the summer of 1998 as well as their refreshing insights into Morocco's political economy.

We have also benefited from the advice and constant encouragement of Eugene Rogan and the critical reviews of two anonymous readers for Cambridge University Press. We are grateful, too, for comments from Catherine Boone, Bradford Dillman, Ira Lapidus, and Alan Richards. We are especially indebted to Anne-Marie Drosso, former student of one of us and wife of the other. As a political economist and multilingual author par excellence, her insights and editorial suggestions vastly improved both the content and the style of the book. The other spouse, Elizabeth Bouri, is an information specialist who greatly facilitated our online research efforts with the Arab Social Science Research web site (*www.assr.org*), which she has designed especially for the needs of social scientists.

Our collaboration in drafting and redrafting our manuscript has been exemplary across three continents – Australia, the Middle East, and North America – facilitated by computer support from Macquarie University and the University of Texas at Austin. We particularly wish to thank John Telec, Paul Lyon, and William Bova for their advice and troubleshooting. We also gratefully acknowledge Macquarie's award of a Visiting Research Scholarship to Clement Henry that enabled us to spend a few weeks together in Sydney during July and August of 1999. A special word of thanks is due to an old friend and colleague, Andrew Vincent, director of the Macquarie University Centre for Middle East and North African Studies, for making these weeks so productive and enjoyable. Henry also wishes to acknowledge an earlier grant from the University of Texas at Austin that enabled him to begin drafting some chapters in the spring of 1998 and a grant from the American Institute of Maghrib Studies for field work in Morocco and Tunisia during the summer of 1998. Finally, we thank Sherry Lowrance and Ji-Hyang Jang, doctoral students in political science at the University of Texas, for assembling and checking some of the economic data, and other members of Henry's political economy seminar, especially Sunila Kale, for their editorial help.

Glossary

Aramco	Arabian-American Oil Company
BDL	Banque du Liban (Lebanon's central bank)
CBRT	Central Bank of the Republic of Turkey
CGEM	Confédération Générale des Entreprises Marocaines
CIM	contract-intensive money (the amount of money held inside a banking system, divided by the total money supply M2)
ECU	European Currency Unit, a basket of European currencies, renamed the Euro in 1999
ESCWA	Economic and Social Commission for Western Asia (United Nations)
EU	European Union
FDI	foreign direct investment
FIS	Front Islamique du Salut (Islamic Salvation Front), outlawed Algerian opposition party
GATS	General Agreement on Trade in Services
GATT	General Agreement on Tariffs and Trade
GCC	Gulf Cooperation Council (Bahrain, Kuwait, Oman, Qatar, Saudi Arabia, United Arab Emirates)
GDP	gross domestic product – "the total output of goods and services for final use occurring within the domestic territory of a given country" (World Bank)
GNP	gross national product – GDP "plus any taxes (less subsidies) that are not included in the valuation of output plus net receipts of primary income (employee compensation and property income) from nonresident sources" (World Bank)
GOE	Government of Egypt
HDI	Human Development Index
HHI	Herfindahl-Hirschman Index, measuring the degree of concentration of an industry as the sum of the squares of the market shares of its competing firms

IIT index	intra-industry trade index
IMF	International Monetary Fund
infitah	"opening" of the economy to international markets, along lines suggested by Egyptian President Anwar Sadat in 1974
ISE	Istanbul Stock Exchange
ISI	import substitution industrialization
KFH	Kuwait Finance House
LE	Egyptian pound
M2	measure of the money supply that comprises transferable deposits and currency outside the banking system and time, savings, and foreign currency deposits
makhzan	Moroccan king's household and ruling center
mamelukes	medieval Egyptian military ruling class, recruited from Circassian slaves; the term is also used by Egyptian critics to denote high-ranking officers and security officials in contemporary Egypt and to associate them with medieval practices
MEED	*Middle East Economic Digest* (London)
MENA	Middle East and North Africa
MNC	multinational corporation
mudir	director, manager
NGO	non-government organization
ODA	Official Development Assistance
OECD	Organization for Economic Cooperation and Development
ONA	Omnium Nord-Africain, a Moroccan conglomerate
OPEC	Organization of Petroleum Exporting Countries
PA or PNA	Palestinian Authority or Palestinian National Authority
PLO	Palestine Liberation Organization
S&P	Standard and Poor's, a business information firm that rates countries and enterprises worldwide for their credit-worthiness and financial performance
SABIC	Saudi Arabia Basic Industries Corporation
SAMA	Saudi Arabian Monetary Agency
SOE	state-owned enterprise
Sonatrach	Société Nationale pour la Recherche, la Production, le Transport, la Transformation et la Commercialisation des Hydrocarbures
UNDP	United Nations Development Program

USAID   United States Agency for International Development
USFP   Union Socialiste des Forces Populaires, a Moroccan
             political party
WTO   World Trade Organization

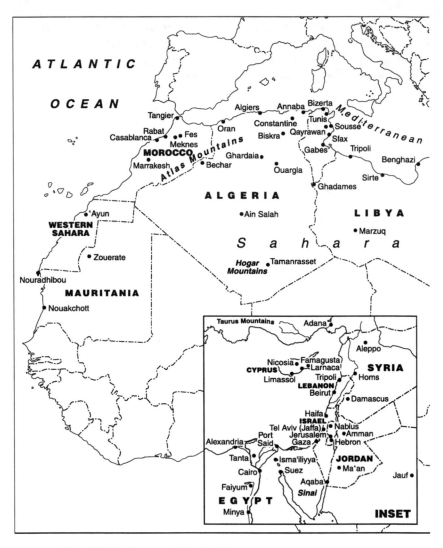

The Middle East and North Africa

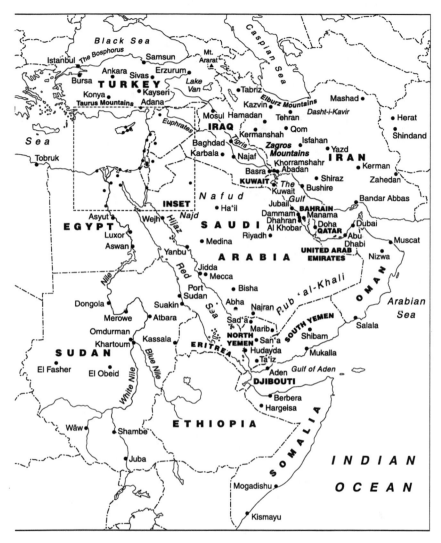

Map (contd)

1 Overview

Some readers may have memories of postwar Alexandria and Cairo or will have read Lawrence Durrell's *Alexandria Quartet* – the tales of a cosmopolitan high society. Egypt appeared in the mid-1940s to be as economically developed as war-torn Greece and equally ready to catch up with the rest of Europe. To the north, Turkey was singled out like Greece for special assistance under the Truman Doctrine (March 1947) and seemed virtually a part of Europe. To the west, in "French" Algeria, Algiers was at least as prosperous as the rest of France, and, further west, Casablanca was home to big French industrial interests poised to transform the picturesque Moroccan protectorate into Europe's California. At the eastern end of the Mediterranean, a newly independent and polyglot Lebanon was fast becoming the West's principal commercial gateway to Iran, Iraq, and the Gulf. Riding on the postwar oil boom in those states, Lebanon would become the Middle East's Switzerland in the 1950s and 1960s and apparently exemplify an easy "modernization without revolution" (Salem 1973). Beneath snow-covered mountains on the unspoiled shores of a clear and relatively unpolluted Mediterranean Sea, Beirut was as pretty as Geneva in those days, at least in the richer parts of the city, and rather more lively than Calvin's home. Inland, to the east of Lebanon's two mountain ridges, the open Syrian economy boomed with new manufacturing and agricultural development in the 1950s (Sachs and Warner 1995: 34). Morocco and Turkey also grew rapidly during this period because their open economies took advantage of expanding world markets. Of all the new states in the region, however, Iraq had the most promising prospects for balanced development. It was endowed with the world's second largest oil reserves, the most water of any country in the MENA including Turkey, some of the richest alluvial soils, a strong British educational system, and a relatively large, skilled workforce. Further east, Iran had thrice the population and a diversified economy with oil reserves only slightly less plentiful than Iraq's and very substantial natural gas deposits as well. Captivated by the cash flows, the young shah would dream of making his country into the world's third or fourth mightiest military power.

But over the decades of the Cold War (1946–1989) various conflicts within the region dashed any hopes of catching up with Europe. Egypt, Morocco, Syria, and Turkey closed their economies to foreign trade and investment, whereas Greece opened up in 1959 (Sachs and Warner 1995: 79). By the end of the twentieth century the only countries in the MENA reaching Greek levels of individual prosperity and welfare were little states that did not even exist in the immediate postwar period. Israel and the Greek part of Cyprus rank just above Greece on the United Nations' Human Development Index. The oil principalities of Kuwait, Bahrain, Qatar, and the United Arab Emirates come well behind Greece. Their populations, including their majorities of expatriates, comprise about 1 percent of the region's 400 million inhabitants. They enjoy "high human development" whereas the other oil-rich states of Iran, Libya, Oman, and Saudi Arabia are mired in the ranks of "medium human development" alongside most of the MENA's less mineral-rich Mediterranean countries. On the periphery, the Sudan and Yemen are at the "low" end associated with the Indian subcontinent and Sub-Saharan Africa.

Table 1.1 presents the information for 1997. It also shows that most MENA countries score lower on the Human Development Index than their adjusted per capita income (calibrated in Purchasing Power Parity dollars) would predict. HDI includes education, literacy, and life expectancy as well as per capita income, and most MENA countries rate relatively low for their income on these other variables. If enrolments in primary and secondary school today contribute to future economic growth, the worst is yet to come. Other growth factors are further causes for concern. The MENA's current situation may deteriorate in the coming decade because investment flows into the region have stagnated, and internal sources of capital tied to oil prices have diminished since the early 1980s. In recent years the region has failed to keep pace with economic development not only in East Asia, but also in much of the rest of Asia, as well as Latin America. Figure 1.1 presents the regional comparisons over three decades, together with the most recent available years. Figure 1.2 also shows that the performance of most individual MENA countries in 1985–1995 was poorer than in previous decades, whether or not they were oil producers. If current trends continue into the twenty-first century, much of the MENA region will slide toward the bottom of world development tables, with potentially serious consequences for political stability.

Table 1.1. *The Human Development Index 1997*

HDI rank		Country	Adult literacy rate (%), 1997	Combined 1st-, 2nd-, 3rd-level enrolment ratio (%)	Education index	GDP index	Human Development Index	Life expectancy index	Real GDP per capita (PPP$)	Real GDP per capita rank minus HDI rank[a]
High	23	Israel	95.4	80	0.90	0.87	0.883444	0.88	18,150	3
	26	Cyprus	95.9	79[b]	0.90	0.83	0.869706	0.88	14,201[c]	6
	27	Greece	96.6	79	0.91	0.81	0.866786	0.89	12,769[c]	8
	35	Kuwait	80.4	57	0.73	0.92	0.833392	0.85	25,314[c]	−30
	37	Bahrain	86.2	81	0.85	0.85	0.831955	0.80	16,527[c]	−8
	41	Qatar	80.0	71	0.77	0.89	0.814055	0.78	20,987[c]	−23
	43	United Arab Emirates	74.8	69	0.73	0.88	0.812217	0.83	19,115[c]	−18
Medium	65	Libyan Arab Jamahiriya	76.5	92	0.82	0.70	0.755763	0.75	6,697[c]	−6
	69	Lebanon	84.4	76	0.82	0.68	0.749385	0.75	5,940	−4
	78	Saudi Arabia	73.4	56	0.67	0.77	0.739612	0.77	10,120	−37
	86	Turkey	83.2	61	0.76	0.69	0.727806	0.73	6,350	−22
	89	Oman	67.1	58	0.64	0.77	0.724615	0.76	9,960[c]	−47
	94	Jordan	87.2	66[d]	0.80	0.59	0.714969	0.75	3,450	2
	95	Iran, Islamic Rep. of	73.3	72	0.73	0.68	0.714699	0.74	5,817[c]	−29
	102	Tunisia	67.0	70	0.68	0.66	0.694838	0.74	5,300	−34
	109	Algeria	60.3	68	0.63	0.63	0.664504	0.73	4,460	−31
	111	Syrian Arab Republic	71.6	60	0.68	0.58	0.663026	0.73	3,250	−11
	120	Egypt	52.7	72	0.59	0.57	0.616487	0.69	3,050	−14
	125	Iraq	58.0[e]	51	0.56	0.58	0.585659	0.62	3,197[c]	−22
	126	Morocco	45.9	49	0.47	0.58	0.582414	0.69	3,310	−27
Low	142	Sudan	53.3	34	0.47	0.46	0.475148	0.50	1,560	−7
	148	Yemen	42.5	49	0.45	0.35	0.44503	0.55	810	18

Notes: [a] A positive number indicates that the HDI rank is better than the real GDP per capita (PPP$) rank, a negative the opposite. [b] UNESCO 1997. [c] Heston, and Summers 1999. [d] Human Development Report Office estimate. [e] UNICEF 1999. Data refer to a year or period other than that specified in the column heading, differ from the standard definition or refer to only part of the country. Data from Human Development Report 1999.

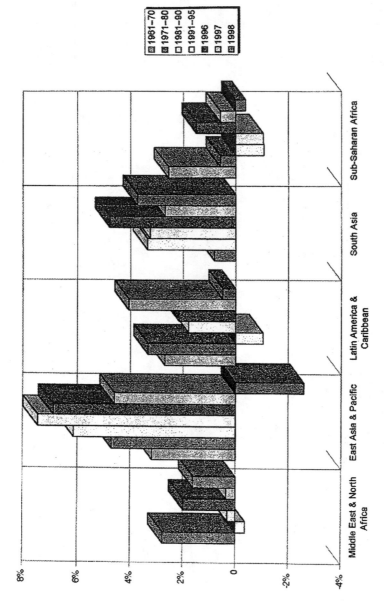

Figure 1.1 Per capita GNP growth rates by region, 1961–1998
Source: World Bank, World Development Indicators 2000 on CD-ROM

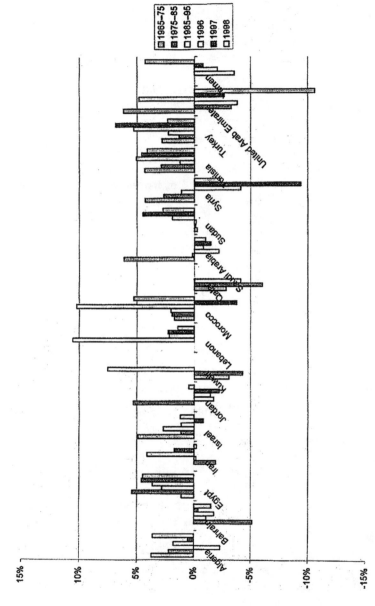

Figure 1.2 Per capita GNP average annual growth rates, 1965–1998
Source: World Bank, World Development Indicators 2000 on CD-ROM

Indeed, much of the Arab world already suffered poverty on levels not far removed from those of Sub-Saharan Africa and South Asia. Table 1.2 presents the sad accompaniment of development, the Human Poverty Index that the United Nations Development Program (UNDP) also publishes annually. The Arab average of 32.4 percent is closer to those of the poorest regions than to Latin America and the Caribbean or East Asia.

This book will assess the prospects for reversing these tendencies and accelerating economic development in light of the major regional and international changes currently influencing the region. The end of the Cold War, the new international economic and political order, the increasing attention of Europe to its "Mexico," and the Arab–Israeli peace process, however precarious, are having a major impact on the region's domestic political economies. All of its regimes are faced with the challenges and opportunities of globalization, yet they also share a defensive legacy ingrained by over two centuries of interaction with major European powers, joined in the past half-century by the United States. Many Middle Easterners view the globalization of finance and business as a threat to their national, religious, or cultural identities comparable to that of an earlier period of globalization prior to 1914, when the foreign intrusions were associated with European imperialism.

Indeed, a complex of political and economic factors is responsible for this region's comparative lack of economic success. Overgrown and inefficient states constitute the primary factor at the national level. In their size and relative involvement in and control over economies, many of these states are comparable to communist states prior to the collapse of the USSR. "To this day," observes the annual review of a leading regional economic think-tank, "the public sector still dominates most MENA economies, far more than in other low and middle income countries in the world" (*Economic Research Forum*, 2000: 11). Despite preponderant positions within their political economies, these states lack the necessary capacity and will to promote sustained and rapid economic growth. Insufficient capacity results from the well-known deficiencies of state management in command economies, while the lack of will results from political calculations taking precedence over economic ones.

Yet the size and nature of Middle Eastern states cannot be understood without reference to the regional, global, and economic contexts which facilitated their creation and within which they presently operate. Just as the global Cold War produced "national security states," so has protracted conflict in the MENA region caused and justified the emergence of states with overdeveloped coercive capacities. Hobbesian regional and

Table 1.2. *Human Poverty Index, 1997*

HDI Rank	Country	Human poverty index Rank	Value (%)	Adult illiteracy rate	% of population dying before age 40	Population without access to: water	health	sanitation	Underweight children under 5	Real GDP per capita (1980–1994 latest) Poorest 20%	Richest 20%	Rich to poor[a]	Below poverty line (%)
23	Israel	–	–	–	2.6	–	–	–	–	4,539	29,959	6.6	–
26	Cyprus	–	–	4.1	3.2	0	0	3	–	–	–	–	–
27	Greece	–	–	–	2.8	–	–	–	–	–	–	–	–
35	Kuwait	–	–	19.6	2.9	–	0	–	6	–	–	–	–
37	Bahrain	10	9.8	13.8	4.7	6	0	3	9	–	–	–	–
41	Qatar	–	–	20.0	4.9	3	0	3	6	–	–	–	–
43	United Arab Emirates	27	17.7	25.2	3.1	3	10	8	14	–	–	–	–
65	Libyan Arab Jamahiriya	22	16.4	23.5	6.4	3	0	2	5	–	–	–	–
69	Lebanon	14	11.3	15.6	7.5	6	5	37	3	–	–	–	–
78	Saudi Arabia	–	–	26.6	5.9	5	2	14	–	–	–	–	–
86	Turkey	24	16.7	16.8	9.6	51	0	20	10	1,292	10,972	8.5	15
89	Oman	39	23.7	32.9	6.4	15	11	22	23	–	–	–	–
94	Jordan	9	9.8	12.8	7.1	2	10	23	9	–	–	–	–
95	Iran, Islamic Rep. of	34	20.4	26.7	9.7	10	27	19	16	1,460	11,459	7.8	–
102	Tunisia	38	23.1	33.0	7.8	2	10	20	9	1,922	12,839	6.7	14
109	Algeria	52	28.8	39.7	9.1	22	–	9	13	–	–	–	–
111	Syrian Arab Republic	32	20.1	28.4	8.5	14	1	33	13	1,653	7,809	4.7	–
120	Egypt	57	33.0	47.3	10.3	13	1	12	15	–	–	–	–
125	Iraq	–	–	–	17.4	19	2	25	23	–	–	–	–
126	Morocco	67	39.2	54.1	11.8	35	38	42	9	1,079	7,570	7.0	13
142	Sudan	61	36.8	46.7	27.1	27	30	49	34	–	–	–	–
148	Yemen	78	49.2	57.5	21.8	39	84	76	39	–	–	–	–
	Arab states		32.4	41.3	13.1	18		29	19				
	Sub-Saharan Africa		40.6	42.4	34.6	50		56	32				
	East Asia		19.0	16.6	7.8	32		73	16				
	South Asia		36.6	47.8	16.1	18		64	48				
	Latin America		14.5	12.8	9.9	22		29	10				

Note: [a] The ratio of the average per capita income of the richest 20 percent to that of the poorest 20 percent.
Source: The Human Development Report CD-ROM

global environments of "war of all against all" further detached the states from their respective societies. Ruling elites seek legitimacy by manipulating symbols and finding scapegoats for any troubles, while also engaging in rent-seeking and misallocating human and physical resources. Moreover, exogenous revenues (or rents) have accrued to these states, freeing them still more from any constraints. Oil rents have been especially critical to the formation of welfare states in the Gulf. They enabled regimes to seek legitimacy by distributing goods and services to people rather than through the more interactive, demanding, and risky approach of taxing them directly and being accountable to them. Volatile oil markets and regional security thus largely condition any internal economic structural adjustment and political reform but are both also largely subject to extra-regional interventions.

The MENA's special colonial legacy

It is not so much Islam that defines the MENA – or Arab culture its heartland – as the tradition of external intervention in the region. The Middle East and North Africa is defined here as extending from Morocco to Turkey along the southern and eastern shores of the Mediterranean and as far east as Iran and south to the Sudan, Saudi Arabia, and Yemen. It is the non-European parts of the old Ottoman Empire, plus its respective western, southern, and eastern peripheries in Morocco, Arabia, and Iran. Leon Carl Brown has succinctly captured its distinctive characteristic:

For roughly the last two centuries the Middle East has been more consistently and more thoroughly ensnarled in great power politics than any other part of the non-Western world. This distinctive political experience continuing from generation to generation has left its mark on Middle Eastern political attitudes and actions. Other parts of the world have been at one time or another more severely buffeted by an imperial power, but no area has remained so unremittingly caught up in multilateral great power politics. (Brown 1984: 3)

In the earlier era of financial globalization lasting until 1914, the encounters tended to produce tensions and fragmentation. The region was too strategically situated to be ignored, yet the Great Powers generally prevented their rivals from definitive conquests while fighting each other for influence, thereby exacerbating internal divisions within the various states or former provinces of the Ottoman Empire. With the discovery of oil in Iran in 1908, then in Bahrain and Iraq in the 1920s and Kuwait and Saudi Arabia in 1938, the region acquired a new strategic importance for international superpowers. During World War I the British coined the term Middle East for their Cairo regional command post. Outmaneuvering their French ally's military and diplomatic administrative bureaux of the "Proche Orient" (Near East), they politically and symbolically redefined the region as if to anticipate the world's energy needs. Oil discoveries, coupled with new transport and communications technologies, spread the stakes of Great Power competition out from the Near East to the Middle East, and eventually to North Africa as well. In World War II Winston Churchill understood the entire region to be Europe's "soft underbelly," and the Allies' campaign to liberate Nazi Europe started in North Africa. The American and British forces converged on Tunisia in 1943, driving Rommel's forces out, before liberating Sicily, Italy, and eventually France.

Outside parties rarely established responsible local government institutions because they were too busy competing with each other for power and influence. In other parts of the world they usually achieved colonial hegemony – the Spanish and Portuguese in Latin America, the British in India and much of North America, and the Dutch in Indonesia. The stakes of conquest were higher in the MENA than elsewhere, however, because it was closer to the European heartland of the Great Powers. And where one power did prevail, the impact upon the local society was often more savage than elsewhere, except in the Americas. The French decimated the Muslim populations of Algeria in the mid-nineteenth century, and the Italians followed suit in Libya after World War I. The British protection of harbors along sea-lanes to India was more benign but concerned only a very small fraction of the MENA's population: Aden, Kuwait, Qatar, and other little Trucial States that comprise the United Arab Emirates today. Britain's control over other parts of the region was either transitory (Palestine 1918–1948) or veiled in various ways (Egypt 1882–1954, Iraq 1918–1958, Iran 1921–1953). French rule over Algeria (1830–1962), Tunisia (1881–1956), and Morocco (1912–1956) was more durable and transparent, but its control of Lebanon and Syria lasted a bare quarter of a century (1920–1946). Italy stayed longer in Libya (1911–1943) but was then displaced by the British until 1951. The United States perhaps never quite crossed the line between technical asssistance and real control over Saudi Arabia, but Aramco, a company registered in Delaware, ran its oil fields until 1990, and the US government helped to establish much of its accompanying state infrastructure.

In short, most of the MENA states were penetrated by a variety of outside parties vying for commercial, cultural, or strategic influence and establishing beach-heads through the various local communities. One widespread effect of these rivalries was to put indigenous business elites at risk. Selective foreign "protection" of local minorities, including grants of foreign citizenship, strengthened them against their local governments and business competitors but ultimately left them vulnerable to retaliation by popular majorities. Another impact was increased sectarianism. Lebanon illustrated how confessional differences, recognized for limited purposes by the Ottoman millet system, were exacerbated by alliances with external powers – the Maronites with the French, the Greek Orthodox with the Russians, the Druze with the British. With the formal freeing of much of the region after World War II, regional powers, including Iran, Israel, and Turkey as well as Arab states, supplemented traditional interventions of the Great Powers vying for influence over their smaller neighbors. The United States, eager to check advances by the Soviet Union, joined the fray and learned to outbid its British and French allies. More external and regional influence peddling and subversion further compounded the divisions of weak states such as Lebanon, the Sudan, and Yemen and provoked others, such as Iraq and Syria, into becoming police states. The rise of transnational Arab and Islamic movements in turn amplified regional and local conflicts.

Whereas colonial rule in the non-Western world usually had a beginning, a long period of insulation from the outside world, and a conclusion, many MENA elites are products of a different legacy. Only the Turks, Algerians, Tunisians, Moroccans, and Israelis can claim to have really won their independence, achieving a degree of national closure, at the expense of either settler or other minorities or, in the case of Israel, the national majority of Palestinians. Others still fear the subversion of foreign powers and interference from their neighbors. Any closure was gained at the expense of local business elites rather than the colonizer. Military coups toppled nominally independent regimes, and then the officers proceeded to restructure their respective political economies. The MENA's special legacy of external intervention has impeded the internal development of public accountability.

The creation of Israel in 1948 also contributed to the militarization of the surrounding states of Syria, Jordan, and Egypt, just as the advent of the Cold War reinforced the Northern Tier of Turkey, Iraq, and Iran. Part of the reason why the economies of the region appear to be so underdeveloped, despite their tremendous mineral resources and proximity to European markets, is their excessive military expenditures over the past half-century (El-Ghonemy 1998: 223–229). The MENA has consistently overspent the rest of the developing world on arms imports. Its strategic location attracted external powers into a variety of formal and informal military alliances, and the easy availability of weapons may have in turn encouraged arms races exacerbating a variety of local and regional conflicts. The MENA's oil resources not only made the region more strategically central to external powers but also largely financed their arms sales.

Consistent with the international model prevailing in the 1960s, most of the MENA states embarked upon policies of import substitution industrialization (ISI). Their statist experiments generally resulted in heavier, more bloated bureaucracies than those of other third world countries and more wasteful projects because the financing was so easy. Oil rents or foreign aid – strategic rents of the Cold War – also supported big military complexes and served to inflate their officer corps. When, shocked by the 1982 international debt crisis, the prevailing international consensus changed in the Thatcher–Reagan years to favor market economies and export-oriented development, the MENA states were slower than others to readjust their economic strategies and structures. Shielded directly or indirectly by the region's oil revenues and strategic rents, they took longer than their East Asian or Latin American counterparts to engage in the various forms of structural adjustment advocated by international financial institutions. The reasons were partly economic: adjustment would be more difficult, the greater the distortions left over from those halcyon ISI times. But the will to change on rational economic grounds also had to be reconciled with political rationality and its imperatives for retaining power.

Virtually all of these regimes suffer deficits of legitimacy (Ayubi 1995; Hudson 1977) and buy support through extensive networks of political patronage that permeate their respective economies through the administration, the banking system, and many "private" enterprises. In these patrimonial regimes private property is not secure from the whims of arbitrary rulers. Many regimes have yet to abandon allocation for alternative strategies of political legitimation, and hence must continue to generate rents that accrue to the state. State–society interaction continues to consist of heavy police control coupled with various forms of patronage to keep the police and other administrations loyal. Some of the MENA's regimes carefully mask their repression with information blackouts that further limit their possibilities for economic adjustment. Indeed their information shyness is becoming a major impediment to attracting capital in global markets. One measure of a regime's political capacity in the twenty-first century is its transparency and openness to new flows of information. On this as on other measures such as the ability to tax its citizens, most MENA regimes display significant limitations. Raising more taxes can stretch a regime's coercive capabilities, and more publicity may embarrass and undermine its patronage networks.

Yet the external rents have diminished sharply. With the end of the Cold War, the MENA lost some of its historic significance as a strategic lightning rod for the rest of the world. Great Powers still do vie for influence and play out their rivalries in the MENA, but some of the geopolitical attention and oil industry interest has already shifted north to Central Asia since the breakup of the Soviet Union. The MENA's strategic rents began to diminish just as oil rents, which peaked in 1981, reached an all-time low in 1986 and, although recovering somewhat in 1999–2000, have in real terms never regained levels achieved in the early 1980s.

Major changes in international financial markets are particularly challenging to the MENA. Most forms of public assistance and foreign aid remained flat or diminished in the 1990s, reflecting the region's declining competitive advantage of strategic situation. While new private flows of foreign direct investment have swamped the developing world, they bypassed much of the MENA. Much of this capital comes from multinational companies accelerating their cross-country invest-ments as they compete in global industries. Since "an estimated one-third of all merchandise trade is actually composed of shipments among the affiliates of a single company, as opposed to arms-length transactions among separate exporters and importers" (Sachs 1998: 98), the MENA is losing its market shares of trade as well as investment to other regions. Indeed, "per capita exports have declined by 5 percent for the MENA region between 1990 and 1995, while they grew by 20 percent for the developing countries as a group" (Alonso-Gamo et al. 1997: 7).

Another surging source of global private capital is portfolio invest-ment, reflecting major changes in the behavior of small savers and institutional investors in Western countries, notably the United States. Instead of placing their funds in commercial banks, savers have pre-ferred mutual funds or shares of publicly traded companies. As portfolio managers packaged "emerging markets" into tradable mutual funds of foreign stocks, countries with established stock exchanges raked in sizable flows of portfolio investment. These flows have also bypassed most of the MENA and its underdeveloped stock exchanges but have encouraged a number of regimes in the region to begin to reform their capital markets to attract this new source of foreign investment.

Regional developments are also prodding regimes to engage in eco-nomic reform. Partnership agreements with the European Union call for a full liberalization of non-agricultural trade by 2010, more or less reinforcing the Ten Commandments of the Washington Consensus (see figure 1.3). An Arab–Israeli peace process threatens some of the vested interests of the Israeli, Jordanian, and Syrian political economies while

States are advised:

1 to reduce the budget deficit to no more than 2 percent of GDP

2 to accord budgetary priority to primary health, education, and infrastructure investments

3 to broaden the tax base, including interest income on assets held abroad, and cut the marginal rates of taxation

4 to liberalize the financial system, at least abolishing preferential interest rates and maintaining a moderately positive real interest rate

5 to adjust the exchange rate to encourage non-traditional exports

6 to liberalize trade, rapidly replacing qualitative restrictions with tariffs and progressively reducing the tariffs to 10 percent (or at most around 20 percent)

7 to remove all barriers to foreign direct investment and enable foreign and domestic firms to compete on equal terms

8 to privatize state enterprises

9 to abolish regulations impeding the entry of new firms or restricting competition and insure that all regulations of a given industry are justified

10 to secure private property rights without excessive costs, for the informal as well as formal sectors.

Figure 1.3 The Ten Commandments of the Washington Consensus
Source: Williamson 1994: 26–28

promoting new interests. The 1993 Declaration of Principles agreed between the PLO and Israel, coupled with the 1994 peace treaty between Israel and Jordan, has resulted in rapidly shifting bilateral and multilateral relations. For the first time since the creation of Israel, tactical regional alliances cross the divide between Arab and non-Arab. The projection of Israeli economic power into the region is becoming a reality to which Arab states are seeking to respond in various ways. Were the peace process to culminate in a normalization of relations between Israel and both Syria and Iraq, the region might lose much of its distinctiveness as a Hobbesian killing field and offer fewer excuses for inflated military expenditures and protected markets. The forced integration of Palestine into the Israeli economy might, however, trigger new resistance among the Palestinians and their neighbors as well.

Forced integration could be seen as a microcosm of precisely the globalization that most regimes fear.

In view of the MENA's legacies of foreign intervention, it is hardly surprising that international financial institutions and foreign donors evoke defensive reactions. IMF observation teams and World Bank missions are all too reminiscent of the European financiers who helped informally to colonize much of the region in the nineteenth century. The USAID mission in Cairo, for example, elicits comparisons with the more successful British advisors a century ago in the ministries of finance and public works. Symptomatically an Egyptian journalist's book about his country's negotiations with the IMF pictures Superman on the cover with a big "IMF" in red letters on his blue uniform (Hilal 1987). While some of the MENA governments have officially welcomed "globalization," their practices reflect ingrained suspicions of foreign advisors and their prescriptions for reform – "iron and arsenic to all, whatever the illness," as an Egyptian minister once complained (Hilal 1987: 171).

The foreign advisors are hardly supermen (or superwomen for that matter). Indeed, they must appear to be apolitical lest they offend their hosts or the board members of their international institutions. They express their "advice" in technical economic policy terms and, even when knowledgeable about the host country's politics, are not usually able to translate the advice into viable political strategies. The "Washington Consensus" promoted by the international institutions and Western donor agencies, albeit in steadily more diluted form as the decade of the 1990s progressed, is a set of ten flexible guidelines for opening up political economies and integrating them into global markets (Naim 2000). John Williamson, who coined the term, explains it to be "the common core of wisdom embraced by all serious economists." He leaves open many controversial questions, including even the size of government and the model of the market economy to be sought, whether "Anglo-Saxon laissez-faire, the European social market economy, or Japanese-style responsibility of the corporation to multiple shareholders" (1994: 18). Yet prescriptions which may be standard economics to academics also carry immediate political implications for power-holders. In the 1990s, indeed, the proponents of reform paid increasing attention to its political prerequisites of efficient, responsive, and transparent institutions (World Bank 1997). All the more reason, then, that the Ten Commandments calling for a liberalization and opening up of the domestic economy spelled imperialism and political as well as economic hardship for many local policy-makers.

Further constraints and opportunities result from MENA countries' global relationships. With increasing differentiation and specialization within the world capitalist system, policies presupposing an insulated national economy must give way to strategic calculations of relationships to global markets. Global political factors are similarly imposing themselves with ever greater urgency on the region's decision-makers. The new trilateral competition between the major blocs of North America, Europe, and East Asia is not as fierce as was US–Soviet competition, but it imposes constraints and provides opportunities to which Middle Eastern elites have not fully responded. They have given considerable thought to Washington or Strasburg, but the Tokyo/Beijing alternative barely enters the discussion at present. It can be expected in future.

The dialectics of globalization

The working hypotheses of this book are that politics drives economic development and that the principal obstacles to development in the region have been political rather than economic or cultural in nature. Political rather than economic factors have been the primary cause of the rate and method by which countries of the region have been incorporated into the globalized economy within the framework of the Washington Consensus. Those political factors result from strategies of incumbent elites seeking to retain power – strategies which bear remarkable similarity to those of the "defensive modernizers" of the nineteenth and early twentieth centuries, faced with similar challenges and opportunities of financial globalization prior to 1914. These strategies of "controlled openings" tend to segment the political economy, so that the degree to which various sectors of the economy are globally integrated varies widely. Further differentiation sustains the globalization dialectic, deepening the objective grounds for dividing populations and their elites into globalists and moralists while opening up new opportunities for potential synthesizers.

The drama of globalization is a continuation of the colonial dialectic played out by earlier generations of indigenous elites. Just as colonialism gave rise to movements of national liberation assimilating Western forms of political organization to struggle against Western domination, so the dialectics of globalization may integrate countries in the region into the world economy while also emancipating them. To do so in the new context is to assimilate, negate, and through the hard work of negation to supersede the Washington Consensus rooted in Anglo-American capitalism – perhaps by "Islamizing" it. Dialectic here is understood to comprise sets of ideas and attitudes defining elite–mass relationships rather than material forces, though economic interests obviously play a part. In a dialectic of emancipation (modeled after Hegel's master–slave relationship) ideas may – but do not necessarily – gain ever wider social audiences, achieving what Antonio Gramsci called hegemony (Lustick 1999). In colonial situations a nationalist elite may mobilize the entire nation, transforming a population defined by colonial borders into a people experiencing civil society.

Schematically the colonial dialectic describes three basic stances (or Hegelian "moments") of a native elite toward the colonizer's political culture. The first stance is that of acceptance associated with efforts to be assimilated into the new elite. But emulating alien values may in turn engender a backlash by those excluded from it. This negative moment of a counterelite asserts its claim to hegemony in the name of indigenous values. Under continued colonial pressure, however, new divisions within this elite may lead to the emergence of an alternative elite that is no longer content to articulate the traditional values of an imagined past. The third moment may more effectively combat the imposition of alien rule by assimilating its positive elements, such as skills and values derived from a Western education, and using them to overcome foreign domination. This deeper assimilation of the colonizer's values plays upon the contradictions of colonialism so as to undermine its authority and achieve independence.

Much of the MENA fell under the influence of Western powers without experiencing the full effects of colonial rule. It was in French North Africa that the colonial dialectic was most fully articulated because the colonial presence was more intrusive and protracted than elsewhere. The schema is best illustrated in Tunisia, where French rule lasted long enough to provoke not only emulation and negation but also a nationalist synthesis, yet was not so overpowering that it altogether undermined the authority of any indigenous elite, as in Algeria. Successive generations of educated Tunisians chronologically expressed the logic of the three dialectical moments. Before 1914 aristocratic Young Tunisians emulated French modernity and sought liberal reforms within the system. After World War I a predominantly urban Destour (Constitution) Party rejected the French Protectorate on traditional and legalistic grounds. Then the Neo-Destour, its successor party, with roots in peasant villages, employed modern political methods to organize the entire country against the French occupation. At independence, in 1956, Tunisia had the most deeply rooted nationalist party and trade union federation of any Arab country.

Tunisia was the exception. When, as in much of the Middle East, the "colonial" domination was veiled in technical and military relationships with outside powers, the colonial dialectic could not be completed for lack of a unifying target of opposition or incentive for emancipation.

Even in Tunisia, the synthesis led to new tensions and contradictions after independence. Habib Bourguiba's successful movement eventually engendered resistance from social sectors and actors who felt excluded. Once in power, the third generation of nationalists became vulnerable to attack by new generations of rejectionists who could point to the internal contradictions between the incumbent elite's ostensible Western liberal values and the regime's authoritarian practices. But Tunisia's Islamist opposition, progressive by Arab standards, is a legacy of Tunisian modernization: Rashid Ghannoushi can be seen as Bourguiba's "illegitimate offspring" (Zghal 1991: 205). Tunisia's special advantages deserve further scrutiny.

The critical factors for Tunisia's success were the duration of the colonial situation (1881–1956) and the capacity of political elites to forge durable linkages with mass constituencies before independence. Colonial conflict was sufficiently protracted and its education benefits sufficiently extensive to enable a modern educated provincial elite (sons of peasant freeholders) to displace the traditional urban elite of absentee landlords, merchants, and religious figures. The new nationalist elite succeeded in mobilizing broad popular support because the continued French presence offered a convenient focus for mobilization and coalition building. The timing was critical. It took three generations of nationalist struggle for the educated sons of the provincial elite to acquire sufficient weight to displace and absorb the other educated children of the traditional urban elite in the new middle classes (Montety [1940] 1973). Their Moroccan equivalents would not have time to achieve such social and political prominence before independence. Other new middle classes, defined as being not only educated but of predominantly provincial origins outside the old elite strata, did not achieve political hegemony before independence. In the rest of the Middle East and North Africa only Algeria, Aden, Egypt, Palestine, and Sudan experienced comparable periods of European (or Israeli) colonization. The colonial situation was too veiled in Egypt, however, and too prone to settler violence in Algeria and Palestine for their respective new middle classes to achieve hegemony. If they were to achieve it there or elsewhere in the MENA, it would be after independence and under less auspicious circumstances. In Palestine, however, the Jewish settlers, detached from Europe yet still mostly European, telescoped their nationalism into a third-moment victory over Britain within a generation.

Pervasive Western influence, first exercised through the Ottoman Empire and then more directly by means of mandates from the League of Nations, usually strengthened the hold of urban absentee landowner-merchants over the countryside. Turkey was the prime exception.

Ottoman bureaucracy contained them, and an Anatolian third-moment elite then displaced traditional authorities and achieved independence in 1923 through a successful war of national liberation. In most countries, however, the emergent elites benefiting from Western education did not have time to displace the old urban ones before independence: in Syria, Lebanon, and Iraq, the prime "nationalists" and beneficiaries of independence were the urban landowners; in Iraq they included urbanized tribal leaders. Despite a lengthier history of Western intrusion, Egyptian nationalism was also dominated by its landowners until divisions in the Wafd presaged the end of the monarchy in 1952.

Except in the Levant, the colonial powers tended to establish monarchies if they were not already in place. In the Persian Gulf the British protected ruling families and even imported the Hashemites from Mecca to Jordan and Iraq. The British also disposed of Italy's former colony by uniting Libya under a new monarchy in 1951. Except in Saudi Arabia, which did not experience traditional colonialism, monarchy was the sign of a colonial dialectic that had not run its full course. Had the French stayed a generation longer in Morocco, they would doubtless have discredited the venerable Sharifian monarchy by overuse against rising social forces. Instead, they accidentally raised its prestige by exiling the sultan to Madagascar in 1953. Conversely, had the French left Tunis for good during World War II, Moncef bey might have kept his throne and prevented Bourguiba from founding a republic. The British and subsequently the Americans also strengthened Pahlavi Iran without ever turning it into a formal protectorate. There as elsewhere, the monarchies had trouble coping with the new middle classes nurtured in Western education. Despite his White Revolution the shah was unable to mobilize support from the countryside to offset them. In Morocco, by contrast, the monarchy came to dominate both the old urban merchants and the new middle classes after independence by manipulating provincial notables to its advantage (Hammoudi 1997; Leveau 1985).

Israel, Tunisia, and Turkey were the only countries where a third-moment elite consolidated itself with independence. Afterwards it would be more difficult for new middle classes, the normal carriers of civil society, to forge durable linkages with other social sectors, whether among peasants, workers, or students. In Iran a genuine revolution was needed to expel the monarchy, but much of the new middle classes then fell victim to the victorious coalition of merchants and religious leaders. Elsewhere they invariably achieved power by plotting within their respective military establishments. Nasser and his Free Officers led the way in Egypt in 1952; after many military coups and countercoups,

Hassan Bakr (with Saddam Hussein) and Hafez al-Asad took power in Iraq and Syria in 1968 and 1970, respectively. The officers in turn suppressed civilian politicians and intellectuals who might have deepened their respective civil societies by creating new associations and political spaces. The degree of oppression or liberality of their respective regimes was a function of the potential oppositions they faced. The extent of their economic intervention and financial repression also reflected the strength of their respective merchants and landowners and the degree to which they had coalesced as a class of local capitalists. Thus intervention was heaviest in Egypt, Iraq, Libya, Syria, and Algeria. In fact it is often forgotten that Algeria's more protracted colonial situation had given rise to higher concentrations of Algerian as well as French settler landholdings than in neighboring Morocco. The economic hand of the military was lighter in the Sudan and Yemen, where capitalism was less developed.

The new dialectics of globalization feeds upon an unachieved colonial dialectic. Its thesis is the Washington Consensus, shared by "serious" economists irrespective of nationality and vigorously, if selectively, imitated by certain of the local business and political elites as well. It seems hardly coincidental that the countries governed by third-moment elites at independence – Israel, Tunisia, and Turkey – were the quickest to adopt the Washington Consensus. Reform teams of technocrats, supported at least initially by their political leaderships, also made some progress implementing various structural reforms in Algeria, Egypt, Jordan, and Morocco. The Washington Consensus, however, engendered significant backlash in these and other countries. The "globalizers" almost inevitably provoke "moralizers," who seek solutions in cultural authenticity by affirming a religious or ethnic identity, or at least by reaffirming traditional nationalism. Since Libya's Muammar Qaddafi began speaking of a "Third Way" in the 1970s, the siren call of a distinctive, unique, culturally authentic model has gained considerable appeal, and writings on Islamic economics have proliferated.

Much like second-moment responses to colonial situations, however, moralism remains abstract and ineffective unless it can contest the global economy on its own grounds. Most of the "moralizers" seem unable to devise effective alternative economic policies. Moralism takes the form either of Arab nationalism harking back to the command economies of the 1960s or of Islamic revivalism. On the nationalist track, Arab economists have unsuccessfully promoted a free trade zone as a counterweight to being integrated piecemeal into the international economy (Bolbol 1999). Mainstream Islamism, on the other hand, seems to be more preoccupied with culture than with economics. The moralizers, whether in government or opposed to it, can put globalizers on the defensive, but they rarely promote alternative policies.

Nor do they have much opportunity to do so. Hesitating moves toward greater political liberalization in the 1980s were sharply reversed in most MENA countries in the 1990s. Tunisia, followed in turn by Algeria, Egypt, Saudi Arabia, Turkey, and Jordan, severely restricted the Islamist oppositions. There could be little overt, public debate between globalizers and their opponents inside and outside their respective governments, and efforts to incorporate mainstream Islamist opposi-tions into the political process ceased, except perhaps in Jordan. Tunisia perfected the art of running a contemporary police state by claiming to be democratic while preemptively harassing, imprisoning, and routinely torturing its opponents and their families (Beau and Tuquoi 1999).

Indeed, the political conditions prevailing in most Arab states since the American-led liberation of Kuwait resemble those of a colonial situation – with the Islamists now playing the role of the erstwhile nationalists. It is an odd reversal of roles, a further unfolding of the colonial dialectic. In colonial situations Islam provided the implicit mobilizing structures of Western-inspired nationalism (articulated in Tunisia, for instance, through the modern Quranic schools), whereas today nationalism acquires an overtly Islamist form. Incumbent rulers, however, are both Muslim and indigenous nationals. They all seek legitimacy as Muslim rulers, even in once "radical" republics such as Syria or Iraq. Most of them therefore feel obliged to tolerate limited public Muslim spaces, such as Friday prayers and *shari'ah* courts, even though the message delivered in those prayers is strictly controlled, as are the judiciaries.

The colonial dialectic, in sum, gave rise to independent states of three different types: praetorian republics (Algeria, Egypt, Iraq, Libya, Pales-tine, Syria, Sudan, Tunisia, and Yemen), monarchies (Bahrain, Jordan, Kuwait, Morocco, Oman, Qatar, Saudi Arabia, and the United Arab Emirates), and democracies (Iran, Israel, Lebanon, and Turkey). The monarchies preserved their traditional elites and capitalist legacies. The praetorian republics tended to reject theirs in favor of new political economies, although there were significant differences between Algeria and Iraq at one extreme and Egypt at the other. The "bunker" states, such as Algeria and Iraq, rule primarily by coercion – from their metaphorical or, in some cases, actual bunkers – because the state lacks autonomy from social formations. The "bully states," such as Egypt, are largely autonomous from social forces, whether traditional or modern, and have relatively strong administrations though they, too, depend principally on military/security forces. The democracies, with the exception of Iran, were more selective in their treatment of local capitalists and landowners. In general the regimes which left their capitalist legacies intact were technically better able in the 1980s and 1990s to cope with the new challenges of globalization; the monarchies of Jordan and Morocco adapted more quickly to the new world order than the more radical praetorian republics. They were generally better able than these republics to harness the power of private capital to their political needs. The praetorian republics and democracies varied considerably in their treatment of earlier generations of agrarian, commercial, and industrial capitalists, but they are all under some local as well as international pressure to come to terms with the Washington Consensus.

The relationships with local capital were largely conditioned by struggles against foreign domination, but they are also qualified by the particular variety of capitalism that the foreigners had introduced. These varieties of capitalism deserve some discussion because they condition the structural power (Winters 1994: 431–432) of local capital – an opportunity as well as threat to these regimes in the new era of globalization. Just as the advanced capitalist countries practice their distinct national varieties of capitalism (Berger and Dore 1996), so their colonial offshoots are developing their own trajectories conditioned by the financial systems they inherited. Most of the MENA's business communities are weak, heavily dependent upon the state, and hardly about to be agents of political or economic change (Bellin 2000: 175–205) at present, but their various legacies point to future possibilities.

Capitalist legacies

The Europeans introduced relatively advanced forms of capitalism into most of the region by the end of the nineteenth century. These consisted of a British model predicated on laissez-faire and an efficient, competitive stock exchange, a German model based on universal banks, and a French model stressing greater state intervention in capital markets. Featuring a weaker private sector more dependent on administrative allocations of credit, the French model did not long survive the departure of its French colonial administrators in Algeria, Syria, or Tunisia and bore little relation to its successor model of state "socialism." Contending British and German models survive, however, where indigenous business classes enjoyed continuity and protection from nationalist revolutions and the confiscation of private property.

Anglo-American capitalism is characterized by laissez-faire, as Williamson observes (1994: 18), and most basically by open competitive capital markets centered on stock exchanges. Commercial banking carries a less significant functional load than in alternative capitalist systems (Zysman 1983). Banks still lend to small and medium enterprises, but they remain subservient to market forces. Retail banks, even in Britain's highly concentrated system, wield little market power because their scope of intervention is limited. Under the impact of financial globalization the compartmentalization between retail banks and merchant banks is breaking down, and new conglomerates are challenging the traditional fragmentation and differentiation of financial markets, in the United States as well as Britain. Financial markets remain highly competitive, however, driven by a multiplicity of actors and regulated so as to insure transparency and to prevent insider trading on stock exchanges so far as possible. Walter Bagehot's *Lombard Street* (1873) captured its underlying logic of competition and exploration. Britain was constantly seeking new outlets for its massive capital accumulation and hence required a decentralized system which rewarded entrepreneurship. Capital-rich America followed suit. In this model the structural power of capital is exercised through financial markets.

A second model, best articulated by Rudolph Hilferding (1910), also stresses relatively autonomous private sector capitalist activity, but of universal banks, not individual investors. This German model is adapted to situations of capital scarcity. In late nineteenth-century Germany the largest and most capital hungry firms, typically in capital intensive industries such as iron and steel, fell under the control of their creditor banks. The borrowing industries and creditors alike became more concentrated as smaller entities went bankrupt or were acquired by the larger ones, and the banks concentrated and merged to defend themselves against industrial mergers. Finally an oligopoly of about six large commercial banks based in Berlin at the turn of the century commanded much of German industry. These universal banks, investing heavily in industry, constituted a model adopted by new generations of foreign capitalists, notably Talaat Harb of Egypt (where British and French capitalism coexisted at the time, see Saul 1997) and Celal Bayar of Turkey (Henry 1996). In the German model a small number of bankers scale the commanding heights of the economy and allocate its finance capital. They consult with their government but retain full autonomy and bargaining power. Here structural power works through people rather than markets: a small group of commercial banker/financiers can threaten to withhold loans and investments if the government does not provide an attractive business climate.

The third model is the traditional Napoleonic one of administrative intervention in the French étatiste tradition. While much of the economy, including the banks, may be privately owned, capital is allocated strategically more by technocrats who know best than by private financiers. The rationing of capital by state officials also, as in the German model, offers protection to capital-scarce economies. The banks, however, are less autonomous and exercise less control, for that matter, over stock markets. These capital markets are less developed than in the Anglo-American model. The structural power of capital is not as easily ascertained as in either the German model, with its small number of financial conglomerates, or the Anglo-American model, with its efficient market responses to new information. Market forces operate but they are subject to greater regulation by the technocrats. The best indicators of structural power are the degree of private ownership of the commercial banks and their financial health. Failing banks and ballooning bad loan portfolios (and precursor signs such as chronically low profitability) suggest either that the technocrats have excessively influenced credit allocation or that the banks have not conducted responsible credit analysis. Contemporary Japan would be an illustration. The structural power of capital is diminished by subsidized credit, but so also is the effectiveness of government to respond to business demands.

The model adopted in a MENA country did not necessarily match that of the politically dominant foreign power. Political domination was usually brief and rarely excluded other foreign capital. French and Belgian enterprises prospered in Egypt under Lord Cromer (1882–1906) more than did British enterprises, and the country remained open to other models as well. The German model proved attractive to Egyptian nationalists and other late developers even after Germany was excluded from the region following World War I. Nor did the French, more exclusively rooted in the Maghrib than the British in Egypt, convert all of the local entrepreneurs to their preferred form of capitalism. Morocco turned out to be "German" despite its French and Spanish colonial past. Its French capitalists had themselves adopted the more advanced German universal banking model by 1912, when most of Morocco became a French protectorate. In Tunisia, by contrast, an earlier generation of speculators had projected a traditional form of capitalism similar to that of French Algeria. The French capitalists in Morocco operated through modern German-style universal banks such as Paribas and developed stronger negotiating stances with their colonial government than did their less dynamic counterparts in Algeria or Tunisia, who depended more on the public authorities.

The German model also traveled to Turkey, despite the fact that the Germans were only one of several principal managers of the Ottoman public finances before World War I. The Germans invested more in productive enterprises than did their rivals and offered a more attractive model for postwar Turkish entrepreneurs than did their British or French competitors. Determined to build a Turkish private sector, Mustafa Kemal Atatürk and his top political economist, Celal Bayar, opted for the German model. Subsequently, during the Depression years after 1931, they espoused étatisme but also continued to develop a private sector along German lines.

Indigenous business communities assimilated the metropolitan models in varying degrees. Many of them consisted of minorities whose ties to foreign powers were distrusted by the nationalist forces that ultimately gained power. Business communities in praetorian regimes experienced sharp turnovers caused by an unstable history of coups and revolutions. In Iraq, for example, families promoted under the Ottoman and subsequently British rulers took refuge abroad. Iraq today has virtually no business class, but rather a collection of new people who are personally connected to the ruler. Without the security to accumulate capital, there can be no capitalism. Between 1915 and 1922 the Ottomans and then the Turks virtually obliterated Turkey's business minorities. Subsequently, however, a new Turkish business class grew up under Mustafa Kemal to absorb and sustain the German model into the 1980s.

Few of the MENA's business communities display as much continuity as republican Turkey's. Nationalist revolutions in the Arab world did not usually result in as much disruption as in Turkey prior to 1923, but they have had less time than the Turks since independence to recover. And Algeria represented even greater disruption in July 1962 than did Turkey in 1922. An entire French colonial economic, political, technical, and administrative elite departed on vacation rather than face independence, and few ever returned. The transition to independence was more gradual in neighboring Tunisia, but most of the Tunisians who replaced the Europeans owed their new economic fortunes more to their political activity and connections than to any tradition of entrepreneurship. Syria also effected a more gradual transition than Algeria, but by the mid-1960s the old Aleppan and Damascene business families had succumbed to Ba'athist domination, subsequently loosened by President Asad's cautious "opening" of the economy in the early 1970s. Nasser's Free Officers also rid Egypt not only of its European and khedivial business communities, but most native Egyptian capitalists as well, although ten years of state "socialism" (1961–1971) did not totally erase the country's capitalist traditions.

The Arab country displaying the most continuous business history is Morocco, where the French presence enabled an indigenous Fassi bourgeoisie to expand into Casablanca and other new centers. French industrial interests were only very gradually Moroccanized in the second decade following independence, principally to the benefit of the monarchy and its entourage of Fassi business groups. They preserved the "German" model of capitalism that had evolved under the Protectorate. In Israel the victorious Labour Party regime preserved Jewish businesses, including those founded and heavily subsidized during the colonial period by the Histadrut, the Zionist labor federation. Israel's original variant of state capitalism is similar to the French model inherited by its neighbors, Syria and Lebanon, from Ottoman times. Independent Lebanon conserved its entrepreneurs, but they converted to an Anglo-Saxon model to satisfy the American multinationals that set up their regional headquarters in Beirut in the 1950s and 1960s.

The capital-rich, whether in Lebanon or the Gulf, tended to adopt the Anglo-Saxon model, whereas the capital-poor entrepreneurs of Morocco and Turkey gravitated toward the German model, and the Israelis toward the more administrative French model. But predatory states deprived many countries of the region of their respective capitalist traditions. By default new entrepreneurs were locked into a "French" tradition of administrative favors, although the capital-rich Gulf states are also promoting a third, Islamic way, which is quite compatible with Anglo-American capitalism. Launched in the mid-1970s, Islamic banking and finance offers possibilities for synthesizing moral demands with those of globalization that will be discussed later in this book. The so-called "Islamic banks" operate in accordance with Islamic law, as interpreted by Muslim legal scholars, and do not accept interest although they recognize the time value of money in other ways (Vogel and Hayes 1998). They have captured substantial shares of commercial banking markets in a number of Arab and Muslim countries.

To summarize, the democracies and monarchies tended to preserve their capitalist legacies better than did the military regimes. Lebanon kept its business elite more or less intact, even through a civil war in the 1970s and 1980s, though it had switched after independence toward a less regulated Anglo-American model more in keeping with the country's role as a trading and financial center for the Middle East. Led by third-moment elites, Israel and Turkey were well positioned to maintain their respective legacies. In Iran a second-moment elite also keeps its indigenous capitalist bazaar, albeit in tension with a strong statist tradition inherited from the shah and expanded after the revolution. The monarchies also keep their legacies. The German model serves the poorer, capital-scarce ones. It facilitates palace control of heavy economic concentrations, whereas wealthier monarchies have more rents to pacify their more numerous and competitive local capitalists and tribal elites. The praetorian republics adopted state capitalism and dismissed much of their private sector legacies from colonial times. Residues of the Anglo-American model survive in Egypt and the Sudan, as do echoes of French capitalism in Syria. But whatever their domestic political constraints and capacities, extra-regional factors push all of the regimes to engage with global capital.

Chapter 2 will further address the extent to which global and regional changes may be leveling the differences between the MENA and other parts of the developing world caused by the MENA's special legacies of rents and foreign intervention. These global and regional changes not only constitute a new impetus for economic development, perhaps reversing recent trends, but also shape the context in which state actors make their political and economic calculations and formulate economic policies. The ebb and flow of relationships with the United States, the European Community, and the Tokyo/Beijing axis may tilt them toward one or another of their respective models of capitalism, but capitalism also has indigenous roots in most MENA countries which must somehow adjust to the realities of globalization.

Varying national responses to the Washington Consensus

The responses of the MENA countries to the Ten Commandments have ranged from eager acceptance, to vociferous rejection, to covert compliance with some of them. Israel, Jordan, Morocco, Tunisia, and Turkey were the first to embark on structural adjustment programs, and their official rhetoric favors free market economies. They were also first to sign on to partnership agreements with the European Union, just as they also led the way with Egypt and Saudi Arabia for the Arab–Israeli economic summits promoted by the United States in the wake of the 1993 Oslo Accords. Although civil war delayed Lebanon's entry into the club of World Bank borrowers, this country also accepts free market principles and has never diverged markedly from them. But however much "sold" on the Washington Consensus, each regime's economic strategy is defensive, reflecting its needs for political survival more than commitment to any economic model. No MENA government has implemented all Ten Commandments of the Washington Consensus, and very few have seriously attempted to implement any of the final four, much less to tax the foreign unearned income of their respective elites (part of commandment number 3).

Monarchies have been friendlier to capitalism than have been other forms of autocracy and also appear, with some exceptions, to be less information-shy than the praetorian republics. Countries endowed with strong capitalist traditions are adapting more easily to the new inter-national order than are those with weak or interrupted traditions of capitalism. Those states, by contrast, that control relatively high propor-tions of total societal resources appear to be more reluctant to undertake reforms that would cause a rapid reduction in levels of state appropria-tion. Patronage networks are likely to constrain economic reform the most in countries with weak capitalist traditions, but they are also likely to be more obstructive in countries endowed with Anglo-Saxon than with German (or French) structures. How these local conditions interact with regional and global changes will be further elaborated in chapter 3. The form and structural power of local capital will be inferred from the structures of the local commercial banking systems that reflect the real economy. Each local financial system is also among the most vulnerable of a country's economic sectors to the forces of globalization and offers ready indicators of its degree of integration into the world economy.

Some praetorian republics, however, destroyed their capitalist legacies altogether, so that while they are free of political constraints on their decision-making, they have little capacity to translate nominal into real reforms. Chapter 4 will examine the dilemmas of adjustment faced by these "bunker states" that have gone furthest in crushing their civil societies and expunging their capitalists, with the primary exemplar country being Algeria.

Most of the MENA countries, however, continue to host both old remnants and new forms of capitalism. Our challenge is to assess their potential for sustaining economic growth in light of existing political constraints and to offer insights into how these constraints might change. Generally, to the extent that they tolerate local capital, the praetorian republics insist on the "French" étatiste variant of capitalism, but, like the monarchies, some of them also tolerate Islamic business enterprises and even engage in a semblance of economic reform along Anglo-Saxon lines, in tune with the Washington Consensus. The special affinities and contradictions between the various political regimes and the capitalist models they are emulating will be the subject of chapters 5 through 7.

The Achilles' heel of many of the regimes trying to emulate the Anglo-Saxon model or to devise a new Islamic one is the free flow of information required by competitive capital markets. Either model really presupposes a degree of political liberalization that could endanger many of the region's political regimes as they are presently constituted. Being information-shy, they may prefer a capitalist model that is less open and more under the control of banks that respect confidentiality.

The German model also carries political risks, however. To the extent that the universal banks acquire real autonomy and independently deploy finance capital to the private sector, they may sweep aside a regime's crucial patronage networks rather than remain part of them. Many of the region's regimes, as presently constituted, could not coexist with an independent business class demanding accountability because they are patrimonial in nature, infecting any significant businesses with their business of politics. A viable Islamic model of capitalism would probably compound the political risks of the other two models. Even more than the Anglo-Saxon model, the Islamic model requires transparency and hence political liberalization. It might also mobilize its finance capital to take over or ravage the patronage networks of incumbent rulers.

Chapter 5 will explore the evolving French model in the less repressive of the praetorian republics, focusing primarily on Egypt but also including Tunisia and the Palestinian Authority. Chapter 6 will investigate how the monarchies have sought differentially to obtain both economic and political benefits from the German or Anglo-Saxon models, with Morocco serving as the exemplar of the poorer monarchies and Saudi Arabia that of the wealthier ones. In chapter 7 the mix of financial models that exists in the democracies – Anglo-American, French, German, and Islamic – will be reviewed within the context of the politics of identity that preoccupy those political systems. It is not possible to predict whether any given regime will change or will instead simply alter the model to fit its political needs at the expense of economic growth. But the longer the region stagnates, the more likely it may be that the Islamic model, a largely offshore and transnational phenomenon at present, will develop its markets in a number of countries and eventually challenge their regimes.

Can transformations be incremental, with incumbent political elites retaining power, or does capitalist development require rapid, even revolutionary change in which the incumbents are swept aside by representatives of a new order? Must that new order be "globalist," imitative of capitalist development elsewhere, or can it be a unique synthesis in which aspects of the MENA's own legacy and endowments are included?

The evidence thus far is insufficient to provide definitive answers to these two questions. Some tentative experiments with economic and political liberalization point to the possibility of them ultimately proceeding successfully and hand in hand. In Morocco reasonably successful incremental liberalization was coupled in the 1990s with gradual political liberalization, suggesting that structural adjustment of the economy and the polity can proceed in tandem under an incumbent, ruling elite. Jordan, which in the late 1980s and early 1990s appeared to be a parallel case of simultaneous economic and political liberalization being engineered from the top, had by the end of the decade reverted to more authoritarian politics, while the only partially reformed economy stagnated.

Throughout the region the political space within which effective syntheses of global and local approaches might be forged has not expanded far or fast enough to permit the requisite dialogues. Stalled economic and political liberalizations, whether in the monarchies or praetorian republics, and rising political frustrations in both, imply that incremental, top-down reform may simply not work. The Algerian case points to the possibility that breakthroughs to a new order could be sudden and dramatic. The political chaos and economic stagnation that prevail there, however, suggest that attempts at dramatic breakthroughs are fraught with peril, especially if they do not result in the consolidation of a new, broadly legitimate political order. In all but the most peripheral of the region's countries, however, the process of change will not be determined unilaterally by contest among domestic forces, for within the developing world, the MENA region still remains the most enmeshed in the geo-strategic consideration of the globe's major actors. The globalization dialectic in the MENA region is thus beset with paradoxes, which will be reviewed in the concluding chapter.

Suggestions for further reading

Richards and Waterbury (1996) comprehensively examine the political economy of the region and are usefully supplemented by El-Ghonemy (1998), while Bill and Springborg (2000) and Owen (1992) present comparative political analyses. For political and economic history see Brown (1984) and Owen and Pamuk (1998), respectively. Berger and Dore (1996) introduce varieties of capitalism.

2   The challenges of globalization

The MENA, which has hesitated more than any other region of the world to adopt the reforms needed to benefit from the new international division of labor, is being pushed ever harder to adopt the Washington Consensus as its basis for formulating national economic policies. Global changes are breaking the cocoon that had once protected the region from major structural changes. Although the MENA continues to attract a disproportionate share of attention from external powers, notably the United States, it no longer receives the abundant strategic and petroleum rents that had previously insulated it from the need to reform. As a result, most of its states are compelled to seek to attract compensatory capital flows, which in turn is driving the process of economic structural adjustment. That this process is proceeding unevenly attests to those states' different internal capacities for reform, the topic that will be taken up in chapter 3.

Strategic rents: foreign aid and arms transfers

The end of the Cold War has had a more direct impact on the MENA than on any other region of the Third World. It simply reconfirmed the MENA's special vulnerability to external interventions rather than putting a halt to them. The United States-led military intervention against Iraq in 1991 would not have materialized without a weakened and complaisant Soviet Union and China's abstention in the Security Council. Nor could the United States have so easily attacked Iraq subsequently, striking without fear of political or military retaliation by any rival power. It is the American monopoly on intervention that is the principal difference between the new world order and the region's previous experiences with foreign powers. Yet historians of the Middle East's exceptionalism have observed that no great outside power long exercises hegemony in this part of the world (Monroe 1981; Brown 1984). In fact America's "moment" may already be passing. France, Russia, China, and possibly Germany and Japan are awaiting their opportunities to develop Iraq's bountiful oil fields, once Anglo-American efforts to isolate Iraq falter and UN sanctions are relaxed. Unilateral American efforts to isolate Iran are further enhancing the influence of the Europeans and Asians. In coming years US involvement in the region may focus less on encouraging an Arab–Israeli peace process than on balancing off other contending mediators.

Whether one or several powers contend for influence in the region, however, the traditional stakes of the game are diminishing, eroding the region's special advantages. Passages from the Mediterranean to India are no longer of much interest to Western Europeans. Aircraft flying from Europe to Asia now over-fly the region rather than refueling in it, new weapons technologies reduce the significance of location, and access to the MENA's abundant oil is, except for the USA, considered almost exclusively in financial terms.

The lowering of the stakes of Great Power military and overall geo-strategic competition is reflected in declines of rents that the competitors had previously paid to states of the region, of which foreign aid is a fair measure. Military and economic development assistance of foreign powers had been one of the mainstays sustaining the region's governments' heavy expenditures in the past, supplementing their other traditional means of subsistence – oil revenues earned directly or indirectly. But neither of these forms of rent has kept pace with the region's expanding needs or the rate of growth of the world economy. The unrelated changes of the end of the Cold War and downturn in oil prices converged to hit this region of the developing world the hardest. The international community diminished official development finance to the Third World just as the prices of internationally traded oil plummeted from their high points in 1981 to new lows in 1986 and 1998. Figure 2.1 traces the evolution of oil rents and aid in the 1990s. Not only did development assistance decline in the 1990s, but the MENA region's share of it declined from 17 percent in 1990 (and an all-time high of 30 percent in 1977) to 9 percent in 1997, reflecting its diminished importance in the world.

Other indicators of the strategic importance of the region are military aid and weapons transfers. During the Cold War the Middle East had been the major recipient of arms from the United States and the Soviet Union, but in the 1990s the picture changed. In nominal dollar amounts, inflated by high prices charged to the Gulf states, the region still absorbed 40 percent of the arms in world trade in 1996 (IISS, 1998), conforming to its stereotype as the world's most tension-ridden region. When measured more accurately, however, Asia has displaced the Middle East as the primary purchaser of arms. According to the

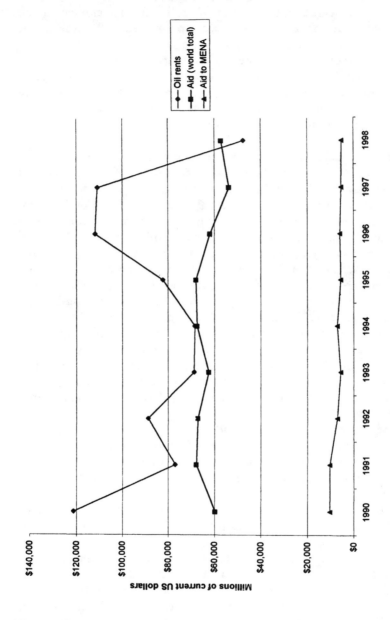

Figure 2.1 Oil rents and foreign aid, 1990–1998

Sources: BP-Amoco world Energy Data 2000; World Bank, World Development Indicators 2000 on CD-ROM

Stockholm International Peace Research Institute (SIPRI), which calculates dollar prices for various major weapons systems, the Middle East and North Africa had only one-quarter of the world's conventional arms imports, whereas East Asia's share was over one-third. Figure 2.2 shows Asia to have dramatically expanded its share in the mid-1990s, whereas arms transfers to the MENA continued to decline after a brief flurry of activity following Iraq's expulsion from Kuwait by the US-led coalition. Despite official American pressures for further arms purchases, the markets in the Gulf are no longer as lucrative for United States weapons manufacturers as in earlier decades. Strapped for cash in the 1990s, Saudi Arabia, the biggest of the Gulf Cooperation Council (GCC) countries marked on the graph, intermittently postponed receiving and paying for arms for which it had contracted. When the price of oil recovered a little, as in 1996 and 1997, the GCC's share of purchases rose, only to collapse in 1998. In 1999 Saudi Arabian arms imports declined to $6.2 billion from $10.8 billion the previous year (IISS 2000).

The region still receives an abnormal degree of attention from the outside world because of its alleged involvement with international terrorism and unconventional weapons of destruction. The White House no longer labels Iran, Iraq, Libya, and Sudan as "rogue states," along with North Korea and Cuba, but as "states of concern" (US Department of State, 19 June 2000). These concerns do not, however, translate into significant strategic rents for allies of the United States in the region. Gone are the Cold War days when the United States bid against the Soviet Union for the favors of their clients. The local allies who still receive American funding, except for Egypt and Israel, were instead subject to cutbacks in the 1990s so that more US foreign aid could flow to the Eastern European and Central Asian countries no longer ruled by the Soviet Union.

Neither the aid recipients, with the exception of Israel, nor the oil exporters allied to the United States share the official American perceptions of the rogue or problem states. The Arab states cannot be counted upon for full support of possible American interventions against other Arab states or even against Iran. However, a reinvigorated peace process between Israel and the Palestinians and agreements between Israel, Syria, and Lebanon might strengthen Arab support of US goals in the region, notably the nonproliferation of unconventional weapons. Conceivably, if the peace process is restored, President Bush might persuade Congress to finance the United States' proposed share of $750 million in a Middle East Development Bank. Such a sum is small, however, compared with the expected inflow of private sector funds that depend

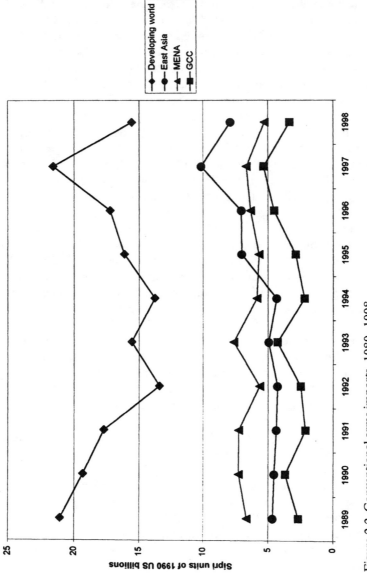

Figure 2.2 Conventional arms imports, 1989–1998
Source: SIPRI 1999

on a timely implementation of structural reforms discussed below. And if the peace process were to collapse, any public US commitment to financing regional development would be unlikely.

The European Union has maintained an interest in the region because its southern and eastern Mediterranean countries remain Europe's "soft underbelly" in a social if no longer in a strategic sense. North Africa and Turkey are contiguous with Europe, and the potential waves of "boat people" and other illegal immigrants from the countries of the southern Mediterranean basin constitute a threat to its social and political stability. North African guest workers in France and Turks in Germany have already ignited racist backlashes that could one day, if allowed to grow, threaten their respective democratic orders. Turkey, a founding member of the Council of Europe as well as of NATO and the OECD, is almost part of Europe, although the European Union only agreed in 1999 to place Turkey on its waiting list and had originally rejected its application for full membership in 1989. The compromise of a Customs Union, launched on January 1, 1996, "gives the Turks closer economic relations with the EU than any other nonmember countries except Iceland and Norway" (Yeşilada 1998: 182–183). In exchange for opening up its markets to Europe, Turkey receives substantial economic assistance as well as full access to European markets including "reciprocal concessions" on agricultural products.

As for the other southern Mediterranean states, the fifteen foreign ministers of the European Union met with their counterparts in Barcelona in November 1995 to launch a Partnership Initiative calling for a free trade zone (for non-agricultural products) by 2010. In addition to Turkey, the prospective partners are Algeria, Cyprus, Egypt, Israel, Jordan, Lebanon, Malta, Morocco, Syria, Tunisia, and the West Bank and Gaza. Libya, until 1999 shackled by UN sanctions, has observer status. The EU supported its Barcelona Declaration with a budgetary commitment over four years (1996–1999) of ECU 4.7 billion (about $5 billion) in grants to finance projects preparing for free trade as well as for other developmental and social objectives. The European Investment Bank, though primarily conceived to finance Eastern European development, committed almost ECU 4 billion in loans.

Europe's new concern with its "Mexico" thus promises some additional public funds to the region. Participation agreements signed with Tunisia (July 17, 1995), Morocco (February 26, 1996), and Israel were fully ratified in 1999–2000, and agreements with Jordan and the Palestinian Authority were about to be. Negotiations with Egypt have been completed, and some of programmed bilateral funds have also reached Algeria, Lebanon, and Syria, without formal agreements. In theory, however, EU support does not offer resources for delaying reform, as traditional strategic rents did. The rapid reformers are supposed to receive greater shares of the allocated funds than the more recalcitrant countries, though size of population (Egypt) and need (West Bank/Gaza) are also taken into account. The funds, however, are limited, and meanwhile the MENA countries are surrendering their preferential access to the EU's agricultural markets, while progressively allowing the EU free access to their markets for industrial products. The countries receiving bilateral assistance are also expected to carry out structural reforms to become more competitive and better able to face the new international competition accelerated by the successful completion of the Uruguayan Round, which is discussed below.

The funding is not particularly generous because MENA is less of a European priority than Eastern Europe and Russia and because the EU is not in a financial position to replace declining American aid commitments to the region. The total of 3.8 billion Euros ($3.2 billion) actually allocated over the four-year period (European Commission 2000) to the entire region is probably less than the foreign exchange that Algerians, Moroccans, and Tunisians working in Europe send back home to their families each year.

Remittances from the region's guest workers in Europe and in the GCC countries are indeed a more reliable source of external income for most MENA countries than any foreign aid. The biggest recipients are Egypt, Turkey, and probably Algeria (where much of the money bypasses official channels). Figure 2.3 shows that Egypt's intake, measured in constant 1995 dollars, increased dramatically after the country's participation in the coalition against Iraq in 1990. The Egyptians were awarded more jobs in Saudi Arabia. But the remittances then tapered off, probably as a result of their Gulf hosts' and Libya's diminishing oil revenues. Turkish remittances, by contrast, have weathered recessions in Europe and kept pace with inflation. So also have North Africa's. Algeria has twice as many guest workers as has Morocco, located mainly in France, but their remittances are largely unrecorded, moving through informal channels. Some of the other Arab states were even more vulnerable than Egypt to declines in oil revenues, war, and local politics. The Palestinians were especially hard hit after their Kuwaiti hosts claimed that their "guests," many of them installed in Kuwait since 1948, had betrayed them during Iraq's occupation. But Jordan, most affected by the influx of the Palestinian refugees from Kuwait in 1991, was receiving more remittances in 1992 than in 1989, the year before the Iraqi invasion. Yemen was another loser in the war. The Saudis expelled at least 750,000 Yemenites in 1990 because their home govern-

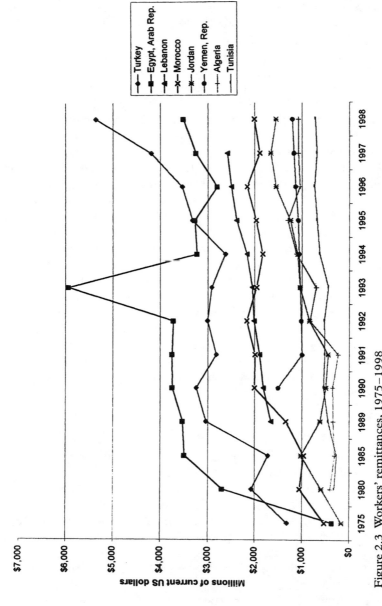

Figure 2.3 Workers' remittances, 1975–1998

Source: World Bank, World Development Indicators 2000 on CD-ROM

ment had tried to be neutral. Yet the remittances declined only by one-third and subsequently held steady.

Remittances act like strategic rents by cushioning the region from the full effects of globalization. Exposed to European labor conditions or to generous pay scales in the Gulf oil states, guest workers have acquired expectations that their home economies cannot match. In much of the MENA, Arab labor is priced out of competitive international markets. Its skills, motivation, and productivity do not keep up with nominal wages, making the MENA's real costs of labor comparatively high by the standards of the developing world. Confined to unskilled tasks in industrial economies, or to protected labor markets at home, workers have little incentive to improve their skills. As noted in chapter 1, the MENA seems to be declining relative to other developing countries on the Human Development Index. This index measures education, longevity, and literacy as well as per capita income, and every MENA country except Israel, Jordan, Lebanon, and Yemen ranks lower on it than on their per capita income scale. Further statistical analysis not included here reveals that only Jordan and Lebanon score higher on the education index than per capita income would predict. The safety valve of labor migration may be sapping efforts to improve labor competitiveness – in a region otherwise characterized by an abundance of cheap labor that should normally benefit from expansions of world trade (Rogowski 1989). The region confronts the challenge of reducing dependence on foreign labor markets before recessions, wars, social unrest, or substitution of local labor closes them down. Remittance "rents" seem bound, like military and economic aid, to diminish in real terms in coming decades.

Oil revenues

The region's other special resource is oil, the value of which has been seriously eroded since the early 1980s. After the dramatic price rises of 1973–1974, the region's economies, except those of Israel and Turkey, were reoriented to the assumption of high petroleum rents or subsidies from rentier states. The shift in international bargaining power from Western multinational oil companies to the Organization of Petroleum Exporting Countries (OPEC) lasted barely a decade, however. By 1983 OPEC was no longer able to set the price for internationally traded crude petroleum because, once supply overtook demand, it could not control the output of its member states. The industrial consumer states had meanwhile not only implemented successful conservation policies, but also gained access to new supplies developed by the multinationals outside OPEC territories. OPEC lost market share in the 1980s without being able to reduce its production sufficiently to keep prices up, and the more market share it lost, the less able it became to protect prices by reducing production. By 1998 the Arab members of OPEC and Iran were responsible for only 34.1 percent of the world's crude oil production although they shared about 68 percent of its proven reserves (BP Amoco 2000). Total revenues accruing to these states diminished from $250 billion in 1981 to about $110 billion in 1998, when better Saudi–Iranian relations enabled OPEC to cut production and drive prices and revenues upward in 1999–2001.

But a dramatic reversal of the slide in oil rents after 1983 remains unlikely. International market forces and security considerations restrict MENA production despite the fact that its costs of production (under $2 per barrel in much of the Persian Gulf) are much lower than those in other parts of the world. Prices need to be above $12–14 per barrel to meet marginal costs of production in the more expensive regions; otherwise the MENA will gain in market share and its potential ability to raise prices. The special Saudi–American relationship contributes to price stability, as was demonstrated in March 2000 when the Saudis responded to President Clinton's urging by increasing output to drive prices back into the targeted $22–28 per barrel range. After Iraq's invasion of Kuwait in August 1990 both countries had been shut out of international oil markets, yet Iran and Saudi Arabia made up the deficits in production with relatively little rise in prices for consumers. In 1999 Iraqi production permitted under Security Council regulations averaged above 2 million barrels per day, approaching pre-Gulf war levels, with prospects for very significant production increases as the US policy of dual containment (against Iran and Iraq) unravels.

International oil prices in turn dramatically affect the budgets as well as international trade balances of Algeria, Kuwait, Saudi Arabia, and other oil-producing states. Table 2.1 shows, for instance, that Algeria's oil and gas revenues constituted about 62 percent of the government's revenues in 1997. Saudi Arabian public finances were even more dependent on oil prices. In 1998 the government's oil revenues were exactly half those of 1997, and total revenues decreased by 31 percent. The budget deficit was 10 percent of GDP (SAMA 1999: 95, 101, 276). Every dollar decrease in the price of a barrel of oil increased the deficit by close to one percent of GDP – and of course the price increases of 1999–2000 considerably relieved the pressure on Saudi public finances. The large oil exporters also depend almost entirely on petroleum to finance their imports. And, as Table 2.1 indicates, oil and gas constitute vital elements in the baskets of exports of most of the smaller MENA

Table 2.1. *Oil revenues 1972–1998 and as percentages of export earnings and government revenues, 1997*

	Oil export revenues (current billion $)			Oil export revenues (constant 1990 billion $)				As percentages of 1997 revenues	
	1997	1998	2000	1972	1980	1986	1998	Export	Government
Bahrain								52	59
Kuwait	11.8	7.9	16.2	8.5	28.8	7.1	6.4	85	81
Oman		5.2						29	74
Qatar	4.0	2.9	6.6	1.4	8.5	1.6	2.4	60	57
Saudi Arabia	45.5	29.4	60.0	14.5	162.7	21.4	23.6	90[a]	75
UAE	13.7	9.3	19.1	3.3	29.9	6.8	7.5	38	70
Algeria	7.5	4.8	10.1	4.2	20.2	4.8	3.9	96	62
Egypt	1.7	0.8						43	
Iran	15.7	10.2	22.0	12.9	20.9	6.7	8.1	79	55
Iraq	4.2	6.1	20.4	4.5	43.6	8.0	4.9		
Libya	9.0	5.5	11.7	9.1	35.3	5.5	4.6	95	
Syria	2.5[b]	1.5–4						63[b]	38
Tunisia	0.5							9	8
Yemen	1.4[b]							95[b]	68

Notes: [a] 1996 [b] 1995
Sources: Feld and MacIntyre 1998: 31, Page 1999: 65, World Bank World Development Indicators 1999, US Energy Information Administration, May 2000

producers as well. During the decade of the 1990s such exports accounted annually for almost two-thirds and close to half of Syria's and Egypt's merchandise exports, respectively.

Trade

The impact of stagnating oil rents is already reverberating throughout the region, affecting not only the budgets of the oil producers, but also the job security of many other Arab nationals employed in the Gulf. Apart from the petroleum sector and its petrochemical derivatives, the MENA apparently has little to offer the world economy. Mineral fuels constitute two-thirds of the region's exports. Its terms of trade, primarily reflecting crude oil prices, are fifteen times more volatile than those of the entire set of developing countries (El-Erian 1996: 141). Its ratio of trade to GDP, a conventional measure of the degree of integration of a country or region into the world economy, is relatively high, but much of it is in exchanges of a single raw material for food and manufactured products. Better measures of integration into the world economy are the respective economies' openness to trade and the degree to which the trade is tied to international production processes. As noted in chapter 1, the region is not keeping up with the explosion of world trade driven by globalized production. However, when the oil revenues are removed from the region's total exports, per capita exports show modest increases in the 1990s, reflecting successes of the early adjuster states discussed further in chapter 3 (see Table 3.1).

The conclusion in 1994 of the Uruguay Round of multilateral tariff reductions has further accelerated the expansion of trade for the developing as well as the industrialized nations of the world. It also eliminates special treatment, however, accorded by industrial countries to their favored former dependencies, as permitted under previous GATT agreements. With the exception of the GCC countries, most MENA countries have benefited from a variety of special trade relationships with the EC, the United States, and Japan, and liberalized trade now threatens their traditional export markets. The European Union's Barcelona Declaration is in part an attempt to compensate for the MENA's losses of special trading privileges. To benefit fully from participation agreements with the European Union, the southern Mediterranean basin countries are required to open themselves to further trade in non-agricultural products. The early adjusters, Israel, Morocco, and Tunisia, have also been the first to undertake the necessary commitments. Tunisia has led the way in an ambitious program, partly financed by the EU, to restructure its enterprises to face up to international competition.

The region hesitates, however, to take advantage of the full range of new trading opportunities offered by the Uruguay Round and by the EC. While the trade regimes of the Gulf Cooperation Council states are relatively liberal, most of the others in the region maintain high tariff barriers. Egypt, Israel, Jordan, Morocco, Tunisia, Turkey, and five of the six GCC states joined the World Trade Organization, but the applications of Algeria, Saudi Arabia, and Sudan were still pending in 2000, and Iran applied only for observer status. Iraq, Lebanon, Syria, and Yemen have not yet applied for any WTO status. Algeria, Egypt, and Jordan are negotiating participation agreements with the EC, whereas Lebanon apparently awaits a Syrian green light for both of them to negotiate their agreements.

With the exceptions of Israel, Turkey, and the GCC countries, even early entrants into the WTO have retained high tariff barriers (see chapter 3). Despite being the first Arab state to sign an agreement with the EU and to join WTO, Tunisia keeps its tariffs higher than the others. Cutting tariffs will also pose special problems for Lebanon, which relies heavily upon customs revenues to finance government expenditures. And it is far from clear to most of the Arab countries whether the benefits of free trade really do outweigh the costs as the IMF and the World Bank claim.

Many of the MENA countries have very few obvious competitive advantages outside the petroleum sector. More free trade will endanger their exports in the short run, regardless of their policy responses. Free trade is also a threat to indigenous manufacturers servicing presently protected local markets. In Egypt, for example, the once export-oriented textile industry now not only is unable to compete on international markets, but is capable of supplying local markets only because they are protected by high tariffs. Significant reduction of tariffs in the absence of major currency devaluation would result in a flood of Asian textiles swamping local markets, a fear shared by many southern Mediterranean countries. Cheap imports could drive many private producers out of business and oblige governments either to increase their burdensome support for public sector textile manufacturers, or to let them go bankrupt, thereby adding to the already large pool of the unemployed.

Any prospective benefits to MENA countries from free trade depend in part on the degree to which they are already engaged in intra-industry trade (IIT), which is the percentage of their total industrial imports and exports that are specialized within given industrial sectors. This IIT index tends to be much lower for the Arab countries than for the members of the European Union. With the exceptions of Oman and Tunisia, Arab countries score lower than their per capita income predicts, either because their trade regimes are more restrictive than the global norm or because their industrial structures (in the oil states) are relatively underdeveloped for their income. Controlling for per capita income, their respective IIT indices were substantially lower than those of a sample of Asian countries, but not of Latin American countries. Table 2.2 indicates, however, that Egypt, Jordan, and Morocco, as well as Tunisia, have substantially increased their IIT since the mid-1980s and are catching up with Turkey, even as Turkey and Israel forge ahead. (Oman's score is inflated by the re-export of tobacco and other products.) A disaggregated view of the Arab countries' IIT indices also shows substantial increases since the mid-1980s in certain manufacturing categories. In particular, chemical products, soaps, plastics, electrical distributing machines, ships and boats, aluminum, lead, leather, clothing, and footwear are all sectors with average Arab country IIT indices of 50 percent or more. In theory these and a number of other sectors could benefit from greater trade liberalization. Economic analysts conclude that "the high levels of IIT in so many 3-digit SITC products suggests that the degree of specialization attained enables Arab

Table 2.2. *Intra-industry trade index*

IIT indices	1984–1986	1992–1994
Algeria	0.051	0.052
Bahrain	0.107	
Egypt	0.102	0.172
Jordan	0.207	0.248
Kuwait	0.192	0.131
Morocco	0.158	0.204
Oman	0.164	0.414
Qatar		0.076
Saudi Arabia	0.047	0.096
Syria	0.143	0.125
Tunisia	0.238	0.301
United Arab Emirates	0.074	0.081
Arab countries (weighted averages)	0.159	0.250
Israel	0.469	0.584
Turkey	0.159	0.284
Industrial countries	0.876	0.878
EU	0.860	0.886
Andean Pact	0.237	0.290
APEC	0.874	0.903
Mercosur	0.428	0.519
NAFTA	0.687	0.773

Source: Trade Analysis and Reporting System (TARS), reported by Havrylyshyn and Kunzel 1997

countries to be competitive in a world market setting" (Havrylyshyn and Kunzel 1997: 21). The Arab countries' IIT indices tend also to be greater for the 10 percent of goods traded among themselves than for their trade with the rest of the world. A further liberalization of intra-Arab trade could therefore enhance the international competitiveness of their respective industrial bases. Israelis, too, view intra-regional trade, currently a very small proportion of the total even for the Arab world, as having tremendous potential in the event of a full Arab–Israeli peace (Rivlin 2000).

The liberalization of trade in services was also included in the Uruguay Round, but the MENA countries shied away in the multilateral negotiations from making voluntary commitments. Algeria, Bahrain, Egypt, Israel, Kuwait, Morocco, Tunisia, and Turkey joined the General Agreement on Trade in Services (GATS), and others have applied, but, of the Arab states, only Lebanon is preparing for eventual negotiations with the EU to liberalize services without referring to GATS' protective clauses. Further liberalization could enhance the region's services and be of special benefit to countries where tourism is important.

Nevertheless, the prescription promoted by the Washington Consensus (and the European Union) of removing or even gradually diminishing trade barriers, whether in goods or services, is threatening to most of the MENA countries, especially to those with the highest barriers and the lowest IIT percentages. Even the wealthy GCC oil exporters, with relatively liberal trade regimes, need to develop more competitive export capacity outside the petroleum sector, where revenues are so unpredictable. How well the MENA countries succeed in becoming more competitive – raising their IIT indices – will depend in part upon the trade liberalization measures they adopt, but also, as the IMF and the World Bank advise, upon complementary fiscal and other macroeconomic and regulatory reforms. Their major related challenge is to attract foreign contributions to the necessary investments in industrial development and renovation and related infrastructure. The specter of volatile oil earnings has inclined even Saudi Arabia, traditionally a reclusive society, to encourage more private foreign direct investment – except upstream in oil exploration and production – and even to promote tourism.

Capital flows

To become more competitive, the MENA needs to be more integrated into global financial markets. Major changes in financial flows to developing countries became apparent in the 1990s. Official public sector assistance to developing countries, fueled by the Cold War, was not keeping up with inflation, whereas the private flows of capital became almost indiscriminate torrents in search of emerging markets until the Asian crises erupted in 1997. Figure 2.4 summarizes the major sources of capital flowing into the developing world from 1990 to 1998.

Official development assistance (ODA) is clearly stagnating and being replaced by the private sector in an expanding pie which increased almost four-fold during these years to just under $340 billion in 1997 and $325 billion in 1998. Total private capital flows to low- and middle-income countries increased from $41.9 billion in 1990 to almost $286 billion in 1997 and $268 million in 1998. The biggest source was foreign direct investment, but portfolio investments in bonds and equities soared from $3.2 billion to over $79 billion in 1997, easily exceeding all forms of public assistance. Commercial bank lending and trade financing slightly diminished, however, as debts were paid off. The banks' share of private capital flows declined from 36 to 15.5 percent from 1990 to 1998.

Yet the MENA region is in large part denied access to the new flows

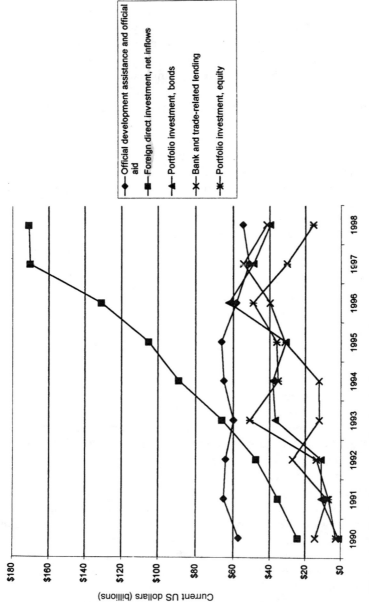

Figure 2.4 Capital resources for developing countries, 1990–1998
Source: World Bank, World Development Indicators 2000 on CD-ROM

of private capital. As the deputy director of the IMF's Middle Eastern Department observed, "the region has attracted a disproportionately small share of recent international equity flows to developing countries . . . and the total flow of private capital (i.e. equity, bond and foreign direct investment) to the region has only been about 2 percent of that going to developing countries" (El-Erian 1996: 141). Figure 2.5 shows just how poorly the MENA region (excluding Turkey) fared, compared with other regions competing for private capital. Its cumulative totals of foreign direct investment, bonds, and equity investments gained in the 1990s are compared with those of other regions of the developing world. The MENA accumulated a little more foreign direct investment than South Asia and Sub-Saharan Africa but tapped less into other sources of private capital than any other region. Its major source of external capital was the diminishing pie of official development assistance, of which it consumed a fair share.

The region fares poorly in part because its trade barriers and other obstacles have discouraged multinationals from investing. Judging from the low IIT indices, there is comparatively little intra-multinational trading with MENA countries, despite the fact that a full third of all merchandise trade is conducted between affiliates of multinational firms (Sachs 1998). Such trade forms a vital part of global production chains, in which MNCs assign specialized tasks in the production of individual commodities to different countries in order to minimize costs. The low IIT indices for the MENA indicate that for the most part MNCs have yet to locate even single links of their production chains there. Investment outside the petroleum and related sectors remains very limited, in part because before the mid-1980s most countries in the region did not need to attract foreign capital. Until the Gulf states' finances were squeezed by declining oil revenues, most of them could count on generous public or private investment flows from these Arab sources. Including workers' remittances, the Gulf states provided $140 billion to other Arab countries between 1973 and 1989, of which over $50 billion constituted official assistance (Boogaerde 1991: 72, 76). Extra rents enabled many of them to postpone internal reforms toward more market-oriented economies open to foreign investors. Even legislation designed, as in Tunisia, to attract foreign investment is often cumbersome. Investment may exclude certain "strategic" sectors, require too many official permits and favors, and still leave investors unsure of being able to repatriate their profits.

Additional political factors also discourage foreign investors. These factors will be examined more fully in chapter 3, but one deserves special mention here: the illiberal, "information-shy" character of most

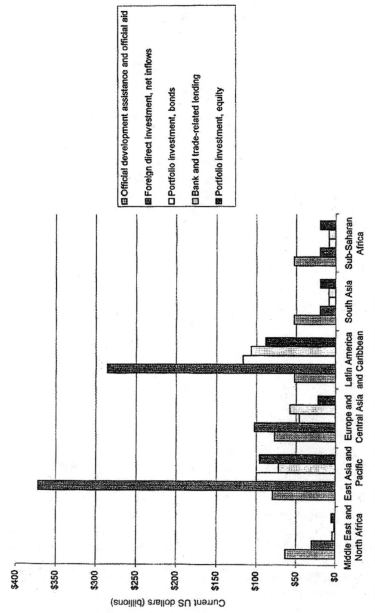

Figure 2.5 Cumulative capital flows by region, 1990–1998
Source: World Bank, World Development Indicators 2000 on CD-ROM

of the incumbent regimes. Investors have information needs that information-shy regimes restrict in a number of ways. In efforts to control all politically related information, they often make it difficult for economic news to be properly disseminated. Moreover, their banking systems, many of them largely state-owned, further constrict the free flow of economic information. The "German" or "French" state capitalism prevailing in much of the region is inimical to the development of stock markets, yet portfolio equity is one of the principal sources of capital in the integrated financial markets of the new world order.

Information needs for attracting private capital understandably vary, depending upon the type of financial flow, whether it be international bank lending, bond issues, foreign direct investment, or portfolio investment in local stock markets. International bankers have the least need of publicly available information. They have their own confidential sources, such as their clients, other banks, local government officials, in-house country risk analysts, teams of external consultants, and expensive country risk publications. Commercial banks used to be the principal source of private capital flows to developing countries, and they carry the fewest potential ripple effects on the political structures of borrowing countries. Although they supported IMF and World Bank policies of economic adjustment crafted in the interests of the creditors in the 1980s, their direct impact upon host political structures is minimal, and the net effect of their loans may have been to delay needed reforms. International bankers prudently avoid any appearance of involvement in host country politics, and governments can rely on their discretion. But unfortunately for information-shy regimes, traditional commercial bank lending is giving way to more open capital markets that require greater transparency if they are to function properly.

All three of these expanding streams of private capital – foreign direct investment, bonds, and portfolio investment in local stock markets – require more publicly available information for the private investors than do commercial banks or foreign aid donors. Portfolio investors and managers are particularly demanding, and probably more so in the wake of the collapse of "emerging markets" in Southeast Asia in 1997. Demands for public information and signals are potentially more troubling and politically destabilizing for information-shy regimes than are the discreet private queries of international bankers or public donors.

While bondholders will be less demanding than shareholders or certain kinds of direct investors, their requirements may still disturb some information-shy regimes. Investors in bonds are principally concerned with the macroeconomic stability of the country issuing or guaranteeing the bond. One sign of future long-term stability and prudent macroeconomic policies of interest to bondholders may be the independence of a country's central bank (Maxfield 1997: 35–37). Just how much central bank independence can be tolerated in most MENA countries, however, is uncertain. Any real independence – and greater transparency of the country's commercial banking system – may expose sensitive political patronage networks, yet international managers of bond portfolios may insist on greater openness, especially in light of recent experiences with the Thai, Indonesian, and other Asian banking systems. Information requirements of bond markets are less demanding than those of stock markets, however, and some illiberal countries, such as Tunisia, have recently raised substantial sums on the Japanese and Eurobond markets.

Portfolio investment in local stock markets is more problematic. In addition to macroeconomic stability, required as a protection against foreign exchange risk, portfolio investors in equities seek active, relatively liquid local markets, displaying a wide variety of traded companies. The region was making some progress by 1997, when it attracted 7.8 percent of the investment in "emerging" stock markets. With Turkey, the region's share approached 10 percent and reached 11 percent in 1998, when the Asian collapse reduced the total equity investment in emerging markets by almost half. In other words, portfolio investment in the MENA substantially diminished in dollar amounts. Indeed its stock markets accumulated under $10 billion in foreign capital between 1990 and 1998, less than Sub-Saharan Africa's. Almost half of it went to Turkey.

Foreign direct investment is the biggest source of capital for developing countries, but, excluding Turkey, the region's share plummeted from 11.6 percent in 1990 to about 3.3 percent in 1997 and 4.3 percent of a much smaller pie in 1998. With the exception of the energy sector, multinationals are deterred from investing because of trade and other restrictions, but also for lack of transparent economic information. Some of the most visible foreign presence, moreover, is not FDI in manufacturing industries, which would increase the IIT indices of MENA countries so that they might better compete in world markets, but rather fast-food chains aimed at local consumers. MENA seems to be hosting its fair share of McDonald's and Kentucky Fried Chicken, but these franchises do not amount to much, if any, foreign direct investment. Rather, they represent a reverse flow of capital to corporate headquarters from the local investors who buy the franchises.

Figure 2.6 looks at the cumulative net flows of capital into the region (including Turkey) from 1993 to 1998, by type of resource and by country. The biggest single flows were $13 billion of foreign aid for

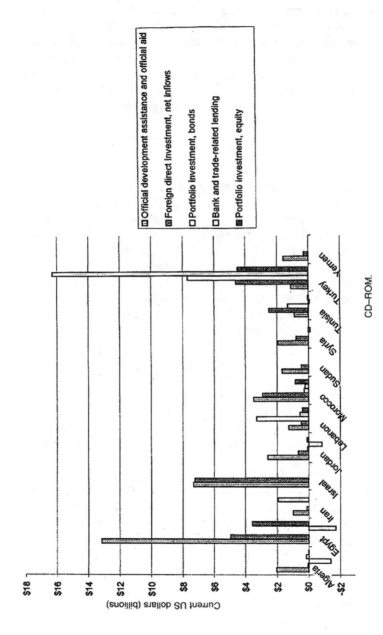

Legend:
- Official development assistance and official aid
- Foreign direct investment, net inflows
- Portfolio investment, bonds
- Bank and trade-related lending
- Portfolio investment, equity

CD-ROM.

Figure 2.6 Cumulative capital flows by country, 1993–1998
Source: World Bank, World Development Indicators 2000 on CD-ROM

Egypt and additional commercial bank lending of over $16 billion to Turkey. Foreign direct investment was much less, although Israel and Egypt, the two largest recipients of foreign aid, led the pack, followed closely by Turkey. The other countries most attractive to foreign direct investment were Morocco and Tunisia, but Syria – and even Sudan and Iran – attracted some investment in their petroleum industries. The stock markets of Egypt and Turkey (and perhaps Israel, for which data were unavailable) were the most successful in attracting portfolio investment. Turkey seemed to be in a league of its own on the bond markets, followed by Tunisia and Lebanon.

Countries with favorable risk ratings for their sovereign long-term debt can issue sovereign bonds as a relatively inexpensive means of attracting portfolio capital. Sovereign bonds are cheaper than traditional forms of lending, but prices depend upon the judgments of the rating agencies, the "new superpowers," as one Lebanese economist complained (Warde, 2000). In the mid-1990s Lebanon, Tunisia, and Turkey scrambled with the other MENA countries to get ratings from Moody's, Standard and Poor's (S&P), and other recognized business authorities. Tunisia, first to make "investment grade," issued sovereign bonds at favorable prices, whereas Lebanon and Turkey had to pay higher risk premiums for their bond issues. Turkey's ratings slipped in the late 1990s, while Lebanon could only briefly hold its unique position "with junk ratings from S&P and Moody's but debt sold at investment grade prices" (*The Middle East Economic Digest* (*MEED*) August 13, 1999, 3). In June 2000 Standard and Poor's placed the latter's sovereign ratings on a "negative credit watch" out of concern for the Lebanese government's ballooning deficits. By 2000 most of the MENA countries had Moody's and other ratings (except Algeria, Libya, Iraq, Sudan, Syria, and Yemen – our bunker states) that facilitated borrowing on the Euromarkets. Only Israel, Saudi Arabia, Tunisia, and some of the smaller Gulf states, however, were up to "investment" rather than a riskier grade. Turkey was hoping to reduce its chronic inflation and improve its credit ratings by implementing a reform program with the IMF that was "seen by many as the country's most credible attempt in years to put the economy back on the right track" (*MEED* July 7, 2000, 36).

Still, just as the MENA is only partially integrated into global trade networks, its financial systems remain relatively insulated from international capital markets. Following IMF interventions in the 1980s to alleviate their unsustainable international debt burdens, many of them underwent some structural adjustment funded by the World Bank. Turkey and Tunisia led the way in the mid-1980s in reforming their respective commercial banking sectors, joined in the early 1990s by Egypt, Jordan, and Morocco. There are limits to the amount of reform some of them could undertake, however, without endangering their political regimes. Turkish financial structural adjustment, for example, stumbled in 1988 over the fate of Ziraat Bankası, the state's huge agricultural bank and extension service, a very important dispenser of patronage at election time. The Washington Consensus favors competitive financial markets and privatization wherever possible, but the governments of Turkey, Tunisia, and Egypt prefer to maintain big state banks and, through them, informal controls over the others. Credit allocation lies at the heart of most patronage systems, so finance is a "strategic" sector that cannot be fully opened to international inspection. Capital markets cannot be fully transparent because the big state banks control much of the finance capital. Consequently foreign capital tends to shy away.

The debt problem

Much of the region, however, including the wealthy oil states, needs to increase its external financing to compensate for adverse trade balances, deteriorating oil revenues, and limited prospects for official development assistance. The alternative to a further opening of MENA's capital markets to the rest of the world is increased debt.

For countries unwilling or unable to issue sovereign bonds at reasonable costs, the alternative to opening themselves to international capital markets is to fall back on the commercial banks, especially the big international ones that specialized in the 1970s in recycling oil revenues for the less transparent economies. As a result of earlier borrowing sprees, much of the region, except the wealthy oil producers, has been under the tutelage of international financial institutions since the mid-1980s, and, as a result, international debt service requirements diminished in the 1990s. One of the largest debtors, Egypt, was also aided considerably as a result of joining the coalition in 1990 against Iraq. Many of its official creditors forgave substantial portions of its outstanding long-term debt, thus lowering its debt service requirements and even enabling the local currency to appreciate, a process further encouraged by high interest rates paid on local currency deposits. The Egyptian experience illustrates major benefits of debt relief for developing countries but, conversely, it offers a warning of the adverse effects to a country's competitive position of a big international debt overhang.

Egypt and many other countries in the region carried heavy debt servicing requirements in the 1980s. For the most part, their situations

Table 2.3. *Debt service as a percentage of exports*

	1988	1990	1992	1994	1996	1997	1998
Algeria	77	63	72	48	28	27	42
Egypt, Arab Rep.	31	22	16	15	13	10	9
Iran, Islamic Rep.	6	3	5	16	28	31	20
Jordan	31	20	20	14	19	17	16
Lebanon	–	3	4	5	6	14	19
Morocco	26	22	41	38	28	27	23
Sudan	17	7	6	1	7	9	10
Syrian Arab Republic	16	23	6	7	4	9	6
Tunisia	22	24	20	19	16	16	15
Turkey	36	29	32	31	22	20	21
Yemen, Rep.	–	6	6	3	2	3	4
Middle East and North Africa	15	15	16	15	13	13	14
East Asia and Pacific	24	16	14	12	12	11	13
Europe and Central Asia	–	–	11	12	11	12	15
Latin America and Caribbean	37	25	26	25	31	36	34
South Asia	22	29	25	25	21	21	19
Sub-Saharan Africa	18	13	12	15	14	15	15

Source: World Bank, World Development Indicators 2000 on CD-ROM

have improved, and the region's debt service ratios to GDP and to exports of goods and services remain substantially lower than Latin America's. Table 2.3 compares their debt service to export ratios with the regional average and with the averages from other regions. By 1998 the Middle East and North Africa was one of the regions least burdened by debt service. Algeria and Morocco were the only countries in the region ever to have traversed the 40 percent line, a red line routinely crossed by big Latin American debtors such as Argentina and Brazil. Algeria again reached the danger point in 1998 because of the decline in its oil and gas revenues that year, but price rises in 1999 would again alleviate its debt service burden in the mid-1990s. Morocco, Turkey, and Iran were still paying back the banks at least 20 percent of their export revenues. Turkey is almost as heavily burdened as Morocco, while Iran also experienced relatively heavy debt servicing in the late 1990s. Erratic macroeconomic management coupled with official United States pressures effectively barred Iran from other capital markets. Lebanon's debt service also mounted sharply in the late 1990s, as the government converted domestic commercial bank debt into cheaper external debt.

Egypt and Tunisia were paying back only 9 and 15 percent of their respective export earnings in 1998. These countries, together with

Jordan and Lebanon, might afford heavier debt burdens, but then they would risk losing the benefits of relatively strong domestic currencies, such as lower inflation rates. With a debt service ratio of only 5 percent, Syria also appears capable of bearing a heavier load of international debt, but its total external debt amounted to 134.8 percent of GDP in 1995. It benefited from bilateral concessional loans, for the most part from Saudi Arabia, Kuwait, and the United Arab Emirates. Syria had also been the largest beneficiary of official assistance from the Gulf states. From 1973 to 1989 it received grants totaling $12.3 billion, $3 billion more than Egypt (Boogaerde 1991: 72). With the shrinkage of their oil revenues, however, these countries no longer appeared to be offering their northern neighbors much aid, whether as grants or subsidized loans.

Governments of course also borrowed from local as well as international markets, and many in the MENA borrowed heavily, as Figure 2.7 reveals. One recent case in point is Lebanon. By 1998 the government's domestic debt amounted by World Bank estimates to 107 percent of GDP. Treasury bills, bought mainly by the commercial banks, still constituted over 80 percent of the domestic debt in early 1999 (Banque du Liban 1999: 20). Despite the government's successful efforts to borrow abroad, financing its deficit still crowded out other borrowers at home. Lending in local currency almost exclusively took the form of treasury bills. Lebanon was caught in a debt trap. Interest expenditure on the national debt was costing the government over 60 percent of its revenues (Banque du Liban 1999: 19). The overall government deficit of over 50 percent of revenues closely reflected the servicing of the national debt and shows no signs of diminishing. The government preferred to increase its external indebtedness because interest rates were lower. Prime Minister Refik Hariri, after regaining office from Salim Hoss, remained committed to a strong Lebanese pound, indeed to an exchange rate pegged to the dollar despite higher local inflation rates. The inflation rate and government deficit, met by printing more money, put considerable pressure on the pound. Kuwait, Saudi Arabia, and the United Arab Emirates had temporarily rescued Lebanon in late 1997 and early 1998 by depositing hundreds of millions of dollars at the Banque du Liban, Lebanon's central bank.

A number of governments in the region would risk being caught in similar debt traps if they borrowed more, though their public finances are not as unbalanced as Lebanon's. Figure 2.7 indicates that the governments of Jordan and Israel are at least as highly indebted as Lebanon. Because of their substantial external as well as internal indebtedness, they have limited financial options and depend upon

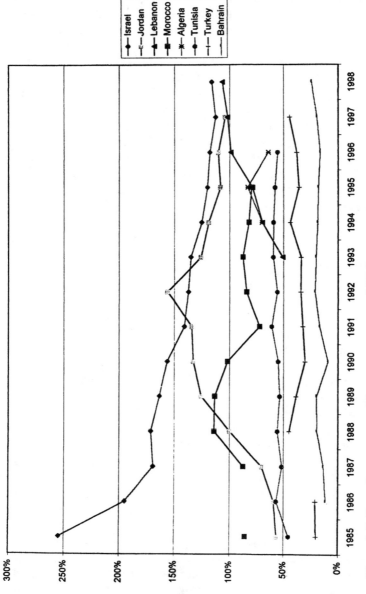

Figure 2.7 Central government debt as a percentage of GDP, 1985–1998
Source: World Bank, World Development Indicators 2000 on CD-ROM

strategic rents from the United States. High interest rates, needed to prop up their local currencies, drove them into recession in the late 1990s. Saudi Arabia, not included in the World Bank data reported in Figure 2.7, was in a more fortunate situation despite the steep fall of oil revenues in 1998. The government financed its deficit by internal borrowing from the commercial banks, rather than racking up external debt. Total government and public sector debt reached only 23 percent of GDP in 1998; in early 1999, as the public sector increased its share of bank credit, the private sector was squeezed a little, but then dramatic petroleum price increases alleviated the situation (SAMA 1999: 51, 53, 276).

Egypt has also significantly increased its domestic debt in the wake of the write-off of much of its external debt, but the exact magnitude of that increase is a contentious issue. The central bank claimed in early 1999 that total governmental domestic debt was LE135 billion ($40 billion), whereas other sources put the figure at LE200 billion, or over 70 percent of GDP. This raises the question of whether part of the attractiveness to Egypt and other countries of substituting domestic for foreign debt is the lack of transparency surrounding internal transactions. Another possible attraction is that the comparatively high interest rates paid for treasury bills and bonds denominated in local currencies guarantee the nominal profitability of public sector banks that in Egypt, for example, purchase virtually the entirety of such offerings. In Lebanon such loans account for well over half the portfolios of the private sector banks owned in part by Prime Minister Hariri, so that in this case, and maybe others, domestic borrowings guarantee profits for those in the government responsible for managing the state's finances.

Most MENA countries are not as heavily indebted both internally and externally as Israel and Jordan. Figure 2.8 presents the present value of the external debt accumulated by each country as a percentage of its gross national product. Only Sudan was carrying more external debt to GNP than Jordan, but Syria, whose domestic banking system was simply an extension of the government, was also heavily extended abroad. The others still have some margin for maneuver and, while awaiting more foreign investment, could take on more debt, either by issuing bonds or by directly borrowing in traditional fashion from the big international banks. But more debt could also jeopardize their competitiveness and hence their attractiveness to global capital, which may be one of the reasons why domestic debt figures are surrounded by considerable ambiguity as MENA governments seek to conceal the real magnitude of domestic borrowings. When external and domestic debt

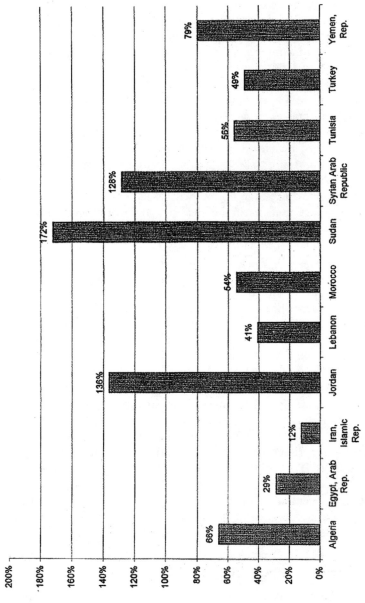

Figure 2.8 External debt as a percentage of GNP, 1998
Source: World Bank, World Development Indicators 2000 on CD-ROM. The debt is expressed as the present value of future expected payments.

reach substantial proportions, even when much of the domestic debt is to the private sector rather than to government-owned banks, further increases risk either being inflationary, putting pressure on foreign exchange rates, or crowding out private enterprises to the detriment of economic growth. Despite their diminishing debt service ratios, for example, Egypt and Tunisia still had "official" external debts in 1998, of respectively, 29 and 56 percent of GDP, and outstanding domestic credit, extended in part to the government and public sector enterprises, amounted to 95 and 53 percent of GDP. By some calculations Tunisia's government debt and external debt were much higher, respectively 72 and 87 percent of GDP (*MEED* May 26, 2000: 36). Algeria, Morocco, and Turkey carried heavier debt servicing obligations of their external debt and were also trying to limit their domestic government borrowing. Most governments in the region, which generally account for a far larger share of total borrowings than do the private sectors of their economies, are trying to reduce their fiscal deficits and borrowing needs, but often with great difficulty.

With many unhappy experiences of international debt in the recent past – and some histories of losses of financial autonomy or outright colonization in the nineteenth century – many countries prefer to find less costly capital in the form of either foreign direct investment or portfolio investment into their local stock markets. Even Algeria and Palestine have established stock exchanges. The mainstream of the Palestine Liberation Organization traditionally favored a liberal economy and had anticipated the experience of self-rule in freewheeling Lebanon. Once it was transformed into the Palestinian Authority as a result of the Oslo Accords of 1993, however, the political imperative to generate patronage for the quasi-state structure caused the new Authority to take measures highly inimical to the interest of business entrepreneurs. Algeria's initiative, coupled with its efforts since 1991 to encourage foreign direct investment upstream in its petroleum sector, is more remarkable. That this former socialist "revolutionary" state should establish a stock exchange is a tribute to the widespread if still abstract and hesitating acceptance of the new global economy in the region. But translating such acceptance at the verbal, theoretical level into actual practice provides a challenge that all are finding difficult to meet.

Pressures for reform

Virtually all the MENA countries have stock markets and new laws to attract foreign investment. They hesitate, however, to implement the reforms that might allow them, as the "serious economists" of the

Washington Consensus intimate, to take full advantage of the emerging global economy. Globalization, which offers numerous advantages to them, also poses very substantial threats. It implies reduced international public assistance, reduced oil revenues, and even reduced arms subsidies. It means opening most domestic markets to foreign competition that is usually better equipped in skills, capital, and marketing power than the local producers. Just as European imports in the nineteenth and early twentieth centuries had destroyed much of the MENA's handicraft industries, so a new wave of competition could annihilate years of independent state-led capitalist development in much of the region, including Israel. The economists advise these governments to privatize their state-owned enterprises (SOEs) in order to stop the hemorrhaging of public funds subsidizing their losses and, more generally, to make their economies more competitive in tradable goods.

Even the GCC states feel the pinch of the global economy, not so much because of low oil prices as because their small populations are growing and seek employment. Declining oil revenues discourage governments, the traditional fountainhead of employment in the Gulf as elsewhere in the Arab world, from more overstaffing. Instead, the governments require their private sectors to hire indigenous staff and limit the employment of expatriates, including other Arabs. Private sectors prefer, however, to limit local hires, viewed generally as less efficient and more expensive than expatriates from Asia. The wealthy Gulf states, so heavily dependent on foreign management and labor, suffer internal forms of colonialism that more indigenous employment may alleviate in the long run. In the short run their private sectors face reduced efficiency and possible declines in their modest manufacturing capabilities if they hire nationals. So, for example, textile plants that have been established in the lower Gulf, and which employ Asian labor almost exclusively, would be forced to close their doors if they had to hire local Arab labor.

The employment situations of the GCC countries amplify the general problem alluded to earlier that faces the region, namely under-qualified and under-motivated labor forces protected by government regulations. Unemployment is higher in the MENA than in other regions of the world, averaging about 15 percent, but reaching about half of the labor force in some of the worst performers, such as Algeria. Better-paid and protected workers tend to be clustered in the state-owned enterprises. It is as difficult for governments to privatize them as for the Gulf states to convince their private sectors to hire nationals. Whether in the Gulf or elsewhere, private sectors are reluctant to hire nationals without appropriate qualifications, lest they lose whatever competitive edge they might enjoy. The way out of the employment dilemma involves a combination of short-term policy changes, such as reversing progressive labor legislation that benefits relatively small proportions of workers, and long-term development strategies, such as reform of the educational systems that fail adequately to educate or even train their graduates. But the short-term policy changes are politically problematic, and the long-term developments will not impact the present generation and are themselves dependent upon policy changes that most governments find it difficult to make.

Globalization, in sum, is becoming associated with new forms of cultural confrontation reminiscent of the colonial dialectic. From Casablanca to Tehran, from Istanbul to Riyadh, the MENA states have already moved into the global economy at least at an abstract level. They all have their stock markets, imported (or locally assembled) cars, cosmetics, and other Western consumer items, and they are developing manufacturing capabilities that may in time withstand global competition. Except in Iraq they also have their Internet service providers. In Israel, Turkey, and some GCC states, the use of the Internet is widespread, as is access to other forms of global electronic communication. In other Arab countries the new users tend to be upper middle class, often with university degrees in science or technology, and associated at least indirectly with local capitalists and high government officials. These are the potential beneficiaries of globalization, sufficiently nimble and polyglot to find niches of comparative advantage in the information age. Certain of the local capitalists and the high government officials can also find their way in the new world order. But the Anglo-American form of capitalism connoted by the stock market is not congruent with their established state capitalist traditions. Governments hesitate to unlock their economic secrets, much less open their protected industries and labor markets to international or internal competition and thereby provoke opposition.

The strategies of incumbent regimes in the region vary considerably with respect to their will and capacity to engage in the reform process. As will be discussed in the next chapter, political considerations take precedence over economic priorities. The early adjusters, despite their cultivated images of openness to the world economy, cannot engage as radically in the reform process as the World Bank recommends without risking major domestic backlashes and/or the prospects of the steady decline of state-controlled resources that underpin the rule of incumbent elites. Even the apparent globalizers in local business communities tend to advocate liberalization for others while trying to protect their own market niches and special privileges. Yet international markets supported and oriented by the industrial powers continue to reshape trade and financial markets in ways that oblige even the most recalcitrant regimes in the region to respond positively, or to face ever bleaker economic prospects.

Suggestions for further reading

Globalization is critically discussed by Gray (1998), Hoogvelt (1997), Mittelman (1996), and Rodrik (1997), while Stallings (1995) shows how Third World responses have varied by region. Gereffi and Korzeniewicz (1994), Goddard et al. (1996), and Sachs and Warner (1995) discuss some of the economic impacts, while Maxfield (1997) and Rogowski (1989) discuss political implications. Concerning the MENA see Shafik (1997 and 1998) and Henry (1996), and for oil rentiers see Karl (1997).

3   Political capacities and capitalist legacies

A state is supposed to be strong and nimble to take full advantage of the accelerated flows of capital, goods, and information associated with the latest post-Cold War spurt of globalization, but few states in the MENA seem to be in the running. Those with the biggest armies and police are still premised on a Soviet–American order that no longer exists. Algeria and Iraq are autodestructing, and Egypt and Syria maintain unsustainable public sectors. These four leading Arab states of the 1960s are hardly alone in the region in bearing the burdens of dubious past economic achievements. More than a decade after the collapse of the Berlin Wall, the MENA still has more state enterprise than most former communist regimes. The latter are labeled "transition economies" in the international lexicon of political economy, whereas few of the MENA countries even rate inclusion in the burgeoning case studies of Third World transitions to market economies (e.g. Haggard and Kaufman 1995: 17), some of which are included in our suggestions for further reading and research.

Israel, Tunisia, Turkey, Jordan, and Morocco have undergone substantial structural adjustment, however, and it is hardly coincidental that they, too, are the most active in forging agreements with the European Union and the World Trade Organization. They score highest on the intra-industry trade index and seem well positioned to further liberalize their trade and capital markets. Yet these early adjusters, like other states, are also constrained by their political and administrative capacities. This chapter therefore tries independently to compare the capacities of the MENA regimes to mobilize resources efficiently and effectively. Also constraining or enhancing their abstract capacities, in addition to the scope and mix of reforms already undertaken, are the capitalist legacies which underpin their civil societies. Whether the legacy was "French," "German," or "Anglo-American" affects the structural power of a regime's local capitalists. The strength of these legacies will be inferred in this chapter from an analysis of their respective commercial banking systems.

This overview of the relative capacities of MENA states and their respective markets to respond to globalization introduces empirical evidence upon which the typology that structures the remainder of the book is based. This typology groups these polities according to their structural features and the degree to which political competitiveness is institutionalized. The results of this categorization suggest support for the principal thesis of this book, which is that the rate of economic growth and integration into the world capitalist economy depends primarily upon any given country's political capacities. In the MENA region such capacities are heavily indebted to the country's colonial legacy and those capacities and legacies in turn are the main determinants of the structural power of capital in the nation-state.

To recall from chapter 1, MENA polities consist of three major types – praetorian republics, monarchies, and, lastly, democracies of varying degrees of institutionalized competitiveness. Each category is in turn composed of sub-types. Praetorian republics are either "bunker" or "bully" states. Praetorian republics ruled by "bullies" have some elements of both civil society and rational-legal legitimacy, which in turn reduce, but do not altogether eliminate, the importance of violence and coercion in political life. The structural power of capital, although negligible in praetorian republics governed by bullies, is noticeably greater than in bunker states, where security of property is insufficient to permit capital accumulation. Consequently the "bully" responses to economic globalization are less brutal than those of the bunkers. The limited capacities of the "bully" states, however, and the structural weakness of capital within them, to say nothing of their own political power requirements, have severely constrained their efforts to globalize. Egypt, Tunisia, and prospective Palestine comprise the "bully" states of the MENA, while Algeria, Iraq, Libya, Sudan, Syria, and Yemen are the bunker states.

MENA monarchies are such largely because the societies in which they persist were not subjected to colonial influence as intense and protracted as those that became republics, where lower strata were mobilized and ultimately removed monarchs or rendered their establishment impossible. Just as traditional political orders in the monarchies were less disrupted by colonial encounters, so, too, their commercial elites typically survived rather than being swept aside by either colonial settlers or radical nationalists. Thus both state and market in monarchies have had greater continuity than their equivalents among the praetorian republics, and the influence of the market over the state is usually greater in the monarchies than in these republics. It is not surprising, therefore, that monarchical polities and economies tend on the whole to be more open and competitive and hence display greater capacities to respond effectively to the challenges and opportunities of globalization. These capacities, however, are in all cases limited by the prerogatives of royal power, intent as it is on retaining its ruling status. The manner in which that power is exercised varies considerably. Among one group of monarchies, including Morocco, Jordan, and Kuwait, power tends to be relatively dispersed and political competition comparatively institutionalized. In the others, the remaining members of the Gulf Cooperation Council (i.e. Bahrain, Oman, Qatar, Saudi Arabia, and the United Arab Emirates), power is more concentrated in ruling families, and political competition is less open, structured, or legitimate.

Finally, the MENA also includes polities that, with qualifying adjectives of various sorts, can reasonably be described as democratic. Turkey and Israel are "ethno-religious" democracies, in which secular Turks and Jewish (especially Ashkenazi) Israelis are privileged participants in their respective political systems, which deny equal rights to Kurds and Islamists (in Turkey) and to Arabs and, in much lesser measure, Sephardim (in Israel). Lebanon is a "consociational" democracy, in which elaborate institutional mechanisms based on elite consensus derived from Ottoman historical models and preserved by the French provide political *modus operandi* to enable competitive religious minorities to cohabit one polity. Conflict arises intermittently as a result of the need to renegotiate those institutional mechanisms, and because of external factors. Lastly, Iran is by name and in fact an Islamic Republic and one in which citizens can change at least part of their government through free and fair elections, hence qualifying it as an Islamic democracy. Befitting democracies, the polities of these four countries are more open, competitive, and institutionalized (with the partial exception of Iran) than those of either the praetorian republics or monarchies, and their civil societies are comparatively well developed. Political openness and pluralism in the democracies accounts in considerable measure for their greater capacity to adjust to globalization, but that capacity is also constrained by the intensity of the political identity questions that continue to bedevil these polities and which generally take precedence over issues of economic management.

That the tripartite categorization of MENA states reflects real political differences is suggested by the correlation between them and the degree to which political rights can be exercised and civil liberties are protected. Freedom House evaluates these two dimensions annually for most countries of the world, assigning numerical values to them, ranging from one (high, i.e., rights can be exercised and civil liberties are protected) to a low of seven. Figure 3.1 summarizes the latest

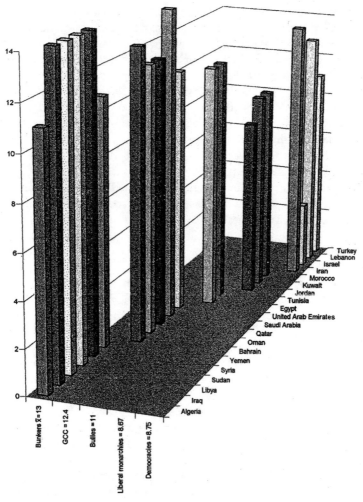

Figure 3.1 Freedom House ratings, 1999–2000
Note: The scores for political freedom and for civil liberties are added
together for each country. The score representing the greatest freedom
is 2, and for the least free it is 14.
Source: Freedom House 2000

available scores for the MENA countries. The four we have labeled as
democratic have an average total score on the two indicators, based on
data for 1999–2000, of 8.75 (and 7.67 without turbulent Iran), whereas
at the other end of the scale the average score for the bunker states is 13.
Arrayed between these two extremes are the three other types of states,

ranked exactly as should be the case if the categories do indeed reflect political reality. The more liberal monarchies that permit a fair degree of political contestation score on average 8.67, followed by the "bully" states which average 11. Finally, for the conservative monarchies that have yet to fully legitimate and institutionalize political competition, the average score is 12.4. In sum, our schema, based on the structure and competitiveness of MENA polities, does indeed appear to reflect those dimensions, while it also arrays their economies in linear progression from those least to those most effective in adjusting to globalization.

All MENA states, however, regardless of how competitive their politics may be, confront major political obstacles that constrain their rate and extent of economic growth. Polities ruled from bunkers have insufficient state capacities, inadequate civil societies, and much too fragmented capitalist legacies to formulate and manage effective strategies of economic development. Praetorian states ruled by "bullies" do have rudimentary civil societies and residual or recently developed capitalists, hence some resources with which to globalize. But the anxious rulers of these states keep the lid on their rudimentary civil societies and hinder their business communities from interfacing productively with international capital. While the monarchies grant a little more space to civil society and tend to have more robust capitalists, they also seek to preserve their personal power by imposing oligopolistic control over the market, frequently through family connections. Such control on private business may be less onerous in monarchies than in the praetorian republics, but it nevertheless impedes the development of free, outward-oriented markets. Finally, the primary business of the MENA democracies is not business, but the politics of identity and the containment or resolution of disputes that flow from those politics. Nevertheless, the freer flow of information in the democracies, their more robust civil societies, and the greater autonomy of their capitalism from the state provide them significant advantages when confronting the opportunities and challenges of globalization.

The state of reform

Most of the MENA states are already integrated into the global economy in the sense of being highly dependent on foreign trade. Except for Egypt and Iran, imports and exports amount to over 50 percent of each state's GDP. Even for Turkey, the other most populous state in the region, they amounted to 54 percent of GDP in 1997 and ranged up to 90 percent for Tunisia and well over 100 percent for Jordan. Real economic reform, however, is evident only in a few of these states. The best indicators of structural adjustment are the extent to which a country has increased its export of manufactured goods and the degree to which it manufactures for international markets. Table 3.1 shows the early adjusters to be altering their economic strategies from import substitution to export-oriented development. Israel, Turkey, and Tunisia more than doubled their exports in manufactured goods from 1987 to 1998, while Jordan and Morocco also target much of their manufacturing on export markets. Israeli manufactured exports consistently comprise roughly 20 percent of GDP. Turkey joined Jordan and especially Tunisia in manufacturing goods primarily for export markets by the end of the decade. Algeria, Egypt, Kuwait, and Saudi Arabia also increased their manufactured exports, for the most part in the petrochemical sector, but these exports remained a small portion of their respective national economies. Egyptian exports rose slightly from 11.2 to 13.5 percent of total value added in manufacturing in 1991 but then declined to 9 percent by the end of the period. Structural adjustment appears to have stalled, despite a doubling of Egyptian manufactures exported during the decade. Only Israel, Jordan, Morocco, Tunisia, and Turkey appear to be developing export-oriented economies.

Average tariff rates, reported in Table 3.1, are another indicator of the degree to which an economy has adjusted to the new international environment. Israel, Jordan, and Turkey lead the way, together with the GCC states, whereas Egypt, Tunisia, and especially Syria maintain relatively high tariff barriers. These Mediterranean countries still have a hard road ahead, for tariff protection is driven by the need to generate state revenue as much as or more than by the desire to nurture infant industries. The Tunisian government, for example, was generating 25.7 percent of its revenues – and almost one-third of its taxes – from customs duties as late as 1996 (see Table 3.4), and Lebanon was even more addicted to them. Participation agreements with the European Community require the southern Mediterranean countries progressively to reduce their tariffs with their major trading partners and to eliminate virtually all of them by 2010. Lebanon reduced many import duties in 2001 but will be in dire straits unless its government can find other means of taxing its citizens. Syria, which has not officially engaged in adjustment programs with international financial institutions, is only slightly less dependent on customs duties than is Lebanon.

Many countries in the region have made progress in stabilizing their economies. Standard indicators of reform include low rates of inflation, relatively balanced budgets, small differences between official and parallel market rates of exchange, positive real interest rates, and low charges of seignorage (a government's income from the depreciating

Table 3.1. *Evolution of manufacture exports, 1987–1998, and effective duty rates on imports, 1997*

| | Manufactured goods exported | | | | | | | | Effective duty rates (weighted, in percent) |
| | (current US $ millions) | | | (as % GDP) | | (as % manufacturing value added) | | | |
	1987	1998	(or latest year)	1987	1998	1987	1998	(or latest year)	c. 1997
Algeria[a]	181	393	(1997)	0.3	0.8	2.1	11.2	(1997)	15.1
Bahrain[b]	122	564	(1996)	3.8	9.7	23.9	59.0	(1995)	5.8
Egypt, Arab Rep.	1,059	1,937		2.6	2.3	11.2	9.1		18.8
Iran									11.1
Israel	7,910	21,134		22.3	21.0				0.7
Jordan[c]	448	867	(1995)	6.9	13.3	60.3	89.2		12.4
Kuwait[a]	682	1,999	(1997)	3.1	6.6	23.7	22.0	(1996)	3.5
Lebanon									14.9
Morocco[a]	1,371	3,449	(1997)	7.3	10.3	40.1	58.5	(1997)	14.8
Saudi Arabia[d]	3,122	5,466	(1996)	4.2	3.9	49.0	43.6	(1996)	10.0
Sudan[e]	2	19	(1996)	0.0	0.3		2.7	(1996)	13.8
Syrian Arab Republic[a]	421	406	(1997)	3.7	2.5				29.7
Tunisia	1,261	4,695		13.0	23.5	86.1	128.9		19.9
Turkey	6,813	24,039		7.8	12.1	38.6	75.3		1.8
Yemen, Rep.[f]		19	(1995)		0.5		4.8	(1995)	9.7

Notes: [a] 1987–1997
[b] 1987–1996
[c] 1987–1995
[d] 1989–1996
[e] 1992–1996
[f] 1995

Sources: World Bank, World Development Indicators 1999 and 2000; Eken et al. 1997: 24

currency it prints and sells to the public). Table 3.2 presents the relevant available information. After the heady price rises triggered by the October War of 1973, the wealthy Arab Gulf states brought their inflation rates under control by the late 1970s. Consumer subsidies subsequently helped to keep their annual cost of living increases minimal. Elsewhere only Jordan, Morocco, Tunisia, and Algeria managed to keep average annual inflation in the single digits. Israel struggled more effectively against inflation than Turkey. Finance Minister Shimon Peres' stabilization program of 1985 curbed Israel's hyperinflation, whereas chronic budget deficits fueled ever-higher rates of inflation in Turkey. Egypt made substantial progress in the 1990s after being relieved of much of its foreign debt servicing. Lebanon also finally after the civil war brought its inflation down to single digits, but its fiscal imbalances spell serious trouble. Another striking macroeconomic development documented in Table 3.2 concerns Syria. It drastically reduced its inflation rate without the help of IMF adjustment programs.

Economic stabilization also requires governments to reduce their budget deficits, with or without official adjustment programs. Algeria, Syria, Yemen, and especially Iran have registered successes, whereas some of the early adjusters, notably Jordan, Morocco, and Turkey fell far short of the 2 percent limit prescribed in the first commandment of the Washington Consensus. Turkey, the biggest delinquent, experienced ever-deeper macroeconomic trouble under a succession of unstable government coalitions until 1999, when an unlikely coalition of ex-socialists and extreme nationalists agreed on an economic program. The basket-case in the region was Lebanon, but the wealthy Gulf states were also unable to control their expenditures or raise new revenues until oil prices soared in 1999–2000. All of them remain heavily dependent on oil revenues, as do Algeria, Syria, and Yemen (see Table 2.1).

Low but positive interest rates are another important sign of good macroeconomic management. In the comfortable days of import substitution industrialization (ISI) the state typically allocated credit to its favored customers at interest rates lower than the inflation rate. Any enterprise being favored with a loan was in effect receiving a gift, even if it eventually repaid the loan. Early adjusters such as Israel were hardly exempt from these practices. Shielded by American aid from undergoing the conventional adjustment processes with the IMF, Israel still subsidized its domestic interest rates until 1995, when they became positive for the first time in the country's history. Turkey, not shown in Table 3.2, slid back into negative rates in the late 1980s after reforming them earlier in the decade, and Jordan was apparently subsidizing its elite of lucky borrowers as late as 1994. Saudi Arabia has kept up the subsidies,

Table 3.2. *Macroeconomic indicators*

| | Inflation (% cost of living) | | Budget deficit (% GDP) | | Real interest rates (% above inflation) | | Exchange rates (official to parallel) | Seignorage (% GDP) |
	average annual 1985–1989	1998 (or latest year)	average annual 1985–1989	1998 (or latest year)	1987	1998 (or latest year)	1998 (or latest year)	average annual 1985–1995
Algeria	9.1	3.80 (1997)		2.9 (1997)	7.1	17.7	0.447	2.7
Bahrain	−1.0	−0.40	−3.6	−5.8			0.989	0.2
Egypt, Arab Rep.	18.9	4.18	−8.1	−1.0	−11.3	9.1	0.991	4.1
Iran, Islamic Rep.	20.5	19.41	−6.5	0.3	–	–	0.365	4.2
Israel	81.8	5.43	−3.8	−1.2	35.2	10.2	0.990	3.0
Jordan	7.0	4.43	−8.0	−6.8	–	8.3 (1997)	0.985	5.6
Kuwait	1.6	0.15	20.1	−5.9	−2.6	2.0 (1995)	0.983	−0.8
Lebanon	–	5.00	–	−15.1	–	10.9 (1997)	0.991	7.7
Libya	–	–	–	–	0.4	–	0.159	1.4
Morocco	4.9	2.90	−5.6	−4.4 (1995)	4.9	8.3 (1994)	0.983	1.7
Oman	–	−0.80	−12.2	−6.9	−1.9	5.5 (1995)	0.986	0.2
Qatar	2.8	2.90	–	−0.1	–		0.995	0.3
Saudi Arabia	−1.2	−0.40	–	−9.4	–		0.991	0.2
Sudan	44.4	17.10	–	–	–		0.906	7.4
Syrian Arab Republic	31.8	−1.20	−2.1	−0.2 (1997)	–		0.209	6.8
Tunisia	7.3	3.10	−5.0	−3.1 (1996)	5.6		0.982	0.8
Turkey	51.1	84.60	−3.5	−8.4 (1997)			1.075	3.0
United Arab Emirates	–	1.60	−0.6	−17.0			0.995 (1997)	1.1
Yemen, Rep.	–	7.90	–	−2.6			0.959	4.8

Source: World Bank, World Development Indicators, 1997, 1999, and 2000; UN-ESCWA 1999: 14

though it does not publish information about interest rates for religious reasons. The kingdom's specialized banks doled out interest-free loans after 1973 as a way of distributing the oil revenues (Chaudhry 1997: 236). Total net subsidized lending of this sort stopped after 1986, when debt repayments exceeded new lending, but new interest-free loans still amounted to 6.7 billion riyals in 1998. Outstanding loans of this type amounted to 149 billion riyals, or almost as much as the credit extended (presumably at positive interest rates) by the commercial banks to the private sector (SAMA, 1999: 46, 83–84).

Another indicator of macroeconomic stability is the degree of coincidence between official exchange rates and informal parallel ones. Table 3.2 presents the ratio of official to parallel rates for dollars in 1997. At the official rate, for instance, one dollar could be bought for about one-fifth (0.209) of the Syrian local currency charged on the black market. It is readily seen that the differences between official and parallel rates were greatest for Algeria, Iran, Libya, and Syria, whereas Sudan and Yemen had reduced theirs through progressive devaluations of their respective currencies. Iraq, not reported, was in worse straits than Libya and Syria. It does not seem coincidental that the black market flourishes in the MENA's bunker states.

A final indicator of macroeconomic balance is seignorage, the money a government makes by making money. Technically it is the annual change in holdings of reserve money. The more money a government prints, the greater its income from this inflation tax. Although imperfectly correlated with inflation, high amounts of seignorage point to macroeconomic instability, suggesting that the government may be compensating for its inability to generate adequate revenues by other means (Snider 1996: 4–6). Lebanon and Yemen, for instance, printed additional money worth up to 10 or 15 percent of GDP in the early 1990s, but had to cut back on this easy way of funding their fiscal deficits in order to bring inflation rates under some control. As Table 3.2 indicates, the only consistently prudent money managers in the MENA have been Tunisia and the GCC countries. Of the early adjusters, Israel and Morocco are developing credible records after profligate pasts, but Jordan and Turkey remain incorrigible, as does Egypt, despite its progress on other dimensions.

An ultimate overall measure of the need for further reform may be the sheer size of the respective public sectors. In the view of the Washington Consensus, public sectors are inherently inefficient and must be privatized as rapidly as possible. From a purely economic point of view the evidence of their poor performances compared with private sector enterprises is overwhelming (Waterbury 1993), although there is no reason to suppose that private sector monopolies would be any more efficient than public ones in achieving public goods. Competitive markets could in theory make public sector firms just as efficient as private ones. The size of a public sector seems less important than market structure and the aggregate agency costs (or costs of supervision, regulation, and incentives) required to keep enterprises efficient, whether they be juridically part of the public or the private sector. Juridical notions also change, leading in Tunisia and Egypt, for instance, to substantial amounts of "privatization" effected without any substantive change of managements, practices, or in some cases, actual ownership (Terterov 2000). Or, if a company really is privately owned, it is not necessarily more efficient. It may be favored over a public sector company if the former is part of a political patronage network; indeed, a public sector manager may favor his private enterprise, or that of his cousin, over the public company – privatizing profits while transferring losses to the public domain.

In the aggregate, however, a predominantly private sector economy is supposed to perform more efficiently than a public sector one. Table 3.3 presents the available but scanty data about public enterprises in the MENA. Of the countries listed, Algeria's public enterprises used to generate the highest proportions of GDP, followed by Sudan, Egypt, and Tunisia. Turkey's public sector contracted to only 5 percent of GDP in the 1990s, but its overall annual losses ("balance before transfers") increased to 5.5 percent of GDP, almost as much as the government's burgeoning fiscal deficit. In the previous decade the Tunisian government bailed out its public sector by an astonishing 7.6 percent of GDP, but no recent data are available. Data are also missing on Iran and Saudi Arabia, but their public sectors are substantial. They consume proportionately as much commercial banking credit as Egypt's public sector. Privatization is on every country's agenda, but results have been meager to date. Turkey has led the way since 1988 in selling off public sector enterprises, followed by Kuwait, Morocco, and Egypt, whereas Iran, Jordan, Tunisia, and the UAE have sold off relatively little. Privatization seems to be as problematic in the Gulf Cooperation Council monarchies as in such countries as Algeria and Egypt. Virtually the entire indigenous labor forces of Kuwait, Qatar, and the United Arab Emirates have government or public sector jobs, as do most Saudis.

The early adjusters are obviously in need of further reform despite their relatively high scores on most of our reform indicators. The three top performers deserve special mention. Israel labors under a heavy public sector burden and still must overcome a reputation for loose macroeconomic management (despite a tighter central bank), chronic

Table 3.3. *State-owned enterprises*

	Economic activity (% of GDP)		Investment (% of gross domestic investment)		Credit (% of gross domestic credit)		Net financial flows from government (% of GDP?)		Overall balance before transfers (% of GDP)		Employment (% of total)		Proceeds from privatization (total $ million)
	1985–1990	1990–1997	1985–1990	1990–1997	1985–1990	1990–1997	1985–1990	1990–1997	1985–1990	1990–1997	1985–1990	1990–1996	1990–1998
Algeria	57.6	–	30.7	–	–	33.5	–	–	–	–	7.2[a]	–	9.30
Egypt, Arab Rep.	–	–	65.5	–	21.5	19.7	–0.7	–	–2.6	–	13.8	–	2,048.90
Iran	–	–	–	–	–	–	–	–	–	–	–	–	7.00
Jordan	–	–	19.3	–	9.9	8.3	–	–	–	–	–	–	63.80
Mauritania	–	–	19.3	–	–	0.1	–	–	–	–	–	–	1.10
Morocco	16.8[b]	–	19.3	–	–	–	0.0[a]	–	–	–	–	–	1,938.90
Oman	–	–	–	–	1.2	1.0	–	–	–	–	–	–	60.10
Saudi Arabia	–	–	–	–	–	14.7	–	–	–	–	–	–	–
Sudan	48.2[b]	–	–	–	18.4	10.0	–	–	–	–	–	–	–
Tunisia	–	–	31.0	–	–	–	7.6	–	–	–	–	–	514.60
Turkey	6.5	5.0	27.1	13.8	6.4	6.0	1.6	0.8	–3.2	–5.5	3.7	2.9	4,616.40
United Arab Emirates	–	–	–	–	–	–	–	–	–	–	–	–	190.00
Yemen, Rep.	–	–	–	–	–	3.0	–	–	–	–	–	–	–

Notes: Data are averages for the periods shown except for proceeds from privatization, for which the data refer to the total for the period
[a] Selected major state-owned enterprises only
[b] Includes financial state-owned enterprises

Source: World Bank, World Development Indicators, 1997, 1999, and 2000

fiscal deficits, and reliance in the final analysis upon continued American subsidies. Turkey faces much greater difficulties in these respects. Tunisia has the strongest record of responsible macroeconomic management and has greater potential than any other country in the region except Israel to be competitive in certain forms of manufacturing. Yet Tunisia continues to hide behind tariff walls and rely on customs receipts for close to one-third of its tax revenues. Its public sector, though relatively small by regional standards, drags down the rest of the economy, but may be too politically costly to sell off. Further adjustment is all the more necessary in the other MENA states if they are to attract the capital needed to control growing unemployment and contain social unrest.

The reform of the state

MENA states vary considerably in their political capacities. By "capacity" is meant the ability of a regime to mobilize public resources and to use them efficiently and effectively (World Bank 1997: 25). The principal component of capacity is the ability to extract taxes. As Ibn Khaldun explained in the fourteenth century, MENA dynasties collapsed periodically because tax bases in this arid region of seasonal migration could not easily support a standing army and self-sustaining infrastructure. Obtaining steady sources of revenue, by hook or by crook, is central to any process of state-building. In the MENA it was primarily foreign powers – Britain, France, and Germany prior to World War I – that completed these processes: within the past century they controlled the entire region's public finances, except those of Saudi Arabia and Yemen.

If the colonial powers utilized revenues relatively efficiently for their own purposes, they hardly cared to promote accountability and transparency, the mainstays of efficiency and effectiveness in the conduct of public affairs. Accountability, including a relatively independent judiciary, is needed to protect property rights and to restrain the arbitrary behavior of public officials. Transparency, which reinforces accountability, also enhances the efficient allocation of resources by enabling markets to function. As the World Bank observes, "A remote and imperious state, whose deliberations are not transparent, is much more likely to fall into the downward spiral of arbitrary rule and decreasing effectiveness" (World Bank 1997: 28). Without information neither markets nor institutions nor public opinion can check the descent.

As presently constituted, few political regimes in the region display the combination of transparency and political accountability needed to attract private capital. Most of what little foreign investment the region does attract goes into sanitized international enclaves such as the petroleum and petrochemical sectors. The biggest challenges to the regimes are internal: to become more accountable and to lift their constraints on the free flow of information. Only then will the necessary external resources become available for economic development.

Israel and Turkey have progressed furthest in these respects, but their political economies, characterized by strong oligopolies and substantial public sectors, limit full disclosure and constrict domestic markets. Both countries are relatively liberal and democratic, although not to their ethnic minorities and, like other MENA countries, they harbor strong "fundamentalist" social forces among their ethnic majorities that may paralyze economic policy and even challenge the legitimacy of their respective regimes. Like the others, their capacity for further reform and integration into the world economy may be constrained by these moralizing challenges to globalization. The influence that globalizers may bring to bear within a given regime depends only in part upon their political resources and strategies of coalition building. More crucial to any economic reform program is the available political and administrative infrastructure and its reflective extensions in civil society. Any reform is conditioned by the state's ability to mobilize resources, by the accountability of its agents to abstract rules and procedures, and by the transparency of the markets that they regulate. Extractive capability (with its associated instruments of coercion), credible institutions, and reliable information channels comprise the three distinct vectors of political capacity.

The extractive capability

It is sometimes argued that the oil-rich states have not developed representative institutions and traditions of accountability because they did not need to extract taxes from their populations. If there is "No taxation without representation," then why bother with representation in tax-free societies? Better still, the oil rentiers could distribute some of the oil revenues to their people as social services and benefices in exchange for acquiescence to patrimonial rule. Oil revenues thus completed the work of colonialism in discouraging the transparency and accountability of government institutions. Usually these vectors of capacity are byproducts, at least in non-colonial settings, of the administrative penetration of a society to extract taxes. For instance, prior to the oil boom in Saudi Arabia, the monarchy was accountable to the merchants. Kiren Chaudhry (1997) argues, perhaps with some exaggeration (Vitalis 1999: 659–661), that the young Saudi state raised revenues by cutting deals with Hijazi merchants to build national markets; a common currency also facilitated the collection of direct taxes such as *zakat*, a Muslim tax on property. It was only with the oil boom that the "central extractive and regulatory bureaucracies" atrophied, as distributive ministries acquired priority over the core Ministry of Finance. A major consequence was a loss of economic information and the transparency needed to make national markets work efficiently. Ideological reliance on "free markets" for distributing oil rents resulted instead in a new class of Najdi capitalists linked by family to the mid-level Najdi bureaucrats who allocated oil revenues to them through state banks.

Most of the other MENA states also indirectly benefit from oil and other rents and are commonly viewed as distributive rather than productive states. They, too, preempt any claims for representation or accountability with "social contracts" promising a variety of social services in exchange for loyalty. According to this view these states face a major crisis because they can no longer deliver the goods. As the rents evaporate, they must tax more and therefore presumably be subjected to greater accountability.

Table 3.4 indicates, however, that most of the non-oil states of the region already tax their citizens "adequately," given their levels of per capita income. Virtually all of them, except Egypt, Lebanon, and Syria, capture over 19 percent of GDP, and only the big oil producers tax much less. The biggest of them, Saudi Arabia, has one of the highest rates of general government consumption in the region, but relies on oil for over 70 percent of its revenues. Its taxation rate is unavailable but might be more meaningfully measured by cuts in subsidized services, such as electricity, rather than by actual taxes. Taxation in Kuwait and the UAE is also negligible. The more diversified and poorer economies of Bahrain, Iran, and Oman tax in the range of 8–11 percent. Algerian non-hydrocarbon taxes are higher, but oil and gas constitute over 60 percent of government revenues (Nashashibi 1998: 24), and the direct taxes shown in Table 3.4 include levies on foreign oil companies.

When compared by type of taxes imposed, some of the MENA states appear to be in the big leagues with high-income OECD countries and East Asian "tigers." Algeria, Egypt, Israel, Morocco, Turkey, and even Yemen raise over 5 percent of GDP from direct taxes, up to half their total taxes. But a finer-grained analysis of "direct taxes" suggests a different picture. Whereas direct taxes on individual incomes are typically some 10 percent of GDP in Europe, in the MENA they tend to be much less. In Egypt and Jordan, for example, taxes on individual

Table 3.4. *Structure of government revenues, c. 1998*

Year		Tax revenues (as % GDP)	Direct taxes (as % GDP)	Non-tax	Direct tax	Sales tax	Social security	Customs	Other
				(revenues as % of total government revenues)					
1996	Algeria	30.7	22.0	4.7	68.3	10.4	0.0	15.5	1.1
1998	Bahrain	10.1	1.7	60.5	6.7	3.7	14.0	12.3	2.8
1997	Egypt, Arab Rep.	16.6	5.7	37.0	21.7	17.2	0.0	12.6	11.6
1998	Iran, Islamic Rep.	11.2	3.2	57.8	12.0	9.2	6.9	9.7	4.4
1998	Israel	36.4	15.4	15.1	36.0	31.0	13.8	0.4	3.7
1997	Jordan	19.8	3.0	25.4	11.4	31.0	0.0	22.7	9.5
1998	Kuwait	1.5	–	–	–	–	–	–	–
1998	Lebanon	12.7	1.5	25.4	9.1	8.4	0.0	44.2	13.0
1995	Morocco	23.8	5.6	16.4	19.8	39.2	6.8	14.8	3.0
1997	Oman	6.4	4.1	74.0	16.6	1.6	0.0	4.4	3.4
1997	Syrian Arab Republic	16.4	7.3	32.2	30.2	20.7	0.0	10.6	6.3
1996	Tunisia	24.8	4.7	16.1	15.7	20.9	16.9	25.7	4.7
1997	Turkey	19.1	7.9	12.9	35.9	43.1	0.0	2.3	5.7
1998	United Arab Emirates	0.7	0.0	77.9	0.0	20.0	2.1	0.0	0.0
1998	Yemen, Rep.	15.2	7.4	62.7	18.2	7.2	0.0	10.4	1.6
1997	Middle East and North Africa	–	–	37.0	15.9	7.6	0.0	10.6	6.3
1997	East Asia and Pacific	–	–	13.6	26.8	29.6	1.2	10.0	4.2
1997	Europe and Central Asia	–	–	9.4	16.7	40.0	27.6	5.4	1.4
1997	High income OECD	–	–	7.1	28.1	26.3	32.7	0.0	3.0
1995	Latin America and Caribbean	–	–	14.2	17.0	38.1	9.2	9.2	3.2
1998	South Asia	–	–	19.0	18.6	32.3	0.0	20.0	4.3

Source: World Bank, World Development Indicators 2000

income and profits are 0.7 and 1.3 percent of GDP, respectively. Moreover, even these minuscule tax collections overstate the actual extractive
capacity because such taxes are imposed almost exclusively on civil
servants, rather than wage- or profit-earners in the private sector. In
Egypt, for example, the taxation authorities receive less than 200,000
tax returns annually from a workforce of some 19 million. The only
meaningful individual income taxes collected are those from civil
servants. Those are simply deducted by the government from the
paychecks it issues. By contrast, the MENA region has the world's
highest rate of indirect taxes imposed on international trade. Except for
some wealthy oil states, it is only Israel and Turkey that essentially
abstain from collecting these taxes that impede globalization, as their
returns from them constitute 0.2 and 0.7 percent of GDP, respectively
(Economic Research Forum 2000: 19–23).

Aggregate tax rates suggest that imposing higher taxes would not
oblige states to become more accountable. A cross-national sample
suggests in fact that gross taxation rates are unrelated to accountability
(Waterbury 1997: 153). But if the measure is direct taxes on individual
and corporate incomes and profits, then the picture might well be
different. Such taxes undoubtedly result in greater resistance by tax-
payers and stimulate demands for accountability and even participation
in decision-making about utilization of tax revenues. It is for this reason,
as well as because of inadequate administrative capacities, that most
MENA states shy away from making concerted efforts to increase their
revenue flows from direct personal taxes. This forces them instead to rely
upon taxes on trade and income generated by the state's own economic
activities. These revenue sources in turn inhibit effective globalization
and avoid stimulating increased demands for "representation."

Accountability and transparency

The transparency and accountability required for economic development in the global economy cannot be directly measured like a regime's
extractive capability. But extraction and bureaucratic penetration leave
other monetary indicators for measuring accountability. One obvious
concomitant of efficient extraction is a common national currency, for it
is easier to collect money than bundles of dates or fractions of a goat.
Paper or electronic transfers are yet another improvement over hauling
sacks of coins or stacks of bills. In the twentieth century the construction
of a state's extractive capability is invariably accompanied by progress in
commercial banking, and banks are predicated on social trust – which
may even survive the collapse of the state, as in Lebanon in the mid-

1970s. The scope and reach of commercial banking systems are easily measured by statistics routinely collected by the IMF since 1948. A recent cross-national study of the political capacity to adjust has used these data as a proxy for institutional credibility and accountability. It roughly reflects our theoretical concern and usefully serves as a starting point for comparing the capacities of MENA countries. The "adequacy of institutions" to protect property rights and to guarantee contracts and the rule of law "can be approximated by the relative use of currency in comparison to 'contract-intensive money'" (Snider 1996: 8) which lies within a country's banking system. As Lewis Snider explains,

Where institutions are highly informal, i.e. where contract enforcement and security of property rights are inadequate, and the policy environment is uncertain, transactions will generally be self-enforcing and currency will be the only money that is widely used. Where there is a high degree of public confidence in the security of property rights and in contract enforcement, other types of money that are held or invested in banks and other financial institutions and instruments assume much more importance. (Snider 1996: 9)

Anyone who has lived in Algeria or Syria may intuitively agree. In each of these countries in the late 1980s the cash circulating outside the banking systems exceeded one-third of GDP. People kept their cash under their mattresses and operated in flourishing informal economies of contraband ("trabendo" in Algeria) goods and undercover services. It may be a conceptual stretch to argue that the ratio of "contractive-intensive money" (CIM) in banks to the total money supply (M2) also measures the more general credibility of institutions and property rights, but the results for the MENA seem plausible at the high and low ends of the spectrum.

As Figure 3.2 shows, the highest performers are the democracies: Iran reaches 90 percent, and the others do considerably better, although Lebanon's numbers may be more exaggerated than others because of the vast amounts of US greenbacks not counted in its currency supply (Corm 1998: 123). The only other countries exceeding 90 percent are the small GCC states. The poorer states, whether monarchies or praetorian bullies, fare about the same, but the bunker states are in a special league. Their low CIM ratios, averaging only 64 percent, reflect political economies that seem to have the least accountable or credible institutions. In other words, if CIM really is a proxy for respect for property rights, then property – the lifeblood of civil society – is considerably more secure in MENA's democracies and in wealthy little oil principalities than in the bunker states. The other monarchies do not appear on the whole to respect property rights more than do the praetorian bullies, but both of these non-democratic forms of govern-

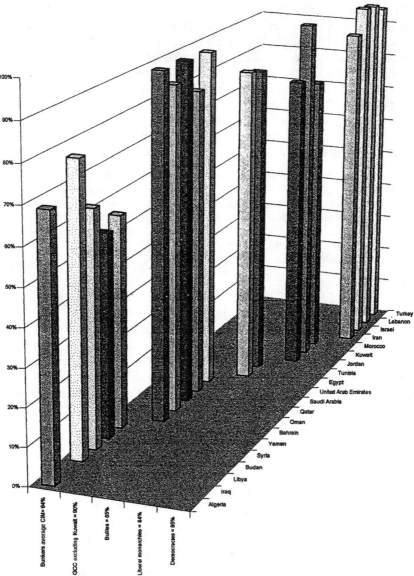

Figure 3.2 Contract-intensive money ratios (CIM), 1997
Note: CIM = (M2 − Cash outside banks)/M2, where cash outside the banking
system is measured in Line 14a by the IMF
Source: World Bank, World Development Indicators 1997 and IMF,
International Financial Statistics, various years line 14a.

ment appear to be significantly more accountable than those led by bunkered elites. If what is really being measured is the informality of the economy, then informal markets seem strongly associated with un-accountable government. A large informal sector also blunts a state's macroeconomic tools and dulls its extractive capability.

Finally, in addition to credible institutions, reliable information is an important dimension of political capacity. Per capita newspaper consumption is judged to be a better indicator of transparency than the broadcast media, radio and TV sets dominated by government propaganda machines. People buy their electronic equipment regardless, whereas they tend not to buy boring government papers in police states. Newspaper readership is also more closely correlated than owning a radio or TV set to use of the Internet. Estimates of Internet usage vary greatly and are rapidly changing as more Arab countries get online, but as of early 2000 Internet usage clustered into the same three groups of countries as newspaper readership. At the high end were Bahrain, Israel, Kuwait, Qatar, Turkey, and the United Arab Emirates. At the low end were Algeria, Iraq, Libya, Sudan, Syria, and Yemen – the bunker states again! Algeria, however, traded places with Morocco in newspaper readership. The press was clearly more interesting and free in chaotic Algeria than in Morocco's controlled pluralistic setting. Figure 3.3 summarizes the information about newspaper readership, showing the bunkers at one end of the continuum and the democracies at the other end – with the exception of Iran. The liberal monarchies average a slightly larger readership than the democracies because Kuwait, with a tiny population and many printing presses, towers over the rest, including Israel, and other little GCC countries also show substantial newspaper consumption, perhaps because of their large expatriate communities. The bullies discourage newspaper readership almost as much as the bunkers. An international press organization consistently rates Tunisia's President Ben Ali among the ten worst enemies of journalism, and in 1997 President Mubarak was also admitted to the select circle of dictators. Tunisia was expelled that year from the World Press Association for failing to defend the freedom of its journalists. The authorities in 1990 had banned what little of an independent press existed and delayed permitting its citizens access to the Internet until late 1997. Another early globalizer, the ostensibly more liberal monarchy of Jordan, was almost as information-shy. It closed its array of independent weekly tabloids in May 1997 on financial grounds. The courts subsequently ruled this to be unconstitutional but most of them had meanwhile gone out of business and the prospect of new, yet none the less constricting, laws discouraged them from returning. Information

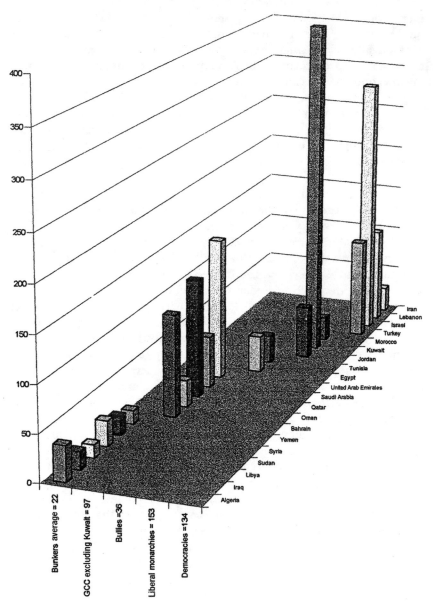

Figure 3.3 Newspapers per 1,000 people, 1996
Note: Newspapers are strongly correlated with estimated Internet subscribers
Source: World Bank, World Development Indicators, 2000

timidity may turn out to be these regimes' Achilles' heels – by deterring the private investment they are trying to attract.

In short, the political and administrative capacities of the MENA present a mixed picture. Figure 3.4 summarizes their standings on the CIM ratio, taxes to GDP, and newspaper readership, our indicators, respectively, of institutional credibility, extractive capability, and transparency. Israel is the only country to rank among the highest on all three dimensions of political capacity. Turkey and Lebanon also rank among the highest on two of the three dimensions, and it is perhaps no coincidence that they are also, with Israel, the most politically pluralistic. Iran, the other relatively democratic state in the region, displays less impressive indicators but may be gaining transparency in ways not yet recorded in formal indicators. Some of the small monarchies of the GCC also seem relatively transparent and accountable, whereas the non-oil monarchies of Jordan and Morocco appear to have less credible institutions as measured by contract-intensive money. Egypt and Tunisia score higher than the bunker states but less than the monarchies on most indicators of capacity. At the low end of the spectrum the bunkers – Algeria, Iraq, Libya, Sudan, Syria, and Yemen – have the largest informal economies escaping administrative control. Algeria and Yemen still enjoy more freedom of the press than the others, but this bottom tier of states also appears most fearful of the Internet. In sum, the data on political and administrative capacities suggest that the democracies are best endowed, that monarchies by and large do better than praetorian republics, and that the bunker states within this latter category have the least developed capacities.

These capacities seem ultimately to depend on the capitalist legacies that the independent states inherited, transformed, or tried to destroy. The states with the lowest political and administrative capacities also turn out to have the most diminished capitalist legacies.

Capitalist legacies

Political capacities are rooted in various colonial capitalist legacies. Independent states transformed and sometimes tried to destroy their imported varieties of capitalism. Whatever the outcome, the structural power of local capital remains a major factor that lengthens the reach and constrains the power of the respective regimes. Structural power strengthens civil society, which is a capitalist construct shaped by domestic and international capital flows as well as by state regulations. While NGOs, political parties, and trade unions are important symptoms of socio-economic preferences and capacities, the driving force of

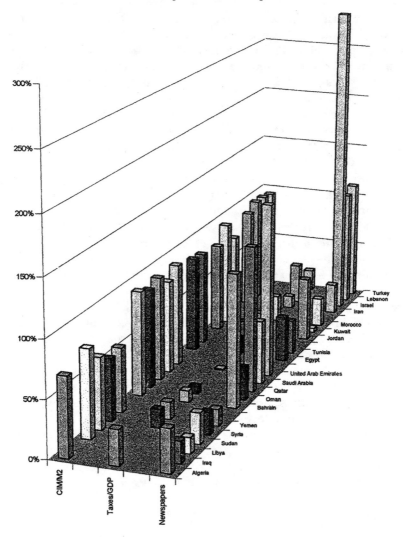

Figure 3.4 Relative political capacities
Note: Newspapers are per 1,000 people
Source: World Bank, World Development Indicators 2000 on CD-ROM

civil society is finance capital. Any winning coalitions of globalizers or
moralizers will depend upon the domestic and international capital they
can mobilize. Put differently, the politics of economic development does
not occur in a vacuum of insulated policy-makers, but instead is driven

by expectations of financial flows and investments of local and foreign business. Such is the structural power of finance capital, which varies considerably, depending on local capitalist legacies. How local capitalists and labor interpret and articulate their interests will in turn condition the processes of structural adjustment and economic reform.

The structural power of local capital can be inferred from the countries' respective commercial banking systems. Commercial banks offer an approximate picture of a country's economy because they finance much of its real assets. An alternative source of finance capital is the stock market, but these markets so central to Anglo-American capitalism are too poorly developed in the region for them to serve as underpinnings of capitalist systems. Table 3.5 compares their capitalization and trading activity with that of stock markets from a sample of countries from other regions. Even in Turkey, where the stock exchange is relatively active, traditional lending remains the principal source of working capital for most enterprises. Primary share issues peaked in 1997 when they comprised 6 percent of the commercial bank credit extended to private sector corporations, but they declined to 1.1 percent in 1998 and 0.2 percent in 1999 before recovering in 2000 (CBRT 2000; ISE 1999, 2000). Firms generally prefer to raise capital through commercial bank loans rather than open themselves up to stock markets where outside investors would require information about their investment. Stock markets require greater transparency than private owners, ever wary of the tax collector, public sector enterprises, governments, and the accounting professions, are ready to provide. Unable to finance their own growth through retained earnings, the enterprises become heavily indebted to commercial banks. These in theory have the power to make or break most businesses.

Commercial banks bear the brunt of business financing for the MENA and indeed for most of the developing world, much as five or six Berlin banks did for the German economy a century ago, when capital was scarce and the banks controlled much of German heavy industry. The German legacy may, as a Wall Street financier predicts, give way in Europe with the further integration of its financial markets to "a new colonization by Anglo-American financial markets" (*The Economist*, April 11, 1998, EMU Survey, 7). In much of the developing world as in Japan, however, commercial banks can be expected to maintain their preeminence, whether along traditional German lines or following the French statist model. The banking structures are the critical channel through which finance capital exercises structural power. Analysis of the commercial banking structures therefore offers a way of mapping the sources of structural power in a political economy.

Table 3.5. *Commercial bank credit and stock market activity, 1998*

	Total domestic credit (% GDP)	Domestic credit to private sector (% GDP)	Market capital (% GDP)	Value traded (% GDP)	Turnover ratio	Listed domestic companies
MENA region	65.2	34.3	26.6	5.8	17.9	1,619
Algeria	45.8	4.6	–	–	–	–
Bahrain	41.8	57.9	18.0	1.5	–	38
Egypt, Arab Rep.	94.9	54.0	29.5	6.1	22.3	861
Iran, Islamic Rep.	46.0	19.3	13.1	1.2	9.3	242
Israel	–	81.9	39.4	11.2	26.4	650
Jordan	91.2	72.7	79.0	8.8	11.6	150
Kuwait[a]	116.8	62.6	8.6	114.5	144.9	74
Lebanon	134.9	74.0	13.8	1.9	12.4	12
Morocco	83.8	50.4	44.1	3.9	10.1	53
Oman	44.7	44.6	29.4	13.0	33.8	131
Qatar[b]	65.4	37.3	–	–	–	–
Saudi Arabia	–	33.3	33.0	10.6	26.9	74
Sudan	6.8	2.1	–	–	–	–
Syrian Arab Republic	28.9	8.9	–	–	–	–
Tunisia	53.2	50.8	11.4	0.9	0.9	38
Turkey	36.6	23.4	16.9	34.5	154.9	277
United Arab Emirates	58.9	59.1	0.1	–	–	44
Yemen, Rep.	35.7	6.3	–	–	–	–
East Asia and Pacific	110.5	103.3	33.0	30.3	124.2	3,702
Indonesia	59.2	53.9	23.5	10.3	59.4	287
Malaysia	159.8	151.1	136.0	39.8	30.9	736
Singapore	86.4	109.7	112.0	60.1	50.5	321
Korea, Rep.	78.1	74.2	35.7	43.0	184.7	748
Thailand	164.9	156.6	31.4	18.6	71.2	418
Latin America and Caribbean	43.7	30.3	20.8	10.7	41.8	2,166
Argentina	32.6	24.2	15.2	5.1	30.2	130
Brazil	54.6	34.6	20.7	18.8	70.9	527
Chile	66.3	61.6	65.9	5.6	7.3	277
Mexico	36.1	19.7	23.3	8.6	28.5	194
Venezuela, RB	18.1	13.4	8.0	1.6	14.2	94
Sub-Saharan Africa	70.9	57.9	80.3	26.3	19.9	1,117
Côte d'Ivoire	28.2	18.6	16.5	0.4	4.5	35
Nigeria	14.2	9.1	7.0	0.4	5.2	186
South Africa	140.0	118.9	127.6	43.8	30.4	668
High-income OECD	140.7	118.8	116.0	95.3	89.5	20,320
United Kingdom	129.5	124.0	174.9	86.0	53.4	2,399
France[b]	103.1	83.6	69.5	40.1	68.7	711
Germany	146.4	119.1	51.3	65.2	144.9	741
Japan	139.4	117.8	66.0	25.1	40.3	2,416
United States	162.2	137.9	163.4	159.8	106.2	8,450

Notes: [a] 1997 data on stock market   [b] 1997 data on bank credit
Source: World Bank, World Development Indicators 2000 on CD-ROM

Types of commercial banking structures

The critical dimensions of a banking system are its autonomy and its degree of concentration as opposed to competition among the member banks. Autonomous and competitive systems exemplify an Anglo-American form of credit allocation, in contrast to the German pattern of autonomous oligopoly or to varieties of "French" state-managed systems. The structural power of capital is greater in autonomous than in managed systems, and in the less competitive, oligopolistic system "concentration . . . clearly increases the power of the concentrated segment of the private sector vis-à-vis the government" (Haggard and Lee 1993: 16). These two dimensions, autonomy and degree of concentration or competitiveness, are ultimately matters of judgment rather than any single, simple measure, but ownership turns out to be a pretty fair indicator of autonomy. State-owned banks tend to follow political orders and reflect the clientelistic practices of their real bosses, whereas privately owned banks tend to distribute their loans and services by more rational business criteria. Commercial banking systems consisting exclusively or in large part of state-owned banks can therefore be considered less autonomous than those that are predominantly privately owned. Adding up the share of assets controlled by the government-owned banks thus offers a rough and ready indicator of autonomy. The indicator of our other dimension, competitiveness, is the banking industry's structure: the greater the number of middling-sized banks, usually, the more they will be competing with one another. The degree of concentration is readily measured and offers a rough mapping of this second dimension. Our preferred measure, the Herfindahl-Hirschman Index (HHI), is the sum of the squares of the shares of deposits held by each bank in the system.

Table 3.6 maps out the MENA's commercial banking systems along these dimensions of state ownership and concentration in order to assess capital's structural power in each country. The banking systems fall into four quadrants (merging the lower right-hand ones) which respectively exemplify an absence of private capital, tendencies toward state-managed "French" capitalism, the concentrated "German" variety, and the Anglo-American model. In each case, however, structural power obviously also depends on the relative financial health of the banks as well as their ownership and concentration.

Although no contemporary MENA system fully replicates imperial Germany's of a century ago, concentrated systems with strong private sector financial performance qualify for structural power. In more étatiste systems the structural power of local capital is more problematic.

Table 3.6. *Ownership and degree of concentration of commercial banking systems*

Ownership	Concentration high HHI[a]>.16	medium	low HHI<.1
Primarily publicly owned	Algeria Iraq Syria Libya Israel Iran	Egypt Sudan Tunisia	
Primarily privately owned	Bahrain Jordan Kuwait Morocco Oman Palestine Qatar	Saudi Arabia United Arab Emirates	Lebanon Turkey

Note: [a] HHI (Herfindahl-Hirschman Index) is the sum of the squares of the banks' market shares of deposits
Sources: Union of Arab Banks 1998; author's data sets of commercial banking systems

It must be inferred from the individual financial performances of the banks as well as from the market shares. To the extent that they are really permitted to compete for loans and deposits, the public sector banks will usually be at a disadvantage, weighed down by non-performing loans from public sector enterprises. Thus an étatiste system can eventually change into the more autonomous and competitive Anglo-American type, as is the intention, if not necessarily the outcome, of the structural adjustment of the financial sector promoted by World Bank programs.

Exclusively public sector banking systems

Since state bureaucracies are usually ignorant of commercial banking practices, they find it difficult to establish publicly owned banks but easy to nationalize existing private ones. Exclusively public sector systems tend by default to be concentrated into a small number of state banks that have absorbed a more complex private sector. In their zeal for bureaucratic rationality the Algerians and the Egyptians in Nasser's "socialist" years specialized their respective banks by sector, thereby breaking with professional banking practices of portfolio diversification. The Iraqi regime went a step further, controlling all transactions through one big state bank until the late 1980s, when a competitor was invented as part of an economic liberalization program. Syria, too, hosted just one big state bank and four small specialized ones, until opening in 2001 to privately owned banks.

In such systems the banks are simply the relays of a central treasury to which the central bank is also subservient. There is no real banking, much less any structural power of private capital. Planners rather than bankers allocate the finance capital, and corrupt officials may siphon off some of it to their brothers or cousins in private enterprises. Any loose investment capital avoids the banking system altogether and simply contributes to a huge informal economy, as indicated by low CIM ratios discussed above. It is hardly coincidental that the low CIM countries, Algeria, Iraq, Syria, and Libya, are also those that have almost exclusively concentrated, public sector banking systems.

Concentrated, publicly owned banking systems also exist in Iran and Israel, but they seem more efficient, using less cash (Figure 3.2), lending more to their respective private sectors (Table 3.5), and supporting active stock markets. Technically Israel's banking system is still almost exclusively public sector because the banks fell under state receivership in 1983 after they had bid up their shares to unsustainable levels on the Tel Aviv Stock Exchange. Earlier, the public/private distinction was never clear in Israel, where Ha'Poalim Bank until recently was controlled by the Histadrut, the trade union federation, and Bank Leumi appeared to be a parastatal emanation of the Jewish National Fund. A prominent Israeli political sociologist argues that Israeli statism dwarfed any real private sector capitalism and stunted the development of civil society until the late 1970s (Doron 1996: 210–212). Ha'Poalim, fully privatized in June 2000, is controlled by a conglomerate, the Arison-Dankner Group, but the Israel's banking authorities are restricting its use of the bank to finance its big construction company (Gerstenfeld 2000: 12). Plans to sell off the government's 43 percent of Bank Leumi and 53 percent of Israel Discount Bank still depended on negotiations with suitable core investors (Berger 2000: 11). If these also turn out to be conglomerates, Israel's system might come to exemplify the German model – with four commercial banking groups dominating the system and pumping substantial amounts of credit to the private sector. Structural power of private capital ultimately will be reflected in the relative health of the principal private sector banks, when and if they are all finally privatized.

Mixed ownership, but still heavily concentrated in public sector banks

In this transitional system the public sector banks still dominate credit allocation and hold 60 to 70 percent of the market. Whether fragmented or concentrated, private sector banks remain locked into the public oligopoly. Efforts to break away from it are likely to be suppressed by a regime intent on preserving its patronage networks, even though they are under international pressure in the MENA, as they have been in Indonesia, to privatize their banks and clean up their portfolios of non-performing loans.

Countries in this category include contemporary Egypt, Sudan, and Tunisia. Most banks are nationalized but seem, except in the Sudan, to finance a substantial private sector (Table 3.5). The structural power of local private capital remains minimal, however, reflecting its fragmentation and subordination to the public sector in the banking system. To the extent that there is any recognizable capitalist system, it is of the "French" étatiste variety. Sudan, since being brought under a bunker capitalist regime in 1989, perhaps no longer really qualifies. Significantly, Egypt and Tunisia are the only two countries in the region whose banking systems were viewed by international business analysts as less "open" in 2000 than in 1996 (O'Driscoll et al. 2000), as their political regimes struggled over reforms. In Egypt and Tunisia stock markets are developing but they remain heavily influenced by the banks and public sector authorities. In Tunisia the central bank's annual report for 1996 reported, for instance, that "the banking system holds more than two-thirds of stock exchange capitalization and over 90 percent of the securities listed on the exchange." The report also noted that "the active role played by the banks" bid up stock prices through the first quarter of 1995 but could not sustain them. In Egypt the dramatic escalation of share values on the Cairo exchange in 1997 resulted primarily from purchases of those shares by the government, mainly through the four public sector banks.

Business lobbies in Egypt and Tunisia do not have independent financial resources. They rely on crony capitalist networks close to their respective political leaders and, to some extent, upon aid from external parties. The United States government, for example, has fostered the creation and/or sustained the operations of several economic policy think-tanks and business associations in Egypt, including the American–Egyptian Chamber of Commerce and the Egyptian Center for Economic Studies. Just as the United States wishes to promote the Washington Consensus in developing countries, so some of these countries with large public sectors wish to project themselves as liberalizing in order to attract foreign capital. Business lobbies in these settings lack autonomy because they have few independent resources and depend largely upon their connections with influential cronies, political leaders, or foreigners for credit and other favors.

Predominantly private sector and concentrated

This category approximates the classic German syndrome if the banks are privately owned and universal, operate like an oligopoly, and provide most of the finance capital to the real economy. However, a high degree of formal concentration is also compatible with the Anglo-American variant of capitalism if it is supported by an active stock market. Britain has a highly concentrated retail banking system, consisting of four big national banks, but the City also features one of the world's leading stock exchanges and many merchant or investment banks. Formal levels of concentration do not indicate how competitive a banking system really is without taking other variables into account. Some of the less concentrated systems may behave as oligopolies and some of the more concentrated ones may behave competitively. In Table 3.6 concentrated systems are defined as having HHI ratios above 16 percent.

The MENA's relatively concentrated, predominantly privately owned banking systems include some, but not all of the Arab monarchies. The rich Arab oil states probably do not need the capital rationing associated with Germany's industrialization a century ago. Their ruling families, however, seek to retain control over budding capitalists by keeping the banks in reliable hands and allocating capital through them. The Saudis set up specialized banks outside the commercial banking system for this purpose, creating a sort of tribal étatisme in the background. Others, notably Bahrain and Kuwait, may be in a process of transition toward the British model of high capitalized stock markets, although turnover rates remain low (Table 3.5). Like Britain, Bahrain has a relatively small number of onshore commercial banks, and its stock market engages other GCC as well as Bahraini companies. In East Asia a more developed "British" illustration would be Singapore.

The most striking illustration of the German model in the Arab world is the Moroccan system, consisting of one relatively large bank about to be privatized and six others that collectively dominate the market (HHI = 17.8 percent, 1997). The Casablanca Stock Exchange is almost as dominated by the commercial banks as is its sister in Tunis. The German model of universal banking had been assimilated by earlier generations of French capitalists who colonized Morocco, and decolonization left the system relatively intact when the monarchy acquired control in 1980 of the Omnium Nord-Africain (ONA), the colonialists' principal industrial conglomerate. The ONA subsequently bought controlling shares of Morocco's best performing bank and minority holdings in some of the others before Morocco embarked in 1991 on financial liberalization and the easing of various credit constraints. In Morocco the commercial banking oligopoly articulates the structural power of private capital but the king reserves enough of it to keep discipline from within.

Other monarchies may be employing similar strategies. Jordan's banking system is almost as concentrated (HHI = 16.5 percent, 1996) as Morocco's. Its two largest commercial banks command about 50 percent of the total deposits. Jordan's stock market has recently been organized to assure greater transparency, but the country is small and capital seems highly concentrated, like Morocco's, in palace circles. In addition to anecdotal evidence, high spreads between the interest banks receive from borrowers and the rates they pay their depositors suggest oligopolistic behavior characteristic of the German model. The major banks do not appear, however, to be linked to conglomerates or holding companies, as they are in Morocco.

The Moroccan variation lends itself to family domination with collusive bankers expected to keep the family business secrets. Paradoxically, in the rich countries, where oil rents have been partially distributed among merchant families, control of a banking system may have less strategic significance than in poorer countries, such as Morocco and Jordan. Kuwait is an obvious example of competitive markets and competitive politics as families compete for influence in commercial banking, on the Kuwait Stock Exchange, and in parliament. In terms of a formal ratio, Kuwaiti commercial banking is slightly more concentrated (HHI = 18.9 percent, 1997) than Jordan's, but its real behavior is much more competitive.

Predominantly private and relatively deconcentrated

The World Bank and other mainstream economists view this "American" structure of commercial banking as optimal for credit allocation because it connotes competitive financial markets. Saudi Arabia, rich in capital like America, appears to be its best exemplar in the region. Its commercial banking system looks similar to Kuwait's, but its formal concentration ratio is lower (HHI = 13 percent, 1997), suggesting a greater potential for competition. Saudi Arabia has ten banks, including a very profitable Islamic one, which is also the world's largest of this type of enterprise and the fourth largest of the kingdom's commercial banks. The largest Saudi bank had only 23 percent of deposits in 1997, and the top four held 60 percent. Except for the smallest of the ten, all appeared healthy and profitable, but information on their spreads is not available. Saudi Arabia's financial system in reality, however, is not fully open to competition. For at least a decade two major conglomerates of Islamic banks have attempted without success to establish commercial banks in Saudi Arabia. Each of them is Saudi-owned, one by a son of the late King Faisal and the other by a self-made businessman. Saudi Arabia's stock market is also thin, despite its relatively high capitalization. Moreover, five specialized state lending agencies still offer concessionary lending for most kinds of private sector business activity, and their outstanding loans in 1998 were about 31 percent of GDP, or almost as much as those of the commercial banks to the private sector (SAMA 1999: 46, 83).

Despite the structural power of capital evident in the commercial banking system, Saudi politics are much less open than Kuwait's, Morocco's, or Jordan's. One reason why civil society in Saudi Arabia has yet to emerge strongly from this material base is that much of that base remains under the direct or indirect influence of the Saudi ruling family and its Najdi allies. The Saudi family, moreover, is far larger than its royal counterparts elsewhere and exerts much more direct control. Nevertheless, the existence of a substantial material base upon which civil society ultimately could draw suggests some potential for political as well as economic liberalization in the future.

Until the 1980s Turkish capitalism seemed largely inspired by the German model, yet its commercial banking system also retained a significant public sector. Turkey's structural adjustment loan for the financial sector was not fully disbursed in 1988 because the government could not carry out certain commitments concerning the reform of Ziraat Bankası, the public sector agricultural bank that holds a quarter of Turkey's commercial bank deposits. Ziraat is also the government's principal patronage vehicle for rallying votes from the countryside. In 2000 Turkey was receiving yet another structural adjustment loan in return for a commitment to reform the bank (*MEED* June 2, 2000: 18). Turkey's commercial banking system features a core of dynamic private sector banks linked to major industrial conglomerates, but it has become considerably less concentrated (HHI = 7.5 percent, 1999) than Morocco's. Despite its historic ties to the German model (Henry 1996: 100–106), Turkey seems to be moving toward the diversified Anglo-American model, as the high turnover rate as well as the capitalization of its stock market shown in Table 3.5 suggests. It is by far the most active market in the MENA and offers an alternative to finance capital dominated by a small number of holding companies and commercial banks. Whether through its business conglomerates represented in the Turkish Industrialists' and Businessmen's Association (TÜSİAD) or through impersonal market forces, private capital seems to have acquired some structural power. TÜSİAD has a much greater voice in economic policies than the Egyptian Businessmen's Association, for instance.

Finally, the least concentrated and apparently most freewheeling banking system in the region is Lebanon's. Despite increases in its concentration ratio since the mid-1980s, none of the eighty banks holds more than 13 percent of the market and the top four had less than one-third (HHI = 6.5 percent, *c.* 1998). Even so, spreads between the going rates for loans and deposits are relatively high, suggesting oligopolistic "cooperation" among this multiplicity of banks. Originally converted during the postwar boom from French- to American-style capitalism, the banking system was becoming more concentrated under the impact of Lebanon's billionaire prime minister, Rafiq Hariri. Coupled with lucrative government borrowing, Hariri's private conglomerate was acquiring control over much of the banking system and the real economy until Lebanon's new president accepted his resignation from office in 1998. The press and judiciary then sniped so much at Hariri's associates inside and outside the government that the threat posed in the mid-1990s to Lebanon's deconcentrated, relatively autonomous system seems to have passed, despite the victory of Hariri's lists in the September 2000 parliamentary elections.

Structural power of capital – summary

From this brief inspection of the MENA's stock markets and commercial banking systems it is possible to come to some preliminary conclusions about the potential of business interests to influence government policies and encourage greater accountability. The greater the structural power of capital, the greater the possibilities that the business community can engage in effective collective action, articulating various sectoral interests, and the greater, too, the resulting developmental capacities of the state. Local capital both reinforces and constrains these capacities. It strengthens them by offering a tax base, information, and economic opportunities, but constrains state choices by presenting a variety of interests to be satisfied.

There will be structural power under any form of real capitalism, whether "Anglo-American," "German," or "French." The "German" and "French" models are currently more prevalent, although the former seems confined to monarchies in which patrimonial controls underlie nascent financial and industrial cartels. The banking system is a major asset for these regimes as long as insiders hold the levers of financial power, for they then extend the regime's reach and patronage networks into the private sector. Because the system rests on oligopoly, however, it is inherently unstable. If opened to international capital, the newcomers could undermine it, or insiders could become more independent and use their financial power to make the regime more accountable.

The "French" model operates under a different set of constraints stemming from the region's legacy of state capitalism, which curtailed commercial banking and drastically limited private capital or eliminated it altogether. Regimes with big public sector banks, including all of the praetorian republics, go through the motions of structural adjustment, but prevent the rise of autonomous private sectors in order to keep control of civil society so as to preserve their own patronage networks. The policy outcomes safeguard the regime at the expense of long-term development.

The structural power of capital is still limited in the region. Only Turkey and possibly Kuwait stand out as financial environments in which private capital enjoys relative autonomy and can support various articulations of business demands. Israel might consolidate a "German" orientation once its banks are privatized or even move toward the Anglo-American model like Turkey. Saudi Arabia's healthy and apparently competitive commercial banking system suggests that it, too, might support a limited articulation of business interests, albeit within a less liberal political framework.

Challenges of globalization

The countries that face the greatest problems of adapting to globalization are those with minimal capacity, small private sectors, and big state banking systems. Civil society is also weakest in these countries, further limiting the potential for effective responses to globalization. Algeria, Iraq, Libya, Sudan, Syria, and Yemen, all praetorian republics ruled from bunkers by political military elites, display the lowest levels of capitalist development. They are also the countries with the largest informal economies. Many of the most dynamic elements of their civil societies have emigrated. While capital flight and labor migration are not confined to these countries, they are its most prominent exemplars. Algerian workers, for example, have a longer history and a more substantial presence in France do than their Moroccan or Tunisian counterparts. Private Algerian capital stays in France, not Algeria, and the real development of the private sector in Algeria, if it is to occur, will depend upon its return. Algeria does have capitalist traditions but they are French, and its painful adjustments to the new world order will be along "French" lines like Egypt's and Tunisia's. Syria, too, enjoys close historic ties with France, while Lebanon, though no longer quite French, serves as a proxy for the old metropole, a haven for private Syrian capital and outlet for a million Syrian guest workers (in addition to the army). But whether these special ties to the former colonial power pave the way to broader globalization, or lock these countries into relations of bilateral dependency, remains to be seen.

Each variety of capitalism threatens the incumbent regimes, but the Anglo-American variety of capitalism being promoted by international financial institutions appears to be the most threatening one. It offers more ready access to foreign capital than do the French or German models, but at the cost of giving up decisive control over the private sector. Turkey has come closest to taking these risks just as it has benefited the most from influxes of foreign portfolio capital as well as other forms of private investment. Lebanon, by contrast, is a parody of the Anglo-American model; until recently, at least, its capital structures were becoming concentrated into those of a banana republic. Ironically the most effective guarantor of the Anglo-American model in the region may be Islamic banks and businesses, whose capacity to mediate with global capital and markets may empower some countries successfully to engage in globalization, a subject to be taken up in chapter 6.

On the domestic front most of the regimes seem to have effectively contained their nascent capitalist classes. Either they tie them into public sector or political networks, as in Egypt, the Palestinian Authority, or Tunisia, where the state still dominates credit allocation, or they give them a semblance of autonomy in conglomerates directly or indirectly under patrimonial control, as in Morocco. There may be some leakage from the monarchial oligopoly in Saudi Arabia, whether to dissidents, such as one of the Bin Laden family, or to new combinations of law-abiding capitalists financed by the relatively competitive banking system.

For most of the MENA the major structural challenges to incumbent regimes lie outside, not inside the respective countries. The globalization of capital has major implications for every political economy in the region, including those traditionally financed by oil rents. Oil revenues are not expected to return to the levels of the boom years, so Gulf states with their burgeoning populations will continue to be strapped for funds for current expenditures and long-term investment. Every country needs either to attract substantial foreign private capital or to incur potentially destabilizing increases of either domestic debt or unemployment. Globalization also works the other way; a major stimulus to Tunisia's financial reform, for example, was the fear of capital flight. Despite controls, it is increasingly difficult to trap capital in any of the MENA states. Estimates of Arab capital invested abroad range from $350 billion to $670 billion, with $500 billion being a commonly accepted figure (World Bank 1995: 6; Al-Hindi 1998).

To attract more of this capital, governments in the region are sprucing up their stock exchanges. Yet the banks, which tend to dominate local stock markets, may resist greater transparency; so also may their political authorities, whose patronage networks would be exposed. Economic and political information do not lend themselves to easy segmentation in MENA political economies. In the smaller states, especially, political and economic elites may be too intermixed for them to accept the transparency of open markets. Yet the regimes face pressures to open up in order to attract more foreign investment.

If the MENA were to gain a fair share of the expanding pie of global capital, the new investments would probably reinforce local capitalists and other elements of civil society more than they would help to sustain their incumbent, information-shy regimes. It is true that the "German" model has been employed in defense of patrimonial rule in Morocco, and even cruder state oligopolies service political networks supporting other MENA regimes. Accelerated global flows of capital, however, would tend to undermine any oligopoly's control of capital markets. If activated sufficiently to attract significant foreign portfolio investment, stock markets would become alternative sources of financing for local capitalists, whom local oligopolists would no longer be able entirely to exclude. As the capital pie expanded, governments would become less able to control its allocation either directly through public sector banks or indirectly through crony capitalist conglomerates. Turkey, the region's bellwether, best illustrates this transition toward more competitive capital markets.

Such transitions, however, are not inevitable. The prospect of attracting more foreign capital will challenge regimes to devise new strategies and frameworks for balancing or playing off local and international capital. The predominantly public sector commercial banking structures of the region's statist and post-statist economies are under siege, as credit rating agencies and international financial institutions call on their governments to clean up their public sector bank portfolios and then privatize them. But besieged regimes will delay, privatize in ways that keep state managements intact, and try through the banks and parastatal investment funds to retain control of stock markets. Rather than develop more transparency, they are likely to engage in rhetoric of economic and political liberalization while trying to coopt foreign as well as local capitalists into their patronage networks. If international portfolio managers bought into Thailand's corrupt and opaque financial markets, then why not into selected MENA countries?

In sum, global capital markets have structural power to which regimes are presently fine-tuning their responses because they need better access to these markets. Most of the regimes hesitate, however, to open themselves to the indiscriminate workings of Anglo-American capitalism and its requirements for timely information and accountability. Yet the hesitations may have severe opportunity costs, by delaying the capital investments and associated economic growth needed to attack the region's unemployment problems and to contain its rising social movements. Moreover, the net effect of global capital's penetration of MENA political economies may well be to tilt domestic power balances more in the direction of civil societies and away from states.

Suggestions for further reading

Ayubi (1995) and Snider (1996) present interesting insights into the political capacities of countries that are of growing concern of the World Bank (1997). Haggard and Kaufman (1992, 1995), Linz and Steppan (1996), and Przeworski (1991) are part of a considerable literature that virtually omits the MENA in discussions of economic adjustment and transitions to democracy. However, Haggard et al. (1993), Leys (1996), Loriaux (1997), Maxfield and Schneider (1997), and Zysman (1983) offer insights into political and economic development in a variety of capitalist contexts.

4   Bunker states

The critical political weakness of the praetorian republics ruled physically or metaphorically from bunkers is that their states have little if any autonomy from traditional social forces that managed, typically during the turbulent nationalist phase that followed the end of colonial rule, to seize control of those states. Algeria's "deciders," for example, represent political clans anchored in both society and state institutions. Saddam Hussein of Iraq, Muammar Qaddafi of Libya, and Ali Abdullah Salah of Yemen rule their countries through military/security/party structures that are in turn controlled by alliances of these leaders' families and tribes. Although Saddam Hussein had relied heavily on tribes and tribal alliances to rule Iraq prior to 1991, since that time the weakening of the state apparatus has resulted in a dramatic increase in tribal power and Saddam's reliance upon it (Glain 2000; Jabar 2000). The Alawi sect, of which Syrian President Hafez al-Asad was a member, has come to control virtually all important state structures in Syria, although other Alawis oppose the regime now led by Hafez's son Bashar (Perthes 1997: 181–184). In the Sudan tribal alliances lurk behind General Omar Bashir's military organization and Hassan Turabi's National Islamic Front, reorganized in 2000 as an opposition party, the Popular National Congress.

In each of these cases except Algeria, the social forces that have penetrated and come to control these states are tribal or religious minorities, typically ones despised by much of the remainder of the population. Their rule is, therefore, seen by much if not most of the population as being fundamentally illegitimate and intended to serve the interests of that social force, rather than the country as a whole. In these circumstances, coercion is necessarily the primary and in some cases, such as that of Iraq or in much of Sudan, virtually the only means by which government can ensure the public's compliance. In Algeria 132 years of colonialism pulverized the social forces, but the national liberation struggle fostered new clans based on friends and cousins.

Bunker praetorian states are in a potential state of war with the societies they rule. These states dare not permit the freedom of information or autonomy of economic action necessary for globally competitive economic growth. Outside the bunkers their civil societies and business entrepreneurs, to the extent they ever existed, have been deactivated, silenced, forced into exile, or eradicated. Just as these states cannot adopt and then implement consistent and effective policies for economic growth, so are their societies too weak to respond quickly and dramatically to opportunities that policy changes, were they to occur, might offer. It is conceivable, however, that bunker states could evolve into a less virulent form of praetorian republic, were the political elite through accommodation or some other means to come to represent a broader coalition of social forces. In this event, they would begin to take on the characteristics of the praetorian republics discussed in chapter 5.

The six bunker states – Algeria, Iraq, Libya, Sudan, Syria, and Yemen – display the least institutional capacity of any of the MENA states to manage their economies. These countries have the largest informal economies, reflected in the relatively high proportions of their money supply which escape their respective banking systems. Tax revenues outside the petroleum sector are low, and some of those revenues are being siphoned off to ruling factions. Official import monopolies largely escape the official controls of economic decision-makers or planners. The technocrats of these regimes have little opportunity to make or even influence policy, as the ruling clans typically filter and distort economic information. No significant economic establishment, public or private, eludes the predatory rulers, although some firms, notably in the petroleum and military industrial sectors, enjoy special protection. Private entrepreneurs may accumulate capital, but only so long as they enjoy the special favor of those who control the military or security services. Indeed, a major difference between bunker state capitalism and its more sophisticated, "French" variant is that the latter's favored entrepreneurs can buy more durable protection.

While indices of domestic violence and disorder mark these MENA countries off from the others, so also do their underlying financial structures. These are less contingent than episodes of civil violence, since they reflect underlying political economies that are difficult to change. Financial data provide a clue to distinguish these bunker states from the rest of the MENA. Specifically, they fall in the bottom left quadrant of Figure 4.1, low with respect to both commercial bank credit allocated to the private sector (as a proportion of GDP) and "contract-intensive money" (CIM as a proportion of the money supply, M2).

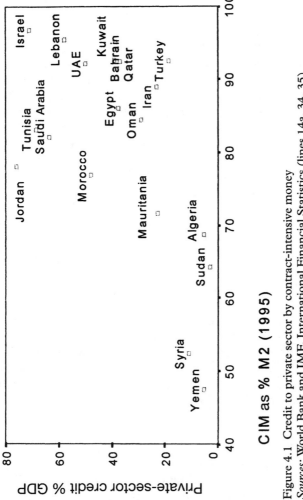

Figure 4.1 Credit to private sector by contract-intensive money
Sources: World Bank and IMF, International Financial Statistics (lines 14a, 34, 35)

CIM, discussed in chapter 3 as a proxy for property rights and institutional credibility, is the proportion of money held inside the banking system, rather than outside it, in the form of currency. As seen in Figure 4.1, the low-CIM countries also have the least viable private sectors underpinning their respective civil societies. Without the shock absorbers of effective political or civic associations, much less the support of private capital, domestic or foreign, adjustment is bound to be rough and the dialectics of globalization less amenable to resolution.

The bunker regimes, however, are under pressure because their dependence, direct or indirect, on oil revenues has rendered them vulnerable and is obliging them to change their ways in order to attract additional external sources of revenue. Yet economic reform is bound to be more painful in the bunker states than in countries already enjoying more integration with the global economy and its financial markets. The bunker states still monopolize oil rents, but any tacit "contract" offering welfare and security in exchange for allegiance has been revised. Their menu of state services has necessarily diminished with the decline in oil revenues, at least on a per capita basis. Their way of keeping up any tacit contract is to increase the value of security – "empowering" themselves by tolerating a small amount of insecurity.

Algeria is the most vivid and bloody illustration of how bunkered elites manipulate economic policy for political ends. Algeria in some respects adjusted far more quickly in the late 1990s than did Egypt or other star pupils of the IMF. The mindless massacres of tens of thousands of civilians enabled the regime to carry out draconian economic policies. The economy has undergone structural change while a hard core of illegitimate military rulers has retained power on the pretext of widespread insecurity. Raw struggles of power between the ruling factions as well as between them and Islamist guerrilla forces diverted attention from the economic policies being implemented with advice from the IMF. Economic policy-makers have enjoyed a relative autonomy of sorts, but virtually no resources in civil society with which to implement economic reforms.

Algeria's bunker

Algeria is, to be sure, an exceptional case, but its very exaggeration sheds greater light on many of the problems faced by other MENA states. It endured the region's most protracted and destructive colonialism. Not only were its indigenous elites suppressed or hopelessly compromised by the French authorities of colonial Algeria; its culture was virtually destroyed. Its own "French" politicians could not negotiate their country's emancipation as did Lebanon's and Syria's urban families, and Tunisia's more broadly based national movement; guerrilla forces overran Algerian civil society. Far from refashioning associational life as in neighboring Tunisia, Algeria's protracted struggle for independence marginalized its small educated elite and destroyed most fledgling organizations, even the Front of National Liberation (whose principal political founder inside Algeria was strangled to death). Deprived not only of its intellectuals but of its high culture as well, Algeria's civil society was among the weakest and most fragmented in the Arab world. Much of it is still located in France and Switzerland, rather than Algeria.

Independent Algeria was militarized from the start, unlike other MENA countries that underwent military coups. The general staff of the external Army of National Liberation seized power in 1962 and placed a prestigious figurehead, Ahmed Ben Bella, in the presidency. When he in turn tried to encourage independent power centers to bring the army under control, Colonel Houari Boumédienne removed him from power. Boumédienne tried to develop political institutions, but he died suddenly in 1978 before his revised blueprint for the Front of National Liberation and various ancillary bodies could be acted upon. The army command, not the civilian leadership, selected his successor, Chadli Benjedid, more or less on the basis of seniority. Chadli's peers then prevented him from consolidating power like his predecessor. As long as the Algerian economy appeared to prosper, the colonels – French-trained professionals as well as former guerrilla commanders – promoted themselves to generals and derived enough legitimacy from embodying the abstract legacy of the revolution to stay comfortably in power. Indeed, Algeria was not perceived from the outside as having a particularly militaristic regime. It did not ever appear to be in the same league as Nasser's Egypt and Baathist Syria and Iraq. The most visible Algerian military leaders were homegrown guerrilla politicians, and their governments were largely composed of civilians. Colonel Boumédienne appeared to be managing a mildly authoritarian administrative state. Military expenditures amounted on average to barely 3 percent of GDP, quite low compared with other bunker regimes or Egypt, Jordan, or Israel. "Algeria today is governed by a complex network of interactive structures that provide institutional stability, direction, and predictability to the political system," a well-informed American academic wrote in the mid-1980s (Entelis 1986: 168). Central government budgets continue to convey this impression: in 1993 the military's share was lower in Algeria than anywhere else but Tunisia and, despite civil war, was barely catching up with Morocco's by 1997. Figure 4.2 presents the available data.

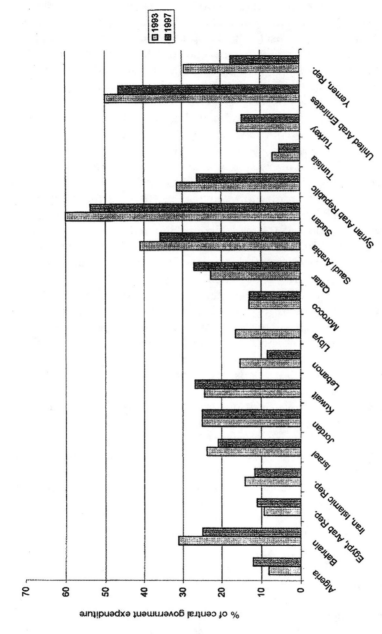

Figure 4.2 Military spending as percentage of central government expenditure, 1993 and 1997
Note: Data on Qatar and Syria are for 1996
Source: World Bank, World Development Indicators 2000 on CD-ROM

From the inside, however, narratives of economic decision-makers record a very different perception of Algeria's system. Two such accounts present the same picture from opposing viewpoints and different positions in the hierarchy. Belaid Abdesselam was Boumédienne's chief architect and manager of the Algerian economy from 1970 to 1977. Ghazi Hidouci was a professional economic planner until 1984, when he was called to head the Department of Financial and Economic Affairs in the presidency. He then served as minister of the economy in Mouloud Hamrouche's government from 1989 to 1991. A third narrative, that of Abdelhamid Brahimi, is politically less informative but offers evidence of the massive corruption implied by the first two accounts. Brahimi was appointed planning minister in 1979, after Chadli Benjedid became president, and he served as prime minister from 1984 to 1988. He publicly declared in March 1990 that corrupt officials and intermediaries had pocketed some $26 billion, the equivalent of Algeria's external debt at the time, in commissions and inflated invoices during the Boumédienne years (Brahimi 1991: 152–155). The timing of his revelation diverted attention to corruption and helped to undermine Ghazi Hidouci's efforts to attack its roots with market reforms.

Belaid Abdesselam views Algeria's industrial technocracy from the summit during the golden Boumédienne years. Like his counterpart planners in Tunisia, Libya, and Senegal (Belkhodja 1998: 78) he was inspired by the French economist Destanne de Bernis' vision of "industrializing industry" and gained Boumédienne's enthusiastic approval. One of a small number of Algerian university students who joined the maquis in 1956, he had political as well as scholastic credentials but had studied medicine, not economics. He oversaw the accumulation of Algeria's oil revenues and their reinvestment in natural gas liquification plants, a step intended to accumulate more export revenues, and in a heavy industrial base, including iron and steel. The vision of an industrialized Algeria was Boumédienne's legitimating myth, much like the Aswan High Dam for Gamal Abdel Nasser. Consequently Abdesselam enjoyed the president's protection.

From his political memoirs (Bennoune and El-Kenz 1990), however, it is clear that Abdesselam's authority was seriously constricted by contending military clans and their business extensions – a set of veritable "mafiosi" in his words. He could sometimes cross one of them, with support from the president, but he dared not provoke them collectively against him. Abdesselam's own following consisted of industrial technocrats, not the regime's core military players. The "turf battles" had a peculiarly Algerian flavor, but they may ring a familiar bell with Syrian or Iraqi insiders. Abdesselam recalls the day, for instance, when the Gendarmerie, backed up by special military units, surrounded the oil fields of Hassi Messaoud. Everybody working in the fields – most of them just wearing shorts in the hot desert sun – was asked for identity papers. Many, including oil executives from Europe inspecting their field operations, were carted off to a police station and held for up to 24 hours or more because they had left their passports back at camp. When Abdesselam protested against this arbitrary and economically destructive police round-up, Bencherif, the minister of the interior and head of the Gendarmerie, primly responded that nobody, not even in the industrial sector, is above the law. Then Abdesselam understood. A few days earlier some crony of an important political personality had asked a European enterprise working with Algeria's national oil company, Sonatrach, whether he could become the firm's representative in Algeria. The Europeans responded that they were agreeable, as long as Sonatrach also agreed. When Sonatrach did not agree, however, the company did not feel obligated to hire him. Abdesselam suddenly understood that Bencherif was teaching the European companies a lesson on that hot day in the oil fields. Sonatrach could not protect them. They had to cut other power centers in on any deals (Bennoune and El-Kenz 1990: II, 43–44). Abdesselam concludes of his experiences as minister of industry and energy,

One is almost up against a system penetrated by a Mafia type of incrustation! When one is responsible for a sector like industry, which engages enormous interests, evidently it arouses much envy and many people want to profit. I have told you how one can get the profits . . . First you have the intermediaries, the compradores who want mandates from large foreign companies to get their percentage on every contract. Then there also has to be complicity within the system. These individuals have to show that they have enough influence within the power structure to influence a deal. All of which necessitates support within the system. If you are opposed to such things and wish business to work normally, you become an adversary. Either you go along with them and get some needed peace or you work according to certain rules and counter certain people's appetites. Then you become an enemy to be shot down. (II, 200–201)

Ghazi Hidouci presents a complementary snapshot of economic decision-making from below during the halcyon years of great industrial projects. Entering the planning ministry as a junior economist at about the time Boumédienne seized power, Hidouci had a backstage view of economic policy-making in Algeria. In theory his ministry was the brain behind Boumédienne's centralized economy. In practice it sat on the margins, consulted about the budgets of the economic ministries but never empowered to engage in real central planning, much less to make other ministries implement a national plan. Inside the planning ministry the macroeconomic planners usually generated three data sets, a relatively prudent one for the president, an "approximately sincere" one for internal usage, and a "highly manipulated" set for dealings with the other ministries (Hidouci 1995: 36). During the 1970s the planning minister, Abdallah Khodja, contested the economic viability of many of Abdesselam's projects. Once the oil revenues surged in 1974, Abdesselam usually had his way, but he symptomatically regarded criticism as a sign that Khodja had the support of powerful cliques of officers and their compradores, or finally of Boumédienne himself (Bennoune and El-Kenz 1990: II, 258). Hidouci, loyal to his minister, describes the clandestine operations of the planners to obtain information about the industrial enterprises and other matters.

In the often empty corridors of the Treasury and Tax [departments of the Ministry of Finance] we developed the habit during these dark years of digging up missing pieces of information on the spot, where the poorly paid, often demoralized bureau chiefs, indifferent to the incongruity of displaying the secrets of prebendal administration, opened up everything to us. It was nevertheless more difficult to penetrate the ministerial cabinets . . . (Hidouci 1995: 39)

Subsequently Hidouci gained access to the inner workings of economic policy-making at the highest levels. He presents a remarkable picture of the climate of mutual suspicion pervading the corridors of power in the mid-1980s. Much of the relevant information was filtered and manipulated; for instance, the personnel files of public sector managers were secrets in the hands of competing security agencies. Part of Hidouci's job was to gather information that could be used against public sector officials, and he had latitude to build his own channels through the banks and enterprises acquired through his years in the planning ministry. Since he did not have access to the security files, he learned "less about interest networks and people than about the administration of things" (Hidouci 1995: 118). Through his own network of former planners and other reform-minded individuals in strategic places, however, he acquired more reliable economic data than that in official reports, which he quickly learned to file without reading (Hidouci 1995: 117).

Algeria's centralized planning was a myth. The reality, once Boumédienne consolidated power, was a centralized system for distributing the rents and prebends, controlled by the presidency and managed by close collaborators in the Ministry of Finance, not Planning. The Ministry of Finance was originally headed by military commanders close to the president. They directly controlled the credit and allocated the grants and subsidies, with little need for administration, much less a banking system. The minister and his personal cabinet made the decisions and left the rest of the ministry in a "shocking state of disrepair" (Hidouci 1995: 39). The French settler assets, virtually the entire modern economy, were up for grabs when almost a million settlers departed "on vacation" before July 5, 1962 – Algerian Independence Day – never to return. Boumédienne brought political order to the anarchic appropriations of the Ben Bella years. After his 1965 coup he distributed the loot so as to pacify the numerous guerrilla commanders and their followers, while he concentrated political power in the hands of his victorious "Oujda clan" (named after the Moroccan city near the Algerian border where Boumédienne had assembled the beginnings of an external army of national liberation before moving to Tunisia in 1958). Once the resources of the European economy were depleted, oil revenues took up the slack. Driven by political considerations, allocations of property, rents, markets, and import licenses had little or no economic rationale. By 1972 Boumédienne had consolidated control over the allocations and also redistributed some of the patronage to the provinces where the prefects enjoyed similar powers independent of the Ministry of Planning and other central ministries.

Abdallah Khodja, denounced as a rightist by Abdesselam (Bennoune and El-Kenz 1990: II, 221), waged a rearguard action until 1974 in favor of a more critical evaluation of industrial projects and greater investment in agriculture. Projects were occasionally stopped or at least delayed, despite pressures from the foreign beneficiaries of the turnkey projects as well as the Ministry of Industry and Energy. Hidouci reports a series of meetings in early 1974 chaired by Boumédienne himself to air the differences between the planners and the industrial technocrats (Hidouci 1995: 65–66). But after a few months oil prices again doubled, terminating any critical economic discourse. "The planners picked up their tools, for nobody was disposed any longer to talk about necessity and economic constraints, and everyone was now supporting adventurism and indebtedness. Expenditure is immediate; management deferred" (Hidouci 1995: 67). Hidouci is "convinced that Boumédienne long believed that progress and modernity could simply be bought from those who had it and that he had no need for entrepreneurs in local markets nor of economic regulation" (Hidouci 1995: 55).

Oil revenues conveniently supplemented the proceeds of the modern economy abandoned by the settlers, rendering economics, in the sense of allocating scarce resources, superfluous for Algeria's political leaders. Algeria, nevertheless, was not a classic rentier state like those of the Gulf Cooperation Council. Until 1972 substantial private sectors of "traditional" Algerian agriculture, wholesale commerce, transport, and small-scale industry survived on the peripheries of the centrally allocated modern sector. "In contrast to the deserts of the Persian Gulf before petroleum, the least developed, where everything was a new creation, in Algeria one destroyed an economy and a preexisting equilibrium to promote a new myth" (Hidouci 1995: 43). The Algerians could then exaggerate their vision of "industrializing industries" well beyond those of other Promethien modernizers such as Bourguiba or Nasser because their oil revenues exceeded the capital available for investment in all but the wealthiest Gulf oil states.

A related impact of Boumédienne's industrial, agrarian, and cultural revolutions launched in 1972 was to drive much of the private sector underground or across the Mediterranean (Hidouci 1995: 73). Figure 4.3 shows Algeria's contract-intensive money ratio increasing in the early Boumédienne years, when he stabilized the political economy, but then contracting in the early 1970s and again in 1979–1980, after Boumédienne's death. Further withdrawals from the banking system occurred in the unstable mid-1980s, when the government was printing money to compensate for the decline in oil revenues. Relative stabilization in the 1990s seems to have been more the result of drastic cuts in the money supply than a sign of public confidence in Algeria's financial institutions. CIM ratios are still low compared with most MENA countries.

Chadli Benjadid, Boumédienne's successor, encouraged economic discourse and criticism of Algeria's industrial experience by appointing Abdelhamid Brahimi to be his planning minister. Boumédienne had himself experienced some doubts about industrializing industry and divided up Abdesselam's ministry, demoting him in 1977 to take charge of the light industries that were supposed to have arisen in the wake of Algeria's heavy industry. Brahimi subsequently carved up Abdesselam's old empire, including Sonatrach, into smaller enterprises. Extracting evidence from the planning ministry, he attacked and discredited the entire experience of industrializing industries. But after Abdesselam and his technocrats were purged, economic analysis had no further place in Algerian policy-making. Hidouci, who remained in the planning ministry until 1984, claims that by this time it did little more than issue national accounts statistics – "to illustrate official speeches about growth in this unconstrained period" – and compile routine public investment programs (Hidouci 1995: 85). Chadli's slogan, "For a Better Life," generated ever more rents from import monopolies tied to military clans – until the oil revenues sharply plunged in the mid-1980s.

Chadli's early reform efforts to cut up the state enterprises and give them greater autonomy amounted to little more than softening them up

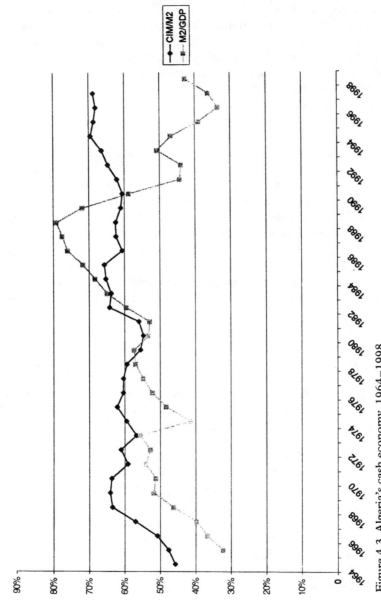

Figure 4.3 Algeria's cash economy, 1964–1998
Source: World Bank, World Development Indicators 2000 on CD-ROM

for the rent-seekers – "assassinating industry," as one purged technocrat exclaimed at an international conference in 1990. The high military command dramatically expanded in numbers and in rank – by 1998 Algeria counted 140 generals – and Chadli could never be more than their front man. Consequently Abdelhamid Brahimi, whom he appointed prime minister in 1983, could not become Algeria's Gorbachev despite his impressive academic and military credentials (a doctorate from Ohio State University as well as previous service as a guerrilla with Chadli inside Algeria). Even when they agreed, neither the president nor the prime minister took decisive action in the face of collapsing oil revenues. Instead of rescheduling the debt, they resorted to more expensive short-term loans in the hope that oil prices would increase. The scarcity of foreign exchange led to widespread shortages of basic consumer items. It also had the interesting effect of extending the state's patronage networks, as a growing group of black marketeers thrived under the protection of the military mafiosi. Algerian dinars circulating outside the banking system jumped in 1986 from 34 to almost 40 percent of the money supply, and foreign exchange cost about four times more on the black market than at the official rate. "Trabendo" (contraband) commerce, already part of Chadli's "Good Life" in the early 1980s, boomed in the late 1980s, further widening the gap between the official and unofficial foreign exchange rates. It would double again – to a factor of 8 and even 9 – after the October 1988 riots finally shook the regime's bunkers.

By sending in the tanks to quell demonstrations in 1988, killing over 600 people in several cities (Hidouci 1995: 162), the army lost any remaining shreds of revolutionary legitimacy and discredited the single-party regime. The civilian edifice, so carefully codified in the 1976 National Charter and "enriched" in the 1986 Charter, was now beyond repair. Until 1988 the real leaders – les décideurs, or "deciders," as Algerians call them – remained faceless, extorting favors from officials much as they had constrained Abdesselam in happier years. Military rule in Algeria, however, was relatively benign. The very fact that a few urban riots shocked the generals into major constitutional and economic reform distinguishes them from the military rulers of Syria (who destroyed a major city in 1982) or Iraq. But the riots and their sequels brought them progressively out of the barracks and into the public eye. From 1989 to 1999 they attempted and failed three times to create new civilian cover for themselves. First, after Chadli introduced a new multi-party constitution, Mouloud Hamrouche led a government from 1989 to 1991 committed to democratic political reforms and economic liberalization. Then, after the military "deciders" made Chadli resign in order to stop the Islamists from winning the legislative elections of 1991–1992, they brought Mohammed Boudiaf back from exile in Morocco.

Boudiaf had quit Algerian politics in 1963 but, as one of the "historic" founders of the FLN, was perceived as a useful figurehead. When he became too popular, assailing corruption, he was assassinated. Finally, with one of their own, retired General Liamine Zeroual, the deciders engineered presidential and parliamentary elections. But in 1998, after barely three years, they obliged their president to resign when he and a possible successor, another retired general, Mohammed Bechtine, appeared to be becoming too independent. New presidential elections in 1999, had they been free, might have preserved at least a fig leaf of legitimacy, but six of the seven contenders withdrew at the last moment in a remarkable display of consensus that the elections were being rigged (*Jeune Afrique* no. 1997, April 20–26, 1999). The winner, Abdelaziz Bouteflika, had served as Algeria's foreign minister from 1963 to 1979 after being a charter member of the Oujda clan. He recovered no more legitimacy than the officers who had brought him out of retirement, and the vote rigging reinforced doubts about the earlier elections of the incumbent parliament and regional assemblies (*El Watan* May 24, 1999). Yet without a cover of legitimate government the "deciders" became more vulnerable to their own internal divisions as their clans openly competed for economic spoils (Addi 1999). And the spoils keep changing with new reforms, destabilizing the clans.

Under Algeria's emergency conditions economic reform was hostage to the officers' hasty efforts to erect political cover. Until 1991, however, reformers still had a chance of extricating Algeria from bunker capitalism without tearing the country apart. The story of its first serious reform effort, while known to Algerian specialists (Entelis and Arone 1992; Corm 1993; Ghillès 1998; Dillman 2000), has not received adequate attention in the political economy literature. Algeria almost succeeded in simultaneously moving to constitutional democracy and a market economy. While its failure illustrates the tenacity of bunker capitalism, it serves also as the rough draft of a dialectics of globalization that may be rewritten elsewhere.

Algerian springtime: reform and democracy (1989–1991)

The reform efforts began by stealth, "putting sand" (Hidouci 1995: 108) into Algeria's dysfunctional administrative engines by offering new sources of information. With Mouloud Hamrouche's transfer from the government to the presidency, however, Hidouci's reform team gained greater leverage. Better informed and weakened by Algeria's deteriorating economic conditions, the president lent them official support in late 1987, less than a year before the October 1988 riots. Parts of the reforms surfaced in seminars and decrees, and the reform team extended its networks across the country beyond the public sector to include "trade union activists, lawyers and judges, the medical profession, private entrepreneurs, and press and culture circles" (Hidouci 1995: 133).

In the reformers' view it was useless to touch up the economy by administrative decentralization and other partial measures, much less control managers by checking on their uses of public equipment – such as automobiles! Selling off parts of the public sector apparently enjoyed some support in 1987 among the top ruling circles of officers and their intermediaries who might benefit (Hidouci 1995: 127), but not among the reform team. Rather, the reformers had a "global institutional and juridical vision" of the necessary changes: to move to "contractual relationships between the administration and the producers of goods and services, including social services, and also to a transparent 'commercializing' of economic transactions" within the public sector (Corm 1993: 13). The virtue of this solution in the late-1980s was its perfect fit with the political liberalization to which the deciders, huddled in the presidential crisis center, had apparently agreed in October 1988 when they called in the Hamrouche team (Hidouci 1995: 161). From the presidency the reformers published and disseminated the *Cahiers* (Hadj-Nacer 1989), five pamphlets giving guidelines for reform, and continued to draft legislation for another year before becoming the official government in 1989; meanwhile a transitional government supervised a constitutional referendum and legalized the components of Algeria's new multi-party system, including the Islamic Front of Salvation (FIS).

The economic reforms were a bold attempt to change the rules governing economic decision-making. Previous efforts under Brahimi to "decentralize" the public sector had not worked because a small number of deciders, including the dreaded Sécurité Militaire (renamed the Département du Renseignement et Sécurité – DRS), kept the real levers of command. Their powerful clans dominated the state monopolies over foreign commerce, domestic credit, and many lucrative domestic markets, as well as the public sector personnel files. Hidouci's solution was to abolish the monopolies, deregulate prices, and establish a framework for each public enterprise, including the banks, to operate as an independent self-supporting firm responsive to market forces. A flexible system of state holding companies was set up in 1988 to replace the supervision of public sector enterprise by parent ministries. Transparency and open markets were intended to curtail the pervasive rent-seeking by eliminating much of the spoils. A gradual devaluation of the dinar was planned to eliminate the gap between official and parallel rates and with it much of the *trabendo* commerce. Foreign direct investment, or Algerians repatriating their capital, was to be encouraged. Algeria, in sum, was to become more openly integrated into the global economy.

The reforms predictably enjoyed little support among public sector officials or labor. The reformers actually attacked Algeria's small private sector for being protected, rather than cultivating its support (Dillman 1997: 171 n. 20). Liberal commentators dismissed the reforms as yet another legalistic exercise (Addi 1991). Despite support from the IMF and the World Bank, the reforms did not receive adequate funding from the conservative French banks because Algeria rejected rescheduling, with the external constraints that it would impose, in favor of an informal "reprofiling" to lighten the servicing of its heavy international debt. In their twenty months in office, however, the reformers did succeed in abolishing the foreign commerce monopolies and establishing a strong central bank to replace the Ministry of Finance's opaque methods of controlling the money supply and credit allocation. Developing a true market economy would inevitably be a slow and painful process. The banks, for instance, could hardly become autonomous agencies overnight when 65 percent of their loans, almost exclusively to public sector companies, were non-performing (Nashashibi 1998: 36); nor could the latter suddenly become operational economic entities in Algeria's tangled, partially deregulated markets. Devaluing the dinar also posed problems. The reformers wished to move decisively to reduce the gap between the official and parallel market rates and shared the IMF's antipathy to inflated official rates. Yet devaluation had to be gradual in order to limit its inflationary impact.

There would appear to be a contradiction between the broad institutional character of the reforms and the narrow political base of those who advocated them. Their only evident support was the president. The parliament, which had been elected when Algeria was still a single-party system, voted through many of the reforms, but it did not represent the country's new political currents. The reformers did achieve some support and understanding among public sector officials, but few of these officials had any practical experience of a market economy. Each public enterprise was to be released from its parent ministry and given its autonomy to operate in partially deregulated markets. But the new "participation funds" established as holding companies to supervise the public enterprises had few staff and little expertise. The annual report of one of them reflected a widespread misunderstanding that they were simply "implementing a new system of economic planning." Obviously it would take many years for new institutions and market-driven behavior to take root in Algeria's vast bureaucracy. Obstacles to change were and remain far greater than in other bunker capitalist regimes, such as Nasser's Egypt. Regimented only for a decade or so (1961–1974), the Egyptians had active memories of a market economy which could facilitate some reform in the 1970s, whereas the Algerians have none.

Yet the Algerian reformers had one tremendous potential source of support in 1989–1990. They enjoyed the tacit blessings of the FIS. The Islamic Front of Salvation has been accused of not having an economic program (Roberts 1994), and indeed its priorities were cultural purification and political power. Their program of March 7, 1989, however, offers an "economic doctrine" calling for a market economy in almost perfect accord with Hidouci's reform program (Al-Ahnaf et al. 1991: 179–187). Originally published abroad after the FIS was officially recognized, the FIS program may have been fabricated after the fact to gain some credit with the reformers. Its official date of publication was the day Abbas Madani assembled a large crowd in an Algiers mosque and, taking other Islamists by surprise, proclaimed the founding of the party (Charef 1995: 39–40). Yet the "economic doctrine" seems consistent with other fragmentary FIS commentaries and with the actions of the party during the reform period. Any formal alliance would have embarrassed both the reformers and the FIS, yet they served each other's political objectives. By defeating the FLN in the municipal elections of June 1990, the FIS strengthened the reformers' hold over the FLN parliament and other ruling circles; by pursuing political liberalization, the reformers opened up political opportunities for the FIS. The tacit alliance fell victim to Abbas Madani's ill-considered call for a general strike in May 1991. Top military leaders, threatened by the economic reforms, seized the opportunity and prevailed upon Chadli to proclaim a military emergency, even though the strike was fizzling out. The reform government resigned in the face of a virtual coup (Entelis and Arone 1992).

What seems most important in retrospect, however, are not the political tactics so much as the fact that the prescriptions for economic reform were almost identical. Like Hidouci, the FIS' economic program attacked Algeria's centralized state economy as "discouraging the spirit of initiative . . . in favor of mediocrity and incompetence . . . penalizing small enterprises . . . In our country industry is actually making the economy more dependent . . ." While in favor of "industrializing industries," as long as they were internationally competitive, "the Islamic Front of Salvation insists that industry, crucial as it is, should never be at the expense of agriculture, as it has been in the past." Khodja and Hidouci had made similar arguments in Boumédienne's time. The FIS, too, opposed industrial and commercial monopolies. FIS not only favored limiting state intervention in the industrial sector and protecting private property but also "watching that the latter not be transformed into monopoly infringing on the public interest, for this would be an open door for economic, political and social parasitism." In addition to specifically Islamic economic reforms such as legalizing *zakat* (Muslim taxes on property for charities) and opening Islamic banks, the FIS joined the reformers in advocating the dismantling of state import monopolies and price controls. "Commercial monopoly should be prohibited except when the State needs to intervene to safeguard major political or economic interests." The FIS advocated export-oriented growth because many of its supporters were in small industry or commerce. Like Hidouci and the International Monetary Fund, the party also specifically favored eliminating the gap between the official and parallel market exchange rates. Hidouci observes that the FIS was happy to let the reformers do the work of economic reform. It did not actively support them but gave them space while focusing its attacks instead on Chadli and the political regime. Observers may claim that the FIS was simply being opportunistic, but apparently the group within the party occupied with economic matters actually favored economic liberalization. The moralizers and globalizers were working together in Algeria at this critical juncture.

The defeat of the tacit alliance between the in-house reformers and a moderate broad-based FIS opposition was by no means inevitable, risky as simultaneous democratic and market reform may be (Przeworski 1991). Most of the FIS leadership had opposed Abbas Madani's call for a general strike and would have preferred to contest the parliamentary elections, originally scheduled for June, with new electoral districting designed to contain the Islamist majority by favoring the countryside over the cities. The reformers would have preferred to postpone the elections, and apparently it was Chadli, not the Islamists, who insisted on the earlier date. Once the general strike was called, a stronger Chadli might have supported the reformers, who were regaining control of the streets, rather than call in the military. In retrospect it is easy to argue that the invisible junta behind Chadli was determined to act to save its clandestine rent-seeking from deregulation and more transparent commercial dealings. Chadli himself had been exposed as an illegitimate beneficiary of agricultural lands restored to their owners in 1986. To intervene, however, the deciders needed the pretext of Madani's Islamist insurgence.

Finally, the specter of a decisive victory by FIS in the 1991–1992 parliamentary elections gave the military the excuse to terminate Chadli as well as the elections. While some political formations in Algeria's burgeoning civil society also favored preventing an FIS victory, the most outspoken of the parties also enjoyed close ties with the deciders. Again Algeria exaggerates the usage made elsewhere of Islamist opposition to buttress authoritarian rule. Once the military lost its constitutional cover, the opposition's resort to guerrilla warfare played into its hands. When in January 1995 the major Algerian political parties, including the FLN as well as the FIS, agreed to the San Egidio (Rome) Platform which would have restored constitutional order, the junta rejected the deal. Even more macabre, however, is the way the guerrilla warfare and counter-insurgency have facilitated Algeria's necessary policies of economic adjustment, now deprived of the buffer of any internal vision of economic reform.

Reforms from the bunker (1994–   )

A variety of governments with various economic policies succeeded the reformers. First, Sid Ahmed Ghozali maintained the IMF program of his predecessors while freezing many of the domestic market reforms and replacing some of the public officials identified with the reform team. He also offered prospects of joint upstream oil ventures to attract international, especially American, capital. Ghozali preserved some continuity as presidents changed, but he was succeeded by his original patron from the Boumédienne years, Belaid Abdesselam, after President Boudiaf's assassination. The new prime minister restored the commercial monopolies, although he also vigorously but unsuccessfully campaigned against the corruption they engendered. Relations with the IMF soured, and for another two years the reform programs stagnated. While fully servicing its external debt – 80 percent of its export earnings – without rescheduling, Abdesselam's government abandoned any semblance of fiscal discipline, printed money to cover widening deficits (Figure 4.3), and tightened price controls while keeping subsidies on basic consumption items amounting to 5 percent of GDP (Nashashibi 1998: 6).

All efforts ceased between 1991 and 1993 to realign Algeria's foreign exchange rate. Despite expansionary fiscal and monetary policies, unemployment increased and there were growing shortages of consumer items. Finally in May 1994, following a drop in oil prices, a balance of payments crisis seemed imminent. Algeria was obliged to embark on another IMF structural adjustment program and finally to engage in formal debt rescheduling. After some quick relief under a one-year stand-by arrangement with the IMF, followed by public debt rescheduling with the Paris Club, it successfully negotiated a three-year Extended Fund Facility in May 1995 and further rescheduled the public debt in July. It concluded a rescheduling of private commercial banking debts with the London Club in September. President Zeroual fielded a succession of governments of varying political complexions, all of which faithfully implemented the IMF program out of necessity, but none of which could project any vision of comprehensive economic reform, much less political institutions to sustain it. For instance, Minister Ahmed Ouyahia, whom Zeroual assigned in 1995 to accelerate the IMF program by imposing greater fiscal austerity, stated in 1998: "We cannot introduce a market economy which is not in working order. If we need it, we will have it but if we do not need it we will abandon it" (Dillman 2000: 142 n. 22).

The IMF proudly reported, however, that Algeria "has adjusted faster" than MENA's earlier starters (Egypt, Jordan, Morocco, and Tunisia) and that its macroeconomic performance had "equaled or even surpassed" them by end of 1996. "Real growth was 4 percent; inflation was declining to single digits, both the budget and the current account posted surpluses; foreign reserves were at five months of imports; and external debt indicators had improved markedly" (Nashashibi 1998: 64). But unemployment was increasing, not decreasing, although government officials, including the security forces, increased between 1985 and 1995 from 4.1 to 4.4 per hundred inhabitants. Government employment was still higher on a per capita basis in Algeria than in Jordan, Morocco, Syria, and Tunisia, not to mention various East Asian states (Nashashibi 1998: 25). A new public works program may have mitigated the effects of adjustment for some, but the real minimum wage "fell sharply during 1994–97" (Nashashibi 1998: 42–44), and the most vulnerable sectors now included the middle classes as well. *El Watan* (May 9, 1999) reported that they were being "laminated" by the rising cost of living without commensurate salary increases. Between 1990 and 1995 over 400,000 Algerians emigrated, including tens of thousands of professionals and managers (Dillman 2000: 143 n. 25). Small private businesses have fled to Tunisia to escape extortion by military clans (Dillman 2000: 58), while others went out of business for lack of credit, being crowded out by the public sector.

The restructuring of Algeria's public enterprises ultimately eliminated many of them. By April 1998 some 800 had been privatized or dissolved, with a loss of 35,000 jobs. State enterprises were subjected after 1994 to tighter budgetary contraints, and the construction sector was especially hard hit, shedding 93,000 workers between 1995 and 1997 (Nashashibi 1998: 50). At least 76 large public companies out of more than 400 were dissolved, with estimates as of April 1998 running as high as 400,000 people thrown out of work (Dillman 2000: 83). In December 1997 250 of the companies were placed on a list to be privatized. Prime Minister Ouyahia, while squeezing Algeria's budget deficit into a small surplus, also cracked down on the public sector managers. Two thousand of them were jailed after 1995, as much for being on the wrong side of power struggles among military factions as for any alleged wrongdoing. One notorious case involved the top management of SIDER, the iron and steel company. Its crime was to have inexpensively imported large quantities of iron bars for reinforced concrete, upsetting monopolies run by people close to President Zeroual (El Kadi 1998: 66). The brother of the manager, however, was an army general who interpreted the attack on his brother as really aimed at himself for having crossed Zeroual on other matters (*Algérie confidentielle* no. 76, June 1996). So many injustices were committed that some of those finally released from prison constituted an "association of incarcerated cadres" in May 1999 (*El Watan* May 23, 1999). Now that Zeroual was out of office, such civic initiative was possible.

The deindustrialization of Algeria is well underway. Algerian sources cited by the IMF indicate that public sector industry, excluding hydrocarbons, produced only 69.3 percent as much in 1997 as in 1987, when they were already well below capacity. The biggest declines came after 1993 (IMF 1998: 44, Table 10). Textile production was down by more than half, and even food processing diminished by 17 percent from 1993 to 1997 despite effective rates of protection in 1996 of respectively 60 and 110 percent in these two sectors (Sorsa 1999: 10). Private industry did not appear to be taking up the slack. As Bradford Dillman explains, "a liberalized economy [is] operating through a circulation of rent between the military, a deficient public sector and a largely commercial private sector" (2000: 3). Structural adjustment is reducing the rents available outside the petroleum sector, by subjecting commercial monopolies to competition. Trade liberalization, also, means fewer rents, although progress remains modest on this front. On a scale of 1 to 10, Algeria's trade regime loosened up from 10 to 8 during the Hamrouche–Hidouci period, and, after closing up again in 1992–1994, opened to 7 in 1997 – a point more than Egypt, Morocco, and Tunisia (Sorsa 1999: 15, 21).

The Algerian political economy, however, is not sustainable in its present configuration. Officers need more patronage to mitigate their rivalries; they have less, making it harder to deter defections except by brute force. With the "traffic accident" of General Fodhil Saïdi a certain line may have been crossed, if in fact Zeroual's rivals eliminated him before he could be promoted from a field command to a strategic post in the Département du Renseignement et Sécurité (*Algérie confidentielle* no. 76, June 1996). With one exception in 1970, operational military commanders have never experienced accidents. Political assassinations have always been directed at retired officers, dissidents, or civilian leaders seeking real power. Lahouari Addi observes that competing clans may be losing some of their mutual solidarity as well as their pecuniary resources. Mohammed Lamari, the chief of staff and major force behind Zeroual's removal, does not come from the Aures region but rather from a coastal city, and he selects his cronies more on the basis of competence and ideological affinity than regional clannishness (Addi 1999). The clans could become too brittle and exposed to survive increased competition over diminishing spoils.

Meanwhile the regime depends on violence to stay in power. Not so much the declining rents as the collective conspiracy to extract them holds the clans together. The major source of regime cohesion remains the war itself. It is really a collection of local wars, paralleling the divided command structures of the army of clans. The Armée Nationale Populaire (ANP) has not fully mobilized to put down the insurgencies. With only 124,000 soldiers, it numbers less than one-quarter of the French army mobilized in the 1950s to defend "French Algeria" against an armed insurgency and has not even "manifested any notable determination to buy the sorts of weapons generally used for this sort of war" (Garçon and Affuzi 1998: 54). Keeping the army small may preserve it better from Islamist contagion. By contracting out some of the counter-insurgency to village defense forces and, since 1997, to Islamist militias, it spreads the mayhem. Whether or not, as ex-Lieutenant Souaïdia (2001) claims, the army deliberately murders civilians, it appears either unwilling or unable to prevent atrocities that have become routine, with estimates of 100,000 dead since 1992. However, the oil fields and the better neighborhoods of major cities have remained relatively immune from the violence; the insurrections cause no particular problem to the regime but justify its professional functions. By 2000 violence seemed confined to the regions of Relizane, in the western plateau, and Medea, south of Algiers, but then it flared up elsewhere.

Higher oil and gas revenues and lighter debt servicing requirements may ease the pressures to adjust. If indeed the low-intensity violence is contained, social pressures will mount, despite the fact that much of Algerian civil society is exiled in France. External pressures, coupled with continued reform, may eventually extricate Algeria from bunker capitalism. President Bouteflika and the deciders headed by General Lamari share a mutual interest in a civil façade serving to cover up the army's role in commerce and politics. The external creditors, including the United States, could impose harsher conditions than in 1994 on future debt rescheduling because the specter of an Islamist take-over of Algeria seems less plausible today. They could insist on further liberalization of trade, deregulation of prices, and privatization, thereby limiting the spoils that contribute to clan solidarity (Leveau 1998). Carrots may be more persuasive than sticks. The deciders indicated the desire to extract themselves from politics in 1999 by retaining a formally neutral position during the presidential elections. They may ultimately be bought off by opportunities to exchange their rents for more permanent acquisitions in Algeria's new private sector. With a measure of security reached through a political settlement, some of the estimated $35 billion (Ghilès 1998: 105) held abroad by Algerian residents might return to the country, along with more foreign direct investment.

Lessons for other bunker regimes

Reform is highly problematic in any bunker regime because economic liberalization requires a change of political system. Reformers within such a regime need outside support. In the MENA, as in Eastern Europe and other transitional settings, the softline reformers need alliances with "moderate" opposition forces that can isolate the hardliners within, while also containing the more radical opposition factions opposed to a political reform process. Under more effective leadership Algeria's FIS could have played such a role in 1991 and conceivably still might. Algeria's situation is extreme, but not atypical of other bunker regimes in the region. With the exception of Sudan, the principal opposition forces to bunker regimes since the 1970s are Islamist. The Algerian case suggests that they can be allies of political and economic liberalization. The economic policy of the FIS translates into the Ten Commandments preached by the Washington Consensus. "Islamism" obviously has no single blueprint, however, and most Islamist movements have little to say about the economy. Bunker regimes, moreover, do not promote political moderation among Islamist oppositions. In other, gentler forms of capitalism, to be discussed in subsequent chapters, alliances with Islamic business sectors have greater chances of success than in bunker states. In Syria, by contrast, the residual private sector's sympathies for the Muslim Brotherhood seem to have positively deterred the regime from further reform since 1991 (Lawson 1992: 130–132; Ayubi 1995: 262–263).

The danger to a bunker regime is that adjustment to the global economy, however economically necessary, will undermine it. These regimes lack strategic depth. There is little civil society with which officers might ally to leverage a reform program. Chadli, Hamouche, and Hidouci tried to pull off an almost impossible stunt. Their implicit ally, the FIS, had little economic base beyond small shopkeepers and *trabendo* commerce. As for Zeroual's reform efforts, maybe "his remarkable political stabilization programme in 1995 was in part a result of his shrewd policy of assuming the same political ground as the FIS. Politically he repositioned himself outside the state while at the same time standing at its centre" (Stone 1998: 252). But there was simply no ground on which to stand.

Civil society, to be sure, is not only a capitalist construct but a public sphere in which political regimes try to project their image of legitimacy. Even the military dictators reach out of their bunkers and, whether or not they have read Jean-Jacques Rousseau, try to "transform might into right." Algeria saw a series of attempts under Boumédienne and his successors to erect a façade of constitutional order so as to camouflage their guns. In Syria, Adib Shishakli (1949–1954) ruled securely behind the scenes, only to fall after his rule became more exposed. His many military successors stumbled until Hafez al-Asad (1970–2000) institutionalized the Baath regime, with its complex of allied parties and associations that enabled his son Bashar to succeed him. In Iraq Saddam Hussein (1968–   ) also commands a complex of civil institutions designed to legitimate his leadership and peerhaps an eventual succession of one of his sons. Saddam Hussein, in fact, rose to power through the Baath Party not the military.

In the Sudan the military has alternated with civilian rule since 1958. After Numeiri's fall and a brief interval of civilian rule (1986–1988), Sudan's military strongman, Omar Bashir, could not rule with military force alone. To legitimate his regime and keep his fellow officers in line, he coopted Hassan Turabi to provide an Islamist cover, but then dismissed him in 1999. Ali Abdullah Saleh has veiled his tribal-military rule of Yemen with the General People's Congress, which has been reinforced, at least in opposition to various rough Yemeni political forces, by tactical alliances with the Islamist Islah Party. In Libya, too, Qaddafi (1969–   ) created a façade of legitimacy. First he created a Libyan Arab Socialist Union modeled after the schema of his late mentor, Gamal Abdel Nasser. When LASU failed, Qaddafi became more creative: the *Jamahuriya* of popular assemblies enabled him as revolutionary leader to retire from all official positions. But Rousseau's lessons about participatory democracy evidently did not inspire him to assume the position of legislator, described in the conclusion of *The Social Contract*, and retire from politics altogether. He might, however, appoint one of his sons head of state, anticipating the succession in Iraq (*Middle East International* no. 620, March 10, 2000: 11).

The visible manifestations of civil society are the media, civic, cultural, and human rights associations, political parties, trade and professional unions, even tribal associations and football clubs. They exist in most bunker states and have positively flourished in Algeria since 1988, when "literally thousands of associations were created" (Zoubir 1999: 36). Yahia Zoubir observes that "civil society has resisted either being reabsorbed by an ascending powerful, authoritarian state or being swept away by yet another populist, totalitarian movement," as he views the FIS (Zoubir 1999: 39). Being the most open and "vibrant" of the civil societies tolerated by a bunker state, in fact, Algeria perhaps also best reveals their limitations. Sandwiched between guerrilla bands and a rapacious counter-insurgency, civil society has no institutional guarantees. While many free-spirited, mostly middle-class Algerians learn the arts of association, their aspirations are constrained by economic as well as political realities. The media and the various associations rest on a very narrow economic base. A private sector of shopkeepers and small enterprises funds some associations, including the FIS, but most politically significant groups, including the press, are funded almost exclusively by the government. In addition to the usual censorship, there are more subtle controls. What is published or not published reflects the balance of power between the clans. Stories of Mohammed Bechtine's abuses of power surfaced in late 1998, for instance, because Lamari clan leaders gave the press the green light to embarrass their rival. This is not to deny the personal bravery of the Algerian press corps: at least fifty-eight journalists have been killed in the line of duty by either security forces or oppositions since 1992. But civil society lacks a private sector base. Thus newspapers connected with leading clans get the subsidies and state advertising accounts, while those of their opponents go bankrupt. Bechtine's own press empire was in a state of collapse after he and Zeroual were removed from office. During the political transition in 1999 some twenty new dailies and weeklies being launched in both French and Arabic, including a specialized business weekly, *Le Capitaliste* (*Maghreb Weekly Monitor* no. 58, May 29, 1999).

The only capital enjoying structural power in a bunker state consists of the rents accumulated by its janissaries and their intermediaries. The bunkers cannot mobilize their business communities or develop durable arrangements with elements of civil society. Without an independent private sector to support it, civil society is largely fictitious or subject to a high degree of manipulation from the bunkers in countries such as Algeria. Libya used to be the *reductio ad absurdum* of a civil society. In 1976 Qaddafi tried to abolish money altogether and destroy the institution of private property on which civil society rests, and "Libyans call the years from 1978 to 1988 the 'dark decade' because of the political repression and the extreme economic hardship" (Al-Kikhia 1997: 94). In 1978 Libya's CIM ratio plummeted to 63 percent but subsequently recovered as the leader's revolutionary appetites waned. Like Algeria under the French, the Libyans had suffered a devastating colonial experience at the hands of Mussolini. While the oil boom of the late 1950s resulted in some capital accumulation by rent-seekers around King Idris, Qaddafi easily leveled the private sector in the early 1970s. At this time Boumédienne was cutting down the remnants of a native Algerian capitalist class left over from the colonial period. In both countries the colonial situation eased the way for bunker capitalism by destroying the elites that might otherwise have articulated a stronger civil society.

In the other bunker states, too, the private sector seems too feeble to support much civil society. Yemen has not one but three scattered bourgeoisies (Chaudhry 1997). Much of the original merchant class escaped the exactions of the monarchy in the 1930s for British protection in Aden. Many of the old landed classes and merchants of Aden and the Hadramout in turn emigrated to Saudi Arabia in 1967, when a radical nationalist faction gained control of the People's Democratic Republic of Yemen. A further wave escaped the state monopolies organized by the Yemen Arab Republic in the 1970s. Many returned with unification in 1990, but the triumph dissipated amid increasing taxation and declining remittances from Saudi Arabia. Yemen's workers also displayed remarkable mobility, departing for Saudi Arabia in the 1970s only to be expelled back home en masse in 1991 – some 800,000 to a million economic casualties of the Second Gulf War. In the Sudan a small, wealthy bourgeoisie is more firmly implanted, but it is overshadowed by a public sector which consumes much of the available credit. Returning to power in 1989, the military cracked down on civil society (Lesch 1996). Rents from cotton exports and arms imports from the Taliban accrued instead to Al-Mahfazah ('The Portfolio'), a business group associated with Hassan Turabi (Hirst 1997). Poor societies with relatively small middle classes such as Sudan or the Yemen, are perhaps more easily plundered than wealthier ones, but Syria and Iraq also lost most of their respective bourgeoisies. In the 1960s successive Baathist revolutions scared away much of Syria's vaunted manufacturing as well commercial entrepreneurship. President Asad's controlled *infitah* (opening of the economy) of the early 1970s, to be sure, did result in an expanded private sector, but it was heavily dependent, like its weaker Algerian counterpart, on military patrons. In the 1970s and 1980s Saddam leveled Iraq's class structure and created new entrepreneurs primarily from his family and village.

Algeria and Iraq have been the bunker states of renown in the 1990s, as their embattled rulers have conducted wars from their literal bunkers against their own people. But in the late 1970s and early 1980s, Syria held the dubious distinction of being the Arab state whose leadership was most hunkered down in bunkers out of fear of attack by its citizens. That Syria ultimately emerged from its civil war with its political elite still intact, but subsequently made little progress in liberalizing its economy or stimulating economic growth, underscores the tenacity of political obstacles that impede effective responses to globalization in the bunker states. The Syrian case suggests that Algeria could win the battle against internal violence, but still lose the war against economic stagnation. In both cases, as in the other bunker praetorian republics, the lack of state autonomy from social forces results in the state becoming an instrument of one or more of those social forces in their domination of others. This in turn prevents those bunker states from developing or implementing economically rational policies. They lack broad, institutionalized support in society, so they must subdue it, which entails extracting resources from civil society both to prevent it from supporting autonomous action and to pay for the coercive capacities of the state. The primary concern of these states, in short, is political control, not economic growth.

Lessons from Syria

From the first post-independence coup d'état in 1949, until 1970, various political movements and cabals of officers, with greater or lesser independence from the religious and ethnic groups of which Syria is constituted, struggled to control the state. Finally, in the late 1960s, army officers drawn from the most "compact" of the religious minorities, the Alawis, who had provided the backbone of locally recruited military forces under the French, gained control of the state. Hafez al-Asad, who ruled Syria for thirty years, quietly overthrew another, more radical Alawi in 1970, after refusing to support his military adventures. Before the end of the decade the Muslim Brotherhood, which represented the majoritarian Sunni Muslim community, began to violently challenge what they saw as Alawi usurpation of "their" state. The denouement came in 1982, when the Brotherhood instigated a mass revolt in the northern city of Hama, hoping thereby to spark unrest in Damascus and throughout the country. In the event their effort failed, in large measure because the regime, deploying troops under the command of kinsmen of the president and including large numbers of other minorities, especially Kurds, pulverized the center of Hama, killing some 20,000 of its inhabitants. For the next several years Sunni Muslim activists were hunted down by the regime, imprisoned, or liquidated. For more than thirty years the Syrian state has been controlled at its apex, in descending order of importance, by the family, clan, tribe, and minority religious sect of the president. Commands of the vital military and security organs are virtually exclusively Alawi preserves, while another religious minority that tends to be favored by the regime, the Christians, provides a disproportionate number of domestic intelligence officers.

In the wake of the 1982 bloodbath, the government embarked upon a hesitant economic reform, necessitated by declining oil prices and made possible politically by the intimidation of the Muslim Brotherhood. The destruction of Hama was fresh in the minds of any Sunni Muslims who might be tempted to use their economic skills and resources to take advantage of the limited economic opening for political purposes. In need of economic assets that the Sunnis possess in greatest measure, the regime essentially struck the same bargain with them as the "deciders" in Algeria have done with Algerian capitalists. That bargain consists of deals between individual Alawi patrons and Sunni capitalist clients, whereby the former provide protection, contacts, and permissions, while the latter do the business, paying their patrons appropriate rents for services rendered. That bargain underpins the political economy of Syria, thereby preserving Alawi rule, but at the cost of more rapid economic growth, as rent seeking, requiring as it does an absence of transparency and accountability and militating, as it also does, against export-led growth, has devoured the country's resources. In the early 1950s Syria's was one of the most rapidly growing economies in the Third World, and most observers judged its prospects to be extremely bright. By the end of the century per capita income was basically no higher than it had been twenty years earlier. Syria had become an economic backwater in a declining region.

Capital has no structural power in Syria because its accumulation is not protected by law or institutions, as reflected in the low ratio of contract-intensive money to the total money supply shown in Figure 3.2. In the decade of the 1990s, only Yemen in the MENA was a worse performer than Syria on this measure, which is a surrogate indicator for the degree of rule of law and security of property. Moreover, although the Syrian ratio has fluctuated somewhat, it was exactly the same in 1995 (the last year for which data are available) as it was a decade earlier, suggesting that the nominal liberalization has not succeeded in inducing those with money to entrust it to official Syrian financial institutions. Even were the rule of law not absent, however, those institutions would hardly be attractive to Syrian capitalists. As a recent comparative study states, "Since the nationalization of banks in the 1960s, the banking system has been reduced to an appendage of the state budget" (Waldner 1999: 122). Table 3.6 reveals that it is also among the most concentrated of the MENA's banking systems.

In Syria the security of property, hardly guaranteed by the legal/judicial system, is sought through personalistic connections. Thus the power and influence of key members of the core of the elite ultimately determine the outcome of even relatively minor property disputes, as claims are pushed up competitive personal networks by the disputants, until one ultimately prevails by virtue of having reached a more powerful patron. Business transaction costs in Syria, like those in Algeria, are extremely high, impressionistic evidence suggesting a qualitative difference between such costs in those two and other bunker states, on the one hand, and the bully praetorian republics on the other. In Syria, transaction costs literally begin at the airport, where those passing through customs and immigration commonly need to expedite the process by paying bribes to officials. Unfortunately, transaction costs do not end there and are so ubiquitous that they are institutionalized at fixed percentages of anticipated gains.

Syria is an information-averse country. All typewriters had to be registered with the government and a sample of their typeface provided until the early 1990s. Fax machines were prohibited until the latter part of that decade and the Internet only became available in the country just prior to Hafez al-Asad's death. The combination of censorship and a dull, state-controlled press reduces newspaper circulation to the second lowest on a per capita basis in the Arab world – only largely illiterate Yemen has proportionately fewer newspaper readers (Figure 3.3). Syrians were cut off from their Lebanese Internet service providers in 1999, although the government projects some web sites.

The Syrian economy remains primarily inward-looking and essentially stagnant. Its effective duty rates in 1997, reported in Table 3.1, were

29.7 percent, the highest in the MENA region. Its manufactured goods as a percentage of GDP were 4.2 percent, which placed it above only war-torn Algeria, oil-rich Saudi Arabia, impoverished Yemen and an almost deindustrializing Egypt. As shown in Table 2.2, it is the only MENA country, other than Kuwait, in which the intra-industry index dropped between the mid-1980s and the mid-1990s, suggesting that Syria was further disconnecting from global industrial trade. The relatively low output of manufactured goods results not from a lack of investment in industry, which has been comparatively substantial, but from an almost complete absence of productivity increases (Waldner 1999: 188). Syria, the region's second largest agricultural exporter with the most rapidly expanding industrial base in the Arab world in the 1950s, had by the 1990s come to rely upon its comparatively meager fuel exports for about two-thirds of its total export earnings. Its dependence is only slightly less than that of the big Gulf exporters, whose fuel exports, however, are many times those of Syria. Per capita GDP was struggling to hold steady at the end of the 1990s.

Syria is not lacking in appropriate factors of economic production. Its endowment of arable land is, on a per capita basis, among the highest in the MENA. Capital flows in the form of geo-strategic rents into the country since 1970, when the current regime took power, have been episodic but substantial. They amounted, for example, to about $2 billion in the immediate wake of the Gulf War, Syria's payment for entering the anti-Iraq coalition. Syria's domination of Lebanon has also generated substantial revenues and provided a sponge to absorb excess Syrian labor. During the 1990s Syria's fuel exports typically exceeded those of Egypt, earning another $2 billion or so annually, which, given a population of about a quarter that of Egypt, is on a per capita basis quite substantial. On human development indicators, including education, Syria ranks on average in the upper half of MENA states.

Based on its endowment of land, labor, and capital, therefore, the Syrian economy should be among the most robust in the region. That it is not results from its very low total factor productivity, which is a measure of the effectiveness with which those factors are integrated for the purposes of production. A result of that low total factor productivity is that industry remains backward, as suggested by the fact that textiles are the only significant manufactured export and are sold principally into Russia and other relatively primitive, low-price markets. The Syrian economy, in sum, is stagnating not because of an absence of factors that make for wealth, but because the utilization of those factors is extremely inefficient.

Paradoxically, if Syria had fewer natural endowments and less ability to generate rents, its economy might have developed more rapidly. But the regime has managed to sustain its almost autarchic economic policy for some three decades precisely because it has been the beneficiary of strategic and petroleum rents and an agriculture that is reasonably productive. Syria is almost able to feed its own population, no small achievement in this region of food dependency. Unwilling for political reasons to unleash its capitalists, who for the most part are Sunni Muslim, the regime has tethered them to the military/security state, using them as cronies in rent-generating activities, primarily through imports of manufactures and exports of raw materials, including agricultural products. The options for Syrian businesspersons are thus to cultivate relations with the Alawi elite and share rents with them, or to conduct as much business as possible beyond that elite's reach, which means outside Syria. Thus Syrian capitalists, who are reputed to be among the most astute in the MENA, have spread their family business conglomerates into the Gulf and Europe, especially the old eastern bloc countries, but their primary base is usually in Beirut, not Damascus or Aleppo. And these family businesses tend to be into trading, with mobile assets, rather than industry. Fixed capital is not safe in Syria, nor is it easy for foreign Arab nationals to establish industrial firms in other Arab states, as they tend to be more at the mercy of those states than are foreign multinational corporations.

The Syrian political economy today, replete with ruling single party and its own cold war, more closely resembles a classic easern bloc, communist one than any remaining in that part of the world. This raises the question of its future, especially if that cold war with Israel were finally to end and/or if private capital were to return to Syria. The "digestion" of Lebanon by Syria over the decade of the 1990s, a country with a once more open economy and which is in some senses Syria's Hong Kong, could be another factor that ultimately might lead Syria to become substantially more integrated into the global capitalist economy.

As is the case with Algeria, it is possible to construct such a scenario without straining credulity to the breaking point. A peace deal with Israel with substantial direct and indirect "peace dividends" for Syria might kickstart a process of economic reform that would be further encouraged by the much more benign regional environment, which, among other things, would reduce the need for military expenditures. President Asad's successor, his son Bashar, even in the absence of peace with Israel might well be tempted to reach out to the various political constituencies, as indeed his father did in tentative fashion upon coming to power in 1970. But such an initiative now, given the forces of globalization, would have to constitute more than "side payments" to those constituencies, as it did back in 1970. In any case the patronage available for such side payments is insufficient, so real concessions in terms of influence over public policy, protection of property rights, and much more unfettered access to the world would have to be made. The key constituency is the Sunni Muslim one, which politically is led by the remnants of the agrarian capitalist class and by the petit bourgeoisie of small shopkeepers and artisans, both categories of which endorse more components of the Washington Consensus than does the present regime.

But the question remains as to whether the gap can be bridged between the ruling social force of Alawis and the ruled Sunnis, Christians, and Kurds, such that any subsequent regime could base its power on coalitions of forces in civil society rather than on instruments of coercion. It could be that in Syria, as in the other bunker states, the antagonisms are too deep, the structures too firmly in place, for a gradual, peaceful transition to more inclusive government and free markets to occur. Fear on the part of the elite that such a process could gain momentum and become uncontrollable may continue to place limits on experimentation, thereby prolonging the country's state of economic and political stagnation. But like colonialism, globalization is a relentless, unforgiving, and still more ubiquitous force, against which Syria has stood longer and more resolutely than most countries in the region, but at an enormous price to the economic well-being of its population. That it can continue to do so indefinitely, now that Asad has passed from the scene, seems unlikely. So the real questions are whether Syria will reach its accommodation in gradual or abrupt fashion, and how extensive that accommodation will be.

Conclusion

Bunker states fragment their upper and middle classes into masses and migrants. Trade unions and business associations exist, but are not permitted to acquire roots in their societies from which to negotiate with governments or render them accountable. Civilian entrepreneurs, whether in business or politics, must remain loyal to their protectors. The one who strikes out on his own for an autonomous power base risks being assassinated like Algeria's Boudiaf or Abdelhak Benhamouda, the head of the labor federation who was also gunned down in ambiguous circumstances after crossing a powerful military faction (*Algérie confidentielle* no. 100, May 1997). No credible economic or political pacts are possible in the absence of credible interlocutors, such as the FIS's Abdelkader Hachani, killed at his dentist's office in downtown Algiers in 1999. It is instead up to the ruling clans to cut their own deals and divide up rents and other economic spoils of domestic and international commerce. When official state monopolies are dismantled, the clans reappropriate the ostensibly privatized and deregulated ones (Dillman 2000: 94–96). In Iraq, Libya, and Syria the clans have imploded into extended families and related tribes of the ruler. In Algeria Mohamed Lamari's military clientele, selected for its competence and conviction rather than roots in the traditionally favored Aurès region (Addi 1999), seems precariously to diverge from the norm of the new *asabiya*, or clan solidarity (Salamé 1990: 61).

The ultimate test of *asabiya* is a succession crisis. Some of the bunker states, whatever their political rhetoric, resemble hereditary monarchies without a private sector. Hafez al-Asad's ultimate triumph was posthumous, passing political power to his son Bashar in June 2000 in a succession that had been deemed "highly unlikely" by one of Syria's best-qualified observers, as well as most people inside and outside the country, only five years earlier (Perthes 1997: 269). One godfather has finally passed the keys to his son, and similar preparations may be underway in Baghdad and Tripoli. The keys of bunker states no longer open many doors, however, because the private sector's treasuries have fled elsewhere along with much of their respective civil societies.

It is not so much declining oil rents as the disconnection between bunkers and their private sectors that explains these regimes' difficulties with globalization. Their officials and entrepreneurs smuggle much of their private capital abroad. Bunker states are not the only ones in the region to be affected by capital flight, but they seem to experience greater difficulty than the others do because their domestic money markets are also less inviting. As their low CIM ratios indicate, they do not have much control over their currency flows. As political economists from Montesquieu to Kiren Chaudhry observe, mobile assets are harder to police than fixed, tangible ones that can be fenced off or occupied. Yemen during the boom years was a more extreme case than Algeria; remittances in the form of various currencies circulated by the money-changers may have exceeded North Yemen's GDP (Chaudhry 1997: 244). With or without booming remittances, however, Yemen's CIM was always low. It reached a new low in 1994, in fact, as Yemen suffered civil war. More ominously, "before, during, and after the war Ali Abdallah Saleh and his faction were purging the key organizations of all opposition groups, arranging for mass and individual assassinations of dissidents . . . and setting up a brutal security state constructed on the model, and, by many informal counts, with the advice of the Iraqi Ba'aath" (Chaudhry 1997: 304). Crackdowns merely decentralized the money-changers' informal system, further rupturing any business–state relations and limiting the bunker's economic capacities. Fierce military and security forces can terrorize merchants or money-changers, whether in Yemen or Baghdad, but the large informal economies defy any sustained economic controls.

The bunker states still have to adjust, as Algeria illustrates, once they become heavily indebted and dependent on imports for their necessities. Lacking in strategic depth, however, the best they can do is to serve as gunships for the IMF. Their nineteenth-century predecessors were the British and French fleets which patrolled the southern Mediterranean, collecting Ottoman debts and establishing colonies or protectorates. In 1995 Algeria adjusted more quickly than its neighbors because it rode roughshod over its budget deficits under cover of an insurrection. Iraq between the Gulf wars also rammed through many reforms of economic liberalization (Chaudhry 1992: 152–158). The chronic civil war and starvation in the southern Sudan allow General Bashir the chance to adjust his deficits, according to a program worked out in 1997 with the IMF. In the Yemen, too, civil war enabled Colonel Saleh not only to crush his oppositions, but also to engage in a major IMF structural adjustment program. Indeed, the only laggards were Libya and Syria, and each had an excuse. Until 1999 Libya was subject to international sanctions, and Syria remained technically in a state of war with Israel. In the event of peace, Syria would be challenged to resume its reforms to attract private investment under Law 10 of 1991.

Most economic reforms of bunker regimes appear to be hollow exercises. The missing piece is the export-oriented private sector that is supposed to benefit from trade liberalization and be the internal dynamo attracting investment and generating employment. In a bunker state, however, any dynamic sector outside the official rent producers must stay underground. In oil rentier states the petroleum sector is an enclave disconnected from the rest of the economy, but other sectors may coexist (Mahdavy 1970). The bunker state, whether or not it also has mineral wealth, is politically as well as economically disconnected from other economic sectors. Efforts of economic liberalization therefore cannot promote greater productivity outside its enclaves. In Algeria manufacturing value added, measured in constant dollars, declined by more than half from 1987 to 1997 (calculated from Table 3.1). Algeria strikingly illustrates the negative impact of economic liberalization and adjustment on economic growth, but neither Sudan, striving despite civil war to exploit its oil resources, nor Yemen, unified largely for the sake of oil, can expect better results. Neither oil nor its related "Dutch disease" but rather politics determines these outcomes (cf. Karl 1997; Ross 1999).

A final point about bunker regimes is that they sharply limit the possibilities of fruitful economic integration with their neighbors.

Algeria shattered efforts in the late 1960s to build a united Maghreb; the final blow was Qaddafi's coup in Libya. The Union du Maghreb Arabe (UMA), proclaimed in 1988 when Algeria and Morocco had repaired their relations, is stillborn. Since Chadli's removal from power in 1992 by his fellow officers, Algerian–Moroccan disputes over the ex-Spanish Sahara have intensified. Relations might again deteriorate as a way for President Bouteflika, fictitiously elected in April 1999, to reinvent a Boumédienne image and acquire some real authority. Syria and Iraq, despite a common Ba'athist legacy, have waged their internal wars since each bunker was consolidated, and the Iraqi bunker is surrounded by hostile neighbors. Libya has been at odds with all of its neighbors; and Sudan has been at loggerheads with Egypt. The political economy of bunker states explains a significant part of the problem. Having castrated their private sectors and civil societies, the bunkers lack the cover of non-governmental intermediaries serving to cushion processes of economic integration and develop mutual interests.

Globalization may strengthen civil society and its underlying financial flows, but these new forces escape the bunkers' reach. These states seem destined to decay amid their internal wars unless they cultivate their private sectors. The longer they stagnate, the greater the social fragmentation and proliferation of social movements in defiance of the economy, and the greater the violence as the movements in turn are suppressed. Algeria may be exceptional only in that it is so close to Europe and has such a vibrant "European" civil society inside and outside the country that the external pressures to change may prove irresistible. Syria and Libya, also facing the Mediterranean, may face greater pressures if their excuses for the bunkers – war with Israel and various economic sanctions, including unilateral American ones – are removed. Syria, like Algeria, has substantial human and capital resources outside the bunkers that might facilitate reform. So for that matter does Iraq, were both the sanctions and the bunkers somehow to be removed.

Suggestions for further reading

The sociological reflections of Ali El-Kenz (1991) deserve all the more attention in light of Algeria's subsequent tragedies. Dillman (2000), Nashashibi (1998), Quandt (1998), and Willis (1996) offer further insights on Algeria. Batatu (1999), Perthes (1997), and Waldner (1999) analyze Syria from a variety of perspectives, while Al-Kikhia (1997) and Vandewalle (1998) focus on another bunker state, Libya. Carapico (1998) and Chaudhry (1997) present contrasting views of Yemen, while Vandewalle (1997) and Zoubir (1999) have edited timely collections of articles on Algeria, Morocco, and Tunisia.

5   Bully praetorian states

Egypt, Tunisia, and the area controlled by the Palestinian Authority are not ruled from bunkers by elites beholden to clans, tribes, or other traditional social formations. In the case of Egypt and Tunisia, and the prospective Palestinian state, the ruling elites are at once both more narrowly and broadly based. Their rule rests almost exclusively on the institutional power of the military/security/party apparatus, but because these elites are not drawn from a clearly identified social formation, they are at least not unrepresentative of their relatively homogeneous political communities. Since the state provides the primary underpinning for these regimes, they have relatively little incentive to build and maintain ruling coalitions based in their respective political societies. The rulers of each of them seem content to restrict their extra-state coalition-building to the placation of rural and traditional elites. Rent-seeking arrangements with crony capitalists are more for the purposes of serving state-based patronage networks than for broadening ruling coalitions.

The differences between bunker and bully praetorian republics, other than that of the key issue of the lack of autonomy of the bunker states from social formations, are not great. The leaders of Egypt and Tunisia, having not been forced to forge societal as opposed to state-based coalitions to come to or maintain their power, lack the political legitimacy that flows, as Max Weber described, from tradition, charisma, or rational-legal procedures. Yasser Arafat used a combination of his coercive capacity based in the PLO, and support from Israel and the USA, as well as political alliances on the ground in the West Bank and Gaza to assert control over Palestine. By virtue of having built those alliances and because of his historical role as state-builder, Arafat personally enjoys considerable legitimacy, but legitimacy that will be hard to bestow on a successor. The Palestinian "state" apparatus has come to supplant the PLO's broader political coalition as the basis for the Palestinian Authority's power.

The rulers of Egypt, Tunisia, and Palestine, dependent primarily upon state-based patronage networks, are thus politically unable to radically downsize their states or dramatically privatize their economies. The Palestinian Authority (PA), for example, is rapidly expanding public employment while subordinating what little private economic activity there is to rent-seeking relationships to key members of Arafat's entourage. In the first four years of its existence, the PA created more than 65,000 government jobs, such that by 1997 the percentage of the labor force it employed (18.7 percent) was virtually level with that of construction (19 percent), making these two sectors the largest employers. In 1998 almost half of all new jobs were in the PA, taking central government employment to more than one-fifth of total employment and accounting for some 60 percent of the PA's budget (Roy 1999: 64–82). But the PA still has some way to go before it reaches Egyptian levels, where total government employment accounts for about one-third of the labor force. Tunisia, heralded as a model for the region by the World Bank, retains a public sector that is among the most costly to the public purse in the MENA.

With insecure political footings in the societies they rule, elites of these bully states are compelled to rely on economically irrational, overgrown governmental and public sectors. They cast about for ways to generate patronage from private economic activities, rather than engage in the political coalition-building that would obviate the need for their leviathans in the first place. But the drain on aggregate economic performance resulting from the gargantuan appetites of these leviathans, combined with the need to garner rents from private economic activity, and reluctance to grant any economic or political space to independent actors, inhibit economic growth. These factors also deter political elites from devising creative strategies that would help perpetuate their rule while encouraging economically beneficial responses to globalization as happened, for example, in Morocco, a case which will be discussed in the following chapter.

Rent-seeking arrangements that have been struck between the political elite and capitalists in Egypt discourage export-led growth, for the elite can rig local but not international markets. Crony capitalists are provided local oligopolies and monopolies that they exploit, leaving the more competitive and risky business of producing for export to those unable or unwilling to strike deals with the political leadership. Unlike the developmental states of Asia, Egyptian policy directs the most capitalized private enterprises to serve local, rather than global, markets, so the country's most dynamic private exporters are, by default, marginal, bit players serving niche markets, seeking to stay as far away from their governments as possible. The vast bulk of the private economy consists of micro-enterprises, large proportions of which are in the informal sector. They lack the capital, technology, productive capacity, and, in the case of informal operations, the legal status, even to consider exporting.

The Palestinian economy is a still more primitive, almost microscopic version of the Egyptian one. Its 60,000 private firms are almost exclusively establishments employing fewer than three persons and capitalized at less than $10,000 (Roy 1999: 71). Since virtually nothing is manufactured or processed for export, the preconditions for which are absent, the patronage that can be extracted by the political elite from aspiring capitalists typically involves the selective use of permissions and regulations for importation. The emerging political economy of Palestine is, therefore, one that appears to be mimicking Egypt's.

Tunisia has enjoyed proportionately greater export success than has Egypt, for its political economy is something of a mix between the comparatively primitive rent-seeking one of Egypt and Palestine, on the one hand, and the more sophisticated, liberal, but still rent-seeking one of Morocco, on the other. The Tunisian ruling elite has retained its overgrown state and public sector for patronage and control purposes. But the domestic market is too small to support any significant manufacturing industry, so the scope for it to generate substantial patronage through rent seeking is limited, although continuing high tariffs suggest that selective permissions for importation still produce a substantial share of patronage resources. Unlike Palestine, Tunisia no longer receives much public foreign assistance, so living off external rents has not been an option. The ruling elite has thus encouraged the development of export manufacturing, but, unlike its counterpart in Morocco, has not succeeded in integrating these activities into a tightly structured oligopoly linked directly to that elite. The Tunisian elite thus remains more wary than its Moroccan counterpart of both civil society and capitalist activity. Lacking the legitimacy and means to direct and to benefit from civil society and capitalist activism, as enjoyed by its Moroccan neighbor, the Tunisian elite hesitates to open any wider the doors to either political or economic competition. The regime thus selectively favors trusted, individual capitalists, rather than capitalism as a concept and practice.

That the economic performance of these bully republics differs considerably, despite the structural similarities of their political economies, attests also to the importance of regional factors for the MENA's economies. The Palestinian economy is hostage to the Oslo peace process, and as that process slowed, so did it. Closure, which was first imposed in 1993 some six months prior to the signing of the Oslo Accords, was intensified during the Netanyahu years (1996–1999), essentially segmenting the occupied territories of the West Bank and

Gaza into collections of small enclaves cut off from the outside world. The World Bank noted in 1997 that the economic situation was so bad "that the hopes for private-sector-led development had to be set aside by the international agencies involved in organizing aid to the Palestinian economy." More than 40 percent of the disbursements by these agencies intended for long-term investment were diverted to emergency budgetary support (Roy 1999: 72). Regional factors worked favorably for Tunisia, on the other hand. Far removed from the Arab–Israeli conflict and only 80 miles from Europe, it was tagged as a "Mediterranean tiger" in the late 1980s as the World Bank and others were looking for success stories to parallel those of the East Asian "tigers." While it has in fact remained an economic pussycat by comparison, it has nevertheless substantially outperformed Egypt in globalizing its economy, thanks in large measure to the eager European embrace, propelled as much by fear of potential North African boat people as by any other considerations. Unable to take to their boats to reach European shores, and situated much closer to the Middle East's "Arc of Crisis," the Egyptians have been proportionately less favored by Europe than have the Tunisians. They have also felt compelled to devote a substantially greater proportion of their budgets to the military.

The capitalist legacies of Tunisia, Egypt, and Palestine also account for some of the variance of their economic performance. The West Bank and Gaza have had far too discontinuous histories and too much conflict for capitalism even to be sustained at the minimal level it had achieved at the time of the "disaster" when Israel was founded in 1948. Egypt's capitalists have not had to deal with occupation and an *intifada*, but the Egyptianized minorities among them, including Jews, Greeks, Italians, Syro-Lebanese, and others, were essentially forced into exile, while the native capitalists were subject to expropriations and other indignities by Nasser's Arab socialism. Still, Egypt's capitalist legacy is both more substantial and more continuous than Palestine's. The Tunisian capitalism that existed at the end of French rule, although substantially disaccommodated by Ahmad Ben Salah's planned economy in the mid-1960s, has remained much more closely linked to the former colonial metropole. Indeed, it is those linkages that account in part for the comparatively rapid rise of Tunisia's manufactured exports over the past decade, but which also pose the greatest threat to them. Having agreed to the EU's terms as laid out in Barcelona in 1995, Tunisia will in the coming decade be losing preferential access to European markets. It will have to open up its nascent manufacturing sector to European competition by lowering its tariffs, which at an average of almost 20 percent in 1997 were only eclipsed by Syria's in the Arab world.

At the core of the explanation of the economic performance of these and other MENA states, however, is the nature of their political regimes. Egypt, Palestine, and Tunisia have different factor endowments and locations, but they share in common rule by elites whose primary base of support is within state structures, rather than in political organizations anchored in society at large. Compelled to service and maintain these structures, these elites are politically incapable of surviving free and fair elections or permitting truly free economic markets to operate. It is thus sufficient to review the experience of Egypt to illustrate how economies in praetorian republics ruled by "bullies" are hostage to their power requirements.

From Paris to tiger along the Nile?

Belle époque Cairo was a "Paris along the Nile," as a recently published book attests by title and by photographs of the city's European architectural legacy (Myntti 1999). A veritable Mediterranean melting pot as Albanians, French, Greeks, Italians, Syro-Lebanese, and others were attracted by the accumulation of wealth first stimulated by the early nineteenth-century reforms of Mohammed Ali, Egypt at nominal independence in 1923 could boast one of the largest, most successful, and certainly most ethnically and religiously heterogeneous capitalist classes in the Mediterranean world. *Mutamassirun*, the Egyptianized foreigners who originally led Egypt's capitalist development under the aegis of British imperial control and French investment, were joined as the twentieth century progressed by increasing numbers of native Egyptians, a process that accelerated as the nationalist movement gained in strength. With the ultimate triumph of that movement under Nasser, most of the *mutamassirun* fled the country, leaving what remained of the capitalist economy in the hands of native Egyptians. But in those hands it did not remain for long, for in the early 1960s the government seized large and even medium-sized holdings of property, stocks and bonds, and other forms of capital that had escaped nationalization until that time. Many Egyptian capitalists joined the *mutamassirun* in exile, external or internal, while the regime-sanctified "national capitalists," who ultimately formed the core of the crony capitalism that first emerged under Sadat, were awarded niches within the public sector dominated economy. But national capitalism was a contradiction in terms, for the economy was as thoroughly socialized as any in the eastern bloc and met the same fate of virtual bankruptcy, only rather sooner.

Faced with an economy that was, as he put it, "below zero," and an Israeli occupation of the Sinai that was corroding what precious little political legitimacy he had, President Sadat, who succeeded Nasser in 1970, saw that he had to come to terms with the USA. To do so would require at least some modification at both the rhetorical and operational levels of the Arab socialism then in effect, a price Sadat was willing to pay as he had never been a supporter of that socialism which had, in any case, run its economic course. So in the wake of the semi-successful October 1973 war, Sadat launched his economic *infitah*, or "opening," which he claimed would wed Arab petrodollars, Western technology, and Egyptian labor and management for the purpose of giving birth to a dynamic, industrialized, mixed public/private economy. The ultimate failure of Sadat's venture resulted from numerous factors, including ever-present regional ones. His controversial peace-making efforts with Israel could not be disentangled from his management of the economy, for they dictated the allocation of scarce material resources to compensate for declining political ones.

But even in the absence of the Arab–Israeli imbroglio, the originally intended pace of Sadat's *infitah* ran far ahead of the resources at the country's disposal. As just mentioned, capitalism and capitalists had been decimated by his predecessor, leaving in the vacuum a constitutional/legal/regulatory structure as inimical to private sector activity as any in the communist world. The legacy of "Arab socialism" in Egypt was a cadre of politically connected public sector managers with little if any private business experience and financial institutions that had been shifted from the German to the French model of administrative control and rendered useless as tools to analyze and encourage economic competitiveness. Lacking experienced capitalists and not having either a civil society accustomed to private economic activity or a legal/regulatory framework which could effectively structure the market, Sadat's *infitah* inevitably foundered. Although awash in capital and enjoying fulsome support from the USA and other Western nations, it could not develop the economy at the pace which its founder had imagined and which the Egyptian public had been promised. On the political front, too, Sadat was in increasing need of new sources of patronage to substitute for the partial dismantlement of the Marxist-Leninist political structures he had inherited from Nasser and to compensate for the loss of resources from the declining public sector.

The answer to Sadat's dilemma was to incubate a system of crony capitalism, key to which was Osman Ahmad Osman, boss of the huge Arab Contractors construction company. Nasser had created a uniquely ambiguous public/private status for Osman's company in order to generate patronage for a limited number of key members of the elite. Sadat elevated this inherited crony capitalist to levels unimaginable under Nasser, to which Osman gratefully responded by generating private wealth and political patronage, and the image, if not the reality, of dramatic and rapid economic development. But the image seemed sufficient at a time when oil revenues were flowing in record amounts and per capita income in Egypt and throughout the MENA was increasing at rates envied by the rest of the world.

Mubarak succeeded Sadat after the high point of oil prices had already been reached and within months of their rapid descent. During much of the remainder of the decade of the 1980s he struggled to keep the ailing economy afloat, threatened as it was with capsize because of its heavy load of external debt. At the end of the decade, when still no major economic reforms had been undertaken, luck of almost the same magnitude as the oil boom rescued the Egyptian economy and maybe Mubarak, whose decision to support the US-led coalition against Iraq netted $25 billion in almost immediate debt relief. This in turn paved the way for an IMF-led stabilization package that by the end of the decade of the 1990s both the IMF tutor and its Egyptian student were heralding as a textbook case of financial reform. Spokespersons for the latter began referring to the "Tiger along the Nile."

Twenty-five billion dollars of sugar coating had made the bitter pill of stabilization very much easier to swallow, but even this was not enough to induce Egypt to ingest the yet more bitter dose of structural adjustment. By the end of the decade the Egyptian leadership, instead of apologizing for the dilatory nature of its adjustment program, was trumpeting the wisdom of its measured pace. It pointed to debacles in Asia, Russia, and Brazil as evidence of the perils of moving too fast, a position which had gained considerable credence among even well-informed, "serious" economists (Richards 1999: 62–71). When Egypt failed to implement its commitment to privatize one of its four public sector banks by the end of 1998, neither the IMF nor the World Bank, nor any of the major bilateral donors, chose to embarrass their budding prize pupil by dwelling on this lapse. It was in fact only one of many departures from promised measures of the structural adjustment program. Such tolerance on the part of international financial institutions suggests once again the importance of regional factors, including strategic rents. The United States in particular had no desire to put the economic screws on Egypt as long as it was being helpful in the bogged-down peace process.

Indeed, if the prize pupil's extra points for political good behavior were not added into its marks, its grades for structural adjustment, economic growth, and integration into the global economy would not be high ones. The state still employs about one-third of the labor force (double the OECD average), a ratio that has not declined under Mubarak. Public employment as a percentage of the total labor force was actually higher by the mid-1990s than it had been in the previous decade (Radwan 1997: 6). The government employs more than half of all workers with post-secondary education. Between 1988 and 1998 the government was the largest contributor to employment growth, as government employment grew at 4.8 percent annually, nearly twice as fast as total employment and contributing 42 percent of net job creation during that decade (EPIC 2000: 2). Government's contribution to GDP "has remained virtually unchanged in the last decade" (Handy 1998: 6). The private sector's share of gross domestic output did not increase during that period, nor have its investments in commodity-producing sectors yet to reach one-third of the total, despite having constituted 32 percent as long ago as 1983 (Ministry of International Trade and Supply 1998: 23). Manufacturing's share of GDP has stagnated. Total fixed investment in industry fell from more than one-quarter to less than one-fifth in the period 1988 to 1996, as public allocations to that sector have declined and not been replaced by private investment.

Privatization of state-owned enterprises, to the extent it has occurred, has not touched the commanding heights of the economy. Egypt not only failed to privatize one of the big four public sector banks before the end of 1998, but in general where privatization has occurred, it has been partial, in most cases not affecting state control nor displacing previous public sector management (Weiss and Wurzel 1998: 105–139). Privatization, moreover, has not been a one-way process. As shares on the Egyptian Stock Exchange commenced a steady descent in 1997, with the average share losing half its value in less than eighteen months, the government first authorized holding companies to buy back shares in their recently privatized companies when they dropped 20 percent below their issue price. When that measure proved insufficient to stop the price decline, it utilized funds in the public sector banks and insurance companies, as well as the government-operated pension fund, to buy at least LE1.5 billion worth of yet more shares, thus effectively re-nationalizing these nominally privatized firms (*Cairo Times* September 17–30, 1998: 17). The prime minister told an audience of National Democratic Party (NDP) leaders in the spring of 1999 that less than 10 percent of state-owned enterprises (SOEs) had been privatized. But even that low figure may be in doubt if the "sale to an anchor investor" of the al Nasr Casting Company is indicative of other such "sales." Although the government claimed it sold the company to an investor for LE48 million in December 1997, the ownership in reality remained with the government. It was transferred from the Holding

Company for Metallurgical Products to the public sector banks that had held most of its debt and to the employee stock association which held a minority stake. Investments in the private sector contributed almost 17 percent to the growth of GDP in 1990, but by 1997 its share had slumped to just over 12 percent (Economic Research Forum 2000: 10).

Persisting state control of the economy has prevented it from becoming effectively integrated into world markets. Egypt is in a small group of less developed countries that is actually "de-globalizing." One measure of a country's integration with the world economy is the sum of its imports and exports as a percentage of GDP. Egypt's declined from 34 percent in 1981–1983 to 23 percent in 1991–1993 (Ministry of International Trade and Supply 1998: 14–15). If the measure is expended to include exports and imports of goods and non-factor services as a share of GDP, Egypt is de-globalizing even more rapidly. In 1985 that index stood at 88 percent, whereas by 1997 it had dropped to 47 percent (Subramanian 1997: 41). The volume of Egypt's exports has declined steadily since 1994. Egypt's share of world exports has also declined, from 0.2 percent in 1985 to 0.07 percent in 1995, while its share of world imports has declined from 0.5 percent to 0.2 percent over that same period. Egypt's market share in the EU fell from 1 percent in 1985 to half that already low level a decade later (Handy 1998: 66). Manufactured goods exported as a proportion of the total value added of manufacturing declined by about 2 percent during the decade that began in 1989, a proportion which was at 9 percent in 1998, compared with 11 percent for Algeria, 58.5 percent for Morocco, 75 percent for Turkey and 129 percent for Tunisia (see Table 3.1). In 1998 tariffs, a major obstacle to export-led growth, were in Egypt "among the most restrictive in the region and higher than in other emerging markets" (Handy 1998: 65). Foreign direct investment contributed 2.4 percent to GDP, but only 1.2 percent in 1997 (Economic Research Forum 2000: 12).

Egypt is also not participating in the revolution in global communications at a level commensurate with its comparative stage of development. As the report of the Ministry of International Trade and Supply previously cited notes, "Egypt lags behind a large number of the comparison countries with respect to most indicators [of information sources]" (1998: 53). It has fewer daily newspapers, televisions, mobile phones, fax machines, personal computers, and Internet hosts per 1,000 inhabitants than almost all comparators among lower- and middle-income developing countries. In 1998 Egypt had only 12,000 private Internet subscribers, in part because the lack of sufficient phone lines resulted in monthly subscription fees of $30–$60, compared with about

$20 in the USA. In any case only some 350,000 computers were in use in the country. Since Egypt does not adequately protect intellectual property rights, including those pertaining to computer software, software manufacturers lose as much as 98 percent of their potential revenues and are understandably reluctant to make new products available in Egypt and the MENA more generally (*Middle East Times* June 6–12, 1997). Although more exposed to global communications than a decade ago, Egyptians are much less well integrated into global communication networks than many of their fellow Arabs, to say nothing of most Latin Americans and Asians.

The textile industry is a microcosm of the globalization challenges facing Egypt and its response to them. It was the focal point of the country's first drive for industrialization, became the backbone of the "socialist" economy and its failed attempt at import substitution, and upon it today rest many of Egypt's hopes for export-led growth. It employs half a million workers, a quarter of all employment in manufacturing. At the beginning of the 1990s it accounted for 30 percent of total industrial, non-oil output and 40 percent of total export earnings. By 1997, however, its share of industrial output had slumped to about one-fifth and its contributions to exports to one-quarter. The accumulated debts of its public sector component, which constitutes 70 percent of the industry, amounted to substantially more than its total fixed assets, suggesting that it was insolvent. The three holding companies responsible for the cotton trade and textile sectors lost LE1.32 billion in 1996/1997 alone (American–Egyptian Chamber of Commerce 1998: 7).

Having failed to sustain its contributions to exports, the industry by the late 1990s was in danger of losing even domestic markets, for, according to the GATT agreement signed by Egypt, the country was to lift the ban on textile imports by January 1998, and that on ready-made clothes by 2003. In order to stop textile imports from "destroying" the industry, as was predicted by the head of the Investor's Division of the Federation of Chambers of Commerce, the Ministry of Supply and Foreign Trade required in 1998 that all imported fabrics have the importer's name woven into them. This "non-tariff barrier to trade," as such methods are called, stopped all imports. This draconian measure protected the predominantly state-owned fabric producers at the expense of the predominantly privately owned garment-manufacturing firms, which had become increasingly dependent upon the much better quality imported cloth, despite the tariff of 70 percent imposed upon it.

Instead of rising to the challenge of globalization, the Egyptian textile industry has been succumbing to it. It has been unable in the 1990s to fill its EU or US quotas under the now expiring Multifibre Agreement, suggesting its lack of competitiveness in these markets, yet the collapse of the eastern bloc sharply diminished Egypt's other, more protected market for exports. In other words, the Egyptian textile industry has lost the contest for textile exports even before the next ratcheting up of global competitiveness in that industry occurs.

As one careful study notes, "the export performance of Egyptian textiles is more constrained by domestic factors than by export market conditions" (Kheir-El-Din and El-Sayed 1997: 4). Those domestic factors relate to the very structure of the industry, "which is character-ized by a heavy concentration of basic production in a limited number of integrated mills and a very fragmented capacity in the downstream garment sector in a large number of private units" (World Bank 1991: 74) The World Bank also noted that "the private units are too small to benefit from economies of scale, while the public sector mills are too large to be managed efficiently." Inefficiencies result in high costs. Lack of modern computer-aided designing in the garment sub-sector results in fabric wastage rates of 17 percent compared with an average rate of 8 percent and time loss 15–25 percent higher than the standard for developing countries (World Bank 1991: 77). The average operating efficiency for spinning in Egypt is less than 60 percent, as compared with a global standard of 85–90 percent. This inadequate performance is due to both poor management and obsolete equipment, with some 850,000 of the total of 3 million spindles in use being uneconomic (USAID 1993b: II-3). Nominally low wage rates place Egypt among the lowest labor cost producers, with a revealed comparative advantage in the vital EU market that is higher for textiles and clothing than that of any other country of the world. Yet, wage costs per worker increased faster in the 1990s than either real production or real value added per worker (Kheir-El-Din and El-Sayed 1997: 7). The labor costs in yarn production are 16 percent of total costs, putting them among the highest percentages for competitive producers. The authors of the most thorough review of the textile sector undertaken in the 1990s observe that "this is ominous for a country that has wage rates among the lowest in the world" (USAID 1993a: II-47). It is ominous because it indicates low total factor produc-tivity resulting from out-of-date technology and bad management, both of which are in turn the products of inappropriate public policies.

The answer to the problems of Egypt's textile industry is not just privatization. Indeed, privatization of SOEs in this industry has stopped, largely because no one wants to buy them in their present form. The private sector, although outperforming the public in terms of its con-tribution to exports in relation to its fixed assets, is not doing particularly well. As the USAID report notes, "In weaving, knitting, dy[e]ing and finishing, and garment manufacturing, privately owned firms are in no better technical condition than the public companies" (USAID 1993a: IV-12). They are more competitive, however, because they pay yet lower wage rates, suggesting that if the textile industry is not completely modernized, its future lies in becoming an ever more marginal sweat-shop. What is true of Egypt is also generally the case throughout the MENA, which actually imports more clothing and textiles than it exports, even though after oil they are its most valuable exports.

The consequences of Egypt's stalled liberalization were by 1999 beginning to erode the accomplishments of the previously successful economic stabilization program. The Egyptian pound came under threat, to which the Government of Egypt (GOE) responded by steadily increasing restrictions on its convertibility. In April and May 1999, the central bank moved to close down twenty-four currency exchange companies on various pretexts, while it also greatly restricted the flow of foreign currency to banks. By May 1999, depositors were being in-formed by their bank tellers that they could not buy even a few thousand dollars with their pounds, while businesspeople were for months turning to what for all intents and purposes was a black market for foreign currency, paying up to LE3.54 for dollars officially pegged at 3.41. In the spring of 2000 the government finally admitted the existence of what it termed a "liquidity crisis," which the president in his May Day speech nevertheless said would not result in a devaluation. The prime minister, echoing the president, claimed that the crisis would be overcome as a result of funds being pumped into the economy by the government repaying its debts to public sector companies, which by early 2000 amounted to some LE25 billion.

As the balance of payments has worsened, the GOE has turned increasingly to issuing domestic paper to cover its budget deficit, and to raising interest rates on pound deposits, thereby further choking off private sector borrowing. Domestic government debt may have reached LE200 billion by 1999, as some well-informed observers claimed, although the central bank, which enjoys virtually no autonomy from the government, held to the figure of LE182 billion, including indebtedness of the public economic authorities (Central Bank of Egypt 1998/1999: 48–49). Egypt, in sum, appeared at the beginning of the new millen-nium to be drifting backwards to the precarious economic state in which it was situated before massive debt relief had bailed it out in the wake of the 1991 Gulf War. As the economy slid downward, the GOE imposed more controls on it, further dampening private activity and isolating it yet more from global markets. This chronicle of poor performance raises the question of why the rapid stabilization of the early 1990s did not lead to a successful structural adjustment, as IMF and World Bank textbook theory would have it.

Impediments to structural adjustment: political deliberalization

As the 1990s progressed, the rhetoric of the regime changed. Having begun the decade with constant reassurances of its intent to democratize, it gradually de-emphasized that commitment and instead spoke increasingly of its sound management of the economy and the measured, steady progress it was making toward economic development and even globalization. This shift in rhetoric may have reflected the belief that more, rather than less, control of the polity would be necessary for the implementation of even the limited structural adjustment that apparently was envisioned.

Whatever the cause, reality matched rhetoric, for as the decade wore on political repression steadily increased. Parliament's approval in late May 1999 of a new law of associations, which further subordinated NGOs to governmental control, amounted to the legislative suffocation of the last remaining element of civil society that was still breathing. Political parties had been choked off gradually during the 1990s. The Muslim Brotherhood was effectively strangled in 1995. During the mid-1990s professional syndicates with political relevance were brought under direct governmental control. The draconian press law of 1995 was amended somewhat in the following year, but it remained highly restrictive. It provided the legal grounds for jailing of several journalists in 1999 and 2000 as a result of their criticism of public figures. The 1995 parliamentary elections were among the most fraudulent in Egypt's modern history, while local government elections in April 1997 were scarcely contested and resulted in the ruling NDP taking virtually all of some 40,000 seats. The government renewed the Emergency Decree in the spring of 2000 and immediately thereafter commenced arrests of potential Muslim Brotherhood candidates in the upcoming fall parliamentary elections.

In the mid-1990s it had been possible to argue that restriction of political freedoms was a result of the GOE's need to combat terrorism. That justification became unsustainable, however, as the insurrection ground to a virtual halt by the end of the decade. Indeed, except for the aberrant attack in Luxor in November 1997, there were no serious terrorist incidents after 1996. The government, in a campaign to recruit tourists, was telling the world by 1998 that Egypt was safer than Europe or North America.

The civilian political system, in short, atrophied in the decade of the 1990s, providing a steadily smaller counterbalance to the military and security-based core of the regime. It is the need to service that base, both directly by facilitating the growth of a military economy, and indirectly through the encouragement of crony capitalism, that accounts in large measure for the failure of structural adjustment to be rapid or thorough, a point to which we shall return below. But even in the absence of these political impediments to structural adjustment, economic reform would still face the challenge of proceeding in the absence of a supporting constitutional/legal/regulatory structure. The standard bearers of the Washington Consensus increasingly recognize good governance to be a prerequisite for successful economic liberalization. Appropriate institutional structures, however, depend for their creation and continued existence on an at least partially competitive political system with some degree of rule of law. That such structures did not emerge in Egypt in the 1990s is one of the costs of political deliberalization and a principal constraint to sustained economic growth.

Constitutional/legal/regulatory structure

Issued in September 1971, and slightly amended in 1980, Egypt's constitution reflects its origins in the very earliest stage of transition away from the command political economy. It expressed various aspirations for a more liberal political system than had been enshrined in the 1964 constitution it replaced, but it provided few institutional manifestations of it nor did it pave the way for a liberalized economy. Article 4, for example, provides that "The economic foundation of the Arab Republic of Egypt is the socialist democratic system based on sufficiency and justice, in a manner preventing exploitation . . ." Article 26 guarantees workers a "share in the management and profits of projects." The constitution is also not "a living document," in the senses that it was either originally written in such a way or subsequently amended so as to provide for and reflect the evolution of the polity or economy, or that all legislation has been brought in line with its provisions. Given the apparent lack of concern to ensure that the constitution reinforces the rule of law or is made consistent with the rhetoric and partial reality of economic liberalization, it is not surprising that substantive law governing the economy also provides an inadequate legal structure for a free market economy.

According to John Bentley, "Egypt's 20-year experiment with socialism and central planning severely and adversely impacted on the ability of Egypt's legal infrastructure to facilitate and encourage private sector economic development . . . Substantive laws were skewed against the free market economy and private sector activity" (Bentley 1994: II, 6). Bentley himself actually played an instrumental role in commencing reform of substantive economic law. The effectiveness of this reform, however, has been impeded by many factors, including the manner in which that law is made. Virtually all legislation is produced in the government itself, with individual ministries assuming primary responsibility for designing the content of proposed bills. Public hearings do not constitute part of the drafting process and only rarely are public hearings used when legislation is being considered in the standing committees of parliament (USAID 1993a: 29). Because many or most of the stakeholders who will be impacted by substantive law play little if any role in its formulation, and because of inadequate drafting procedures, numerous outright mistakes occur. Mahmoud Fahmy, Secretary General of the Maglis al Dawla (State Council) and architect, personally, of much of the legislation associated with economic reform, once observed that a key piece of legislation "violates the constitution because it introduces articles with no legal precedents; its articles furthermore contradict other existing laws" (*Al Ahram Weekly* November 19–25, 1998: 22).

The rule of law in broader terms is hindered by the inadequate capacities of the courts and judiciary. Having been seriously degraded during the Nasser era, they have never been adequately overhauled and upgraded. In the meantime, the caseload of all courts has dramatically increased. In 1998, for example, some 32 million legal cases were filed, meaning that, statistically speaking, virtually every Egyptian is involved in a new legal matter each year, for each case naturally requires a plaintiff and defendant. Deterioration of the court system has caused potential litigants of higher status to seek to avoid those courts altogether, typically by resolving disputes through arbitration. Most foreign business enterprises operating in Egypt, for example, insist upon arbitration clauses in all contracts in order to avoid having to settle disputes before Egyptian courts. Nathan Brown has observed that the "most obvious loser is domestic business. Less able in constructing private arbitration systems, but equally repelled by slow litigation procedures, owners of small businesses have few attractive options" (Brown 1997: 234).

With regard to regulatory bodies, which are an essential adjunct of privatization in some sectors, including public utilities, they are in their infancy and it is not clear that the government is going to facilitate their emergence or effective performance. In telecommunications, for example, the regulatory body that was created for the privatized mobile phone network was simply a vehicle for direct control by the minister of telecommunications, who has ensured that the state monopoly over the use of phone lines remains highly profitable. Consequently international charges remain among the most expensive in the world. The two companies awarded contracts to share oligopolistic control over mobile phones were owned by leading crony capitalists, further reinforcing the need, and underscoring the absence of effective regulation of this vital sector. A comparative study undertaken by a consultant to USAID of the legal/regulatory regimes of Egypt, Israel, Morocco, Tunisia, and Turkey revealed in 1997 that Egypt's was the least effective by a very substantial margin. Turkey's and Israel's were the most effective, and Morocco's and Tunisia's were close behind (USAID 1997: 21).

Executive branch

Of the three branches of government, the executive was most affected by the imposition of the command economy in the 1960s. The high status and legal standing of the judiciary and court systems protected them in part from the ravages of "democratic centralism," and the political standing and potential utility of the parliament also cushioned it from the heaviest blows. The executive, over which the government had direct, undisputed control, became its principal tool for achieving two major objectives – control/surveillance of the population, and cultivation of support through the distribution of patronage. Consequently, the nominal core purpose of this or any executive branch, namely, implementing public policy, was relegated to secondary importance. Little has been done to rehabilitate the executive, to say nothing of modernizing it or redefining its mission from that assigned during the Nasser era to one of supporting economic structural adjustment. It remains, therefore, a major obstacle to more rapid economic growth.

The legacy of the control function is still intact and is suffused throughout the executive branch. Although new, functionally specific administrative bodies were created during the Nasser era in order to control the population, including a vast array of domestic intelligence services and barracked police forces, probably the more serious, residual problem is that posed by the redefinition of the mission of the normal civilian bureaucracy. The Ministry of Local Administration, for example, was assigned the task of controlling local politics and elections, as were, in some measure, the Ministries of Agriculture and Agrarian Reform. The Ministry of Insurance and Social Affairs was made into an organization to oversee activities of voluntary associations, while the various public sector companies were given the task, among others, of mobilizing their labor forces for electoral purposes. The vast bureaucracy and public sector were, in other words, given over to ensuring that there be no autonomous, voluntary activity, a preoccupation that persists.

The second function – that of distributing patronage – has also been preserved. The entire administrative structure was converted to this purpose, for in the first instance patronage meant government jobs, which rose from a few tens of thousands when Nasser took power, to some 3 million when he died, to over 5 million when President Mubarak assumed power. In rural areas government employment typically accounts for more than half of employment outside agriculture. The Minister for Administrative Development, whose task it is to reform the executive bureaucracy, estimates that although "there are five million civil servants in Egypt, there are only two million jobs" (Abu Amer 1998: 2).

The centralized, internally autonomous nature of the executive bureaucracy renders not only efficiency, but also transparency and accountability, almost impossible to achieve. Because the implementation of virtually any aspect of public policy typically requires inputs from various units, and because there are few mechanisms to coordinate those inputs because no actors want to surrender any degree of autonomy, lest their turf be negatively affected, implementation suffers. In the bureaucratic maze through which virtually any public policy matter must pass, transparency vanishes and accountability becomes impossible to enforce.

With the exception of the administrative courts under the Council of State, there are no effective mechanisms to ensure accountability. The Central Organization for Audit, which for some twenty years was the chief means by which parliament could hold individual members of the executive accountable, including high ranking ones, was transferred in June 1998 to the presidency.

The military

The primary economically relevant assets of the military are its direct control of land, labor, and capital, its economic relationships with the state and with domestic and international private capital, and the opacity with which it conducts its business. With regard to material resources, the military controls vast tracts of valuable land, much of it along Egypt's coastline or the Suez Canal, in prime tourist development sites. The conversion of such land originally assigned to the armed forces, either as bases or zones of operation, into other uses provides a major source of revenue directly to the military. It also enables it to enter into joint ventures with public sector and private developers, thereby forging linkages with strategic elites.

The military also controls a large pool of manpower, only a portion of which is absorbed by the primary function of defending the nation. Another significant proportion is utilized in various productive activities, including the raising of crops and livestock, construction of roads, bridges, and buildings, operation of manufacturing plants, and provision of human services, particularly that of health care. Not only do the military directly control what is probably the largest single pool of skilled manpower in the country, but it also deploys the capital required to establish various enterprises and enjoys the freedom to seek technology through joint ventures and other arrangements with multinational firms. It is hardly surprising that it seeks to modernize its enclave economy, but seeking and doing are two different things.

The military is not the vanguard of a technological revolution in Egyptian manufacturing industry. Just as there are incentives for it to modernize, so are there disincentives. Many if not most of its efforts in manufacturing appear to be direct spin-offs from relatively low-level military technology, or joint ventures with private sector Egyptian firms. They are advantageous to both sides not because of the military's high tech capacity, but because the military has access to subsidized inputs. Spin-offs include the production of household cutlery and aerosol canisters for shaving cream in a plant designed to manufacture bullets – hardly the equivalent of the Teflon spin-off from missile nose cones, except that the end use of both products is in the household, not in the laboratory or in industry.

The existence of "free" labor is also a disincentive for technological modernization. Military production plant 200, which produces the M1-A1 tank, for example, commenced production with 6,000 employees. General Dynamics, the US company under whose license and partial supervision the tank is produced, has steadily pressured the Ministry of Military Production to reduce staffing there to 1,200, but has managed to bring it down only to 4,000. Informed US sources estimate that the plant could now operate with as few as 200 personnel.

The underlying problem of the military economy is that in the nether world of economic subsidies and lack of transparency, real and accurate cost accounting is impossible, so that incentives for efficiency are lacking. The microeconomic setting within which production and other decisions are made is "irrational" in the sense that management is inherently incapable in the absence of a price mechanism of assigning true costs to production inputs, however rational it may be for the military to cut costs and become more efficient.

The World Bank, which gathers data on just about every facet of the Egyptian economy, reports nothing about the military's role in the economy, although some of its personnel apparently think that role is quite important. In a presentation to a US government audience in 1998, one of its economists speculated that as much as one-half of manufacturing industry was controlled by the military and claimed that the military was a principal obstacle to privatization in Egypt. At present the military economy itself appears to be in a proto-privatized state, having forged alliances with domestic and multinational private firms. Joint ventures with multinational automobile companies, for example, are partnerships between the military and those companies. They do not constitute true privatization, to which the military economy is unlikely to be subjected for several reasons. First, the centrality of the military to national security means that it is not directly analogous to the civilian public sector. Those with institutional interests in preserving military control will be able to invoke the national security issue with considerable persuasive effect. Second, the state will remain the primary customer of the military public sector, so that market pressures for privatization are largely lacking. Third, the military is a much more powerful political actor than the public sector, hence more capable of defending its interests. Fourth, the patronage dispensed through the military public sector is an important means of maintaining the loyalty of the officer corps and hence is vital to the ruling elite; the rulers will exert little pressure to privatize unless the patronage can be privatized as well. Finally, as long as crony capitalism remains ascendant, a topic to which we shall now turn, the economic interests of the most powerful of the business elite are not in contradiction with those of the military, for indeed, they are in business together. It is only over the long haul that the economic forces theoretically generated by implementation of structural adjustment would become sufficiently coherent and autonomous of the state for them to exert real leverage on civil–military relations and to restrict the role of the military in the economy.

Crony capitalism

Over the years the Nasserist state built up a civilian edifice that both camouflaged the vital role of the inner military/security elite, and performed various technical and political functions. But throughout the Nasser era, all important economic and political decisions were made by the president and/or those entrenched in the military or security forces. Sadat sought to expand the roles and power of the civilian political edifice, in part because of his personal background (he had spent much more time in civilian than in strictly military politics, as he was only briefly a serving officer), in part because his primary opponents were entrenched in the military and security forces, and in part because the image he sought to project required more civilian window dressing. He may also have realized that a more open economy was a prerequisite for rapid economic growth, for he did initiate a stillborn structural adjustment. Sadat, in sum, liberalized both the economy and polity, while engaging in sultanistic politics of dividing and ruling the "mamelukes" controlling the forces of coercion, gradually reducing their direct roles in both the economy and polity.

But the "mamelukes" were compensated for their loss of direct control by the provision of new, indirect rewards through patronage derived from quasi-privatized economic operations, many of which were placed under the military. Although Nasser had permitted and possibly even facilitated a few such relationships, such as those that tied Osman Ahmad Osman to himself and key members of the military elite, Sadat proliferated them, vastly expanding Osman's (and thereby his own) patronage networks, while adding a few new, smaller versions of Osman. As a result, the military/security core elite acquiesced in their nominal loss of power and permitted the rehabilitation of the civilian political system, while establishing methods of remote control that ran through the political economy. Ultimately, however, Sadat's political liberalization fizzled, partly as a result of his peacemaking with Israel, which imposed too heavy a burden for the fledgling system to bear. In the final years of his life he fell back on the military and security forces, over which by then he had established unchallenged control. One of his key instruments in so doing was his vice-president, Hosni Mubarak, an officer well known for his organizational skills in controlling military personnel.

Mubarak is president essentially because Sadat appreciated that he combined a lack of market-oriented political skills with an ability to control a top-down organization behind the scenes. Sadat needed an organization man, but one whose lack of public appeal would render it impossible for him to challenge the incumbent. Mubarak thus inherited the presidency when he had already established reasonably firm behind-the-scenes control of the military and security forces, but he had no political standing whatsoever. He thus spent the first decade of his rule acquiring some trappings of civilian political legitimacy, while further cleansing the military and security of possible challengers. Appreciating that clubs were trumps and that by about 1990 he had firm control of those clubs, he progressively devalued investments in the civilian political fig leaf, justifying political repression explicitly on the grounds of fighting terrorism and implicitly as a prerequisite for economic reform.

In reality, however, control of the "mamelukes" in the military and security forces requires material resources, which in turn has dictated Mubarak's strategy toward the economy, hence of the polity. In order to secure his direct, personal control over the sources of patronage, he dismantled some of the Osman empire that was the key to Sadat's patronage network. He fostered the creation of several additional Osman-like empires, based primarily on construction, an undertaking that provides ample opportunities for generating capital. Leading contractors have access to both public land and public capital (through state-owned banks), require governmental licenses and other approvals, and provide endless opportunities for sub-contracting into labyrinths where public monies can never be traced. Thus crony capitalism, which was almost in the singular under Sadat, became "cronies capitalism" under Mubarak, starting first with Osman and his clones, and then spreading out into various other sectors of the economy.

As in Indonesia, Tunisia, or Palestine for that matter, crony capitalists in Egypt are the instruments of powerful political forces lurking in the background. Chief among them are the president and his family, the key member of which is the older son, Ala'. Through family members Mubarak has mediated business relations with many if not most of the leading cronies, of whom there are some two to three dozen. The Mubaraks provide the necessary rent generating facilities, such as access to satellite communications, monopolies over telecommunications markets, or contracts for services to SOEs, while the cronies do the rest. But the Mubarak family is not the only actor in the system. Powerful active and retired military and security generals also have their own cronies. So the Bahgat Group, for example, is tied to military officers who have provided Ahmad Bahgat both access to military factories to assemble electronic goods and protection from others who might want to assemble competitive appliances, by closing the factory gates to them. The automobile industry replicated this model, but without closing the door so tightly to imports, which became a problem in the late 1990s as the currency became steadily overvalued, thus sucking in ever more imports. Finally, in early 1999 the crony capitalists, backed by their protectors in the regime, leaned on the Ministry of Trade, through the presidency, to issue Decree 619, which prohibited entry into Egypt of trans-shipped goods, thereby significantly reducing auto imports, most of which are trans-shipped through third countries.

Mubarak, in sum, has diversified the crony capitalist system he inherited from Sadat, and reaped considerable benefits by so doing. He has gained direct or indirect control over the flow of resources, such that his dominance over the key elite is unchallenged. He has been able to present, more or less convincingly, accomplishments of crony capitalism as manifestations of Egypt's economic liberalization, thereby reducing pressure to really liberalize. His strong position on both counts has enabled him to deal harshly with the civilian political system, partly ignoring it and partially dismantling it.

But the economic price of Mubarak's political success is high. Inward-looking crony capitalism, coupled to the military economy and the leviathan government with its still large public sector, generates the patronage and provides the controls required for the regime to retain its support within the state, while contemptuously ignoring or repressing what little autonomous political life remains. But this nexus of cronies, officers, bureaucrats, and public sector managers is inherently inward-looking, as it feeds off rents that can only be provided by the monopolies and oligopolies of a protected economy. In 1982 Egypt exported goods worth $8.6 billion and Turkey $9.2 billion. In 1999 Turkish exports had risen to $52 billion, while Egypt's had increased to only $14 billion. Virtually 100 percent of revenue collected through direct taxes, some LE28 billion, by 1999 went to pay interest on the steadily rising public debt. In that year imports amounted to $17 billion and exports to $4.4 billion, a ratio of about four to one, whereas five years previously those figures were $10.6 billion and $3.3 billion, respectively, for a ratio of about three to one. The steadily more negative balances of trade and payments, and associated need for governmental borrowing, presage an economic crisis.

In the meantime, however, the steady slide toward insolvency places stress on the linkages between the cronies and their patrons, as the former can take their money and run, while the latter are rooted in the Egyptian state. When a threat to the Egyptian pound materialized in February 1998, for example, Mubarak called in thirty-one of the key cronies and told them that if they dollarized their holdings he, who had put them in their Mercedes automobiles, "would put them back on bicycles." As if to underline the extreme mobility of capital generated by crony capitalism, Osman's death in the summer of 1999 stimulated a stampede of family and other claimants to Aachen, Germany, where the granddaddy of Egyptian cronies had stashed his fortune. No doubt it constituted a considerable portion of the $50–$80 billion the World Bank and other sources estimate Egyptians hold abroad, which in turn is only 10–15 percent of total Arab holdings outside the Arab world, if the estimate of $500 billion of such holdings is correct.

The limited power of capital

The very magnitude of flight capital from the Arab world and the MENA generally, for which savings abroad are equivalent to 90 percent of the region's GDP, the highest ratio in the world, suggests the relative weakness of capitalism therein (Yousef 1998: 14). In the case of the bully capitalist states, both the historical legacy and present regime strategy ensure that emerging capitalists lack the power to act autonomously from the state, to say nothing of inducing the state to provide the hypothetical level economic playing field.

As regards the historical legacy, Egyptian and Tunisian capitalists were both much weakened at the hands of their radical nationalist states, although the decimation of nativized foreigners that occurred in the former did not take place in Tunisia, nor were the nationalizations so thoroughgoing. Palestinian capitalists are, for the most part, outside Palestine and seem intent on remaining so unless and until the "investment climate" becomes more favorable. The uneven resuscitation of capitalism in Egypt and Tunisia has been too incomplete and too discontinuous to generate a new class of independent capitalists, although private capital accumulation is accelerating in both, as suggested by the rising share of profits and rents and declining share of wages in both economies. But accumulations of capital do not translate into political power. While regimes in bully states are not as hostile to capitalist accumulation as they tend to be in bunker states, bully regimes jealously guard their monopoly on political power. As Jean-Pierre Cassarino observes with regard to Tunisia, "The 'challenges of globalization' . . . have encouraged the emergence of a group of highly visible entrepreneurs . . . but in doing so [have] strengthened their connection with the state, through the distribution of financial resources, 'titles of nobility,' and media visibility." He further notes that "As for the government, there is no question that by mobilizing the 'Captains' of these corporate groups, it enhances its control over economic liberalization . . ." (Cassarino 1999: 69–72).

Both impersonal and personal methods are used to restrain the political autonomy of capital, as evidence from Egypt suggests. The financial sector remains under close and centralized governmental control. The central bank is neither autonomous by statute nor effective in practice, having neither changed its organizational structure nor added to its staff of only some 200, despite the expanded roles nominally assigned to it by economic liberalization (Caprio and Claessens 1997: 27). Almost three-quarters of bank deposits continue to be held by banks 100 percent owned by the government, with the bulk of remaining deposits in the twenty-three joint venture banks at least partially owned by the big four public sector banks. In Indonesia, by comparison, deposits in government-owned banks dropped from above 80 percent in 1988 to less than half some six years later (Caprio and Claessens 1999: 25). Mahmud Abd al Aziz, chairman of the biggest public sector bank, the National Bank of Egypt, is also chairman of the biggest "private" bank, the Commercial International Bank (CIB). Confidence in the banking system, as one observer tactfully remarked, was much eroded in the 1980s and is still "not commensurate with the ensuing stabilization" (Subramanian 1997: 26). Some 30 percent of the loan portfolios of the four public sector banks are estimated to be "non-performing" (Mohieldin 1995: 20). Public sector textile firms alone owed the banks LE6.3 billion in 1997, non-performing loans that will, most probably, never be repaid. In 1993 at the start of the privatization program the government stated that the public sector had a total debt of LE66 billion. Since that time debts are generally thought to have increased, but in 1998 the Central Auditing Agency in its report to parliament noted that, as of June 1996, the public sector owed banks LE26.9 billion, further increasing the informed public's skepticism about the reliability of the government's financial reports. This skepticism is underscored by Egypt's relatively low CIM/M2 ratio, as shown in Figure 3.2. The significance of that ratio is suggested by the 1998 annual report of the central bank. It noted that the value of paper money circulating in Egypt exceeds LE30 billion, or about LE500 per capita. Two-thirds of the country's quarter of a million firms that employ fewer than ten people do not maintain bank accounts.

The banking sector's lack of autonomy from the government was underscored in 1998 and 1999 by a series of scandals involving half a dozen parliamentarians from the ruling party who utilized their governmental connections to plunder the public sector banks or joint venture banks in which they have an interest. The former chairman of parliament's Planning and Budget Committee, who had also been minister of aviation and tourism, was finally taken into custody in August 1999, along with another parliamentarian who was the son of a former minister of local administration. These members and their colleagues were charged with having arranged loans exceeding LE100 million without the provision of collateral. This signal that the government was finally bowing to pressure to do something about this long-running scandal caused three others to flee the country, to which the government responded by barring four more members of parliament, fifteen businessmen, and thirteen bankers from leaving the country (*Al Ahram Weekly* August 5–11, 1999: 8). But the state obviously decided that it would be better to expedite the escape of one of the really big fish caught up in the loans scandal, lest the ensuing trial bring to light embarrassing information. Alia al Ayouti, the former managing director of Nile Bank who was under investigation for defrauding her own bank of several hundred million Egyptian pounds, was issued a travel permit days prior to her arrest by the outgoing attorney general, Raga al Arabi.

The relative weakness and government control of the banking sector reflect the financial sector more generally. The three large state-owned insurance companies control 90 percent of the market directly and own shares in joint venture companies that control another 8 percent (Westley 1998). Public finance is extremely concentrated, such that virtually all allocations of public money for civilian purposes, even those by local governments, must be approved at what in practice is the prime ministerial level. Central bank auctions of governmental treasury bills are nominally open to all bidders, but in reality restricted to the public sector banks. "The Egyptian banking system's support of the private sector has been quite limited . . . the amount of credit to it lags even within the Middle East region." Caprio and Claessens go on to note that even some of the so-called "transitional economies," such as Poland and Romania, are allocating proportionately more capital to their private sectors than is Egypt (1997: 25).

The nominal representation of an Anglo-American capitalism in the financial sector, the stock market, in fact more closely resembles the French model of administrative control. Small investors are notable in their absence from the market, in which thirty companies account for over half of total capitalization, of which only fifteen "effectively grant investors free entry and exit." The market accounts for a minuscule 0.77 percent of the capitalization of emerging markets (*Al Ahram Weekly* November 5–11, 1998: 8). In the first half of 2000 two companies, one of which was a proposed media city on Cairo's outskirts that was still in the planning stages and the other one, Mobilnil, one of the country's two mobile phone companies, accounted for more than half the Cairo exchange's turnover. The government is the largest player on the exchange, using public monies in an attempt to manipulate share prices.[1]

---

[1] Based on the calculation that it could maximize its return from privatizations of SOEs by driving up the price of shares, the government began in 1997 to purchase large amounts of those issues, which for some months did have the desired effect. But within a year this strategy backfired, in part because the magnitude of governmental purchases scared off private buyers and because the government itself, under financial pressures, was unable to sustain its purchasing. By early 1999 the share prices of two-thirds of privatized companies were below their issue price, a factor which contributed to the further deceleration of the privatization program.

The market itself has been plagued with scandals of insider trading, lack of transparency, and inadequate regulation, as well as rapid turnover in key positions. Three officials succeeded one another in the chairmanship of the exchange in less than two years up to 1999, and one of them was forced out for attempting to enhance the transparency of share trading and corporate financial reporting (*Financial Times* January 15, 1999: 40). An advisor to the minister of public enterprise was forced to resign when it was revealed that he was using the confidential information of that ministry to speculate on the market. One of the top 100 investors in the market is an "official responsible for restructuring public sector companies undergoing privatization" (Mostafa 1997b). In May 2000 investors "fed up with the lack of clarity governing stock transactions . . . protested in front of the Egyptian stock exchange headquarters" (Abdel-Razek 2000). The particular source of aggravation was that insiders had dumped vast amounts of Mobilnil shares just prior to the release of disappointing reports on earnings. Investor disenchantment with the inefficient and even rigged market has been manifested by flight from it. Of fifty-seven public sector companies whose shares were floated on it during 1999, the share prices of forty-three had fallen by 75 percent or more within six months. (Essam el-Din 1999: 5). The commanding heights of the economy, in sum, even though they are not so commanding by the standards of many other emerging economies, remain under at least indirect governmental control.

In the case of the Islamic financial sector, in which the potential for conversion of capital into autonomous political resources is much greater, the degree of governmental control is qualitatively higher. The "informal" component of that sector consisted of so-called "Islamic investment companies" that proliferated in the mid-1980s and came to control a very substantial share of private savings, largely by serving as channels for remittances from the Gulf. The government cracked down on it in 1988, but depositors were still struggling to obtain some portion of their frozen funds a decade later. The inordinate delay suggested that the government was purposely seeking to deter citizens from making such investments in the future, were the opportunity to arise.

The formal Islamic sector, which consists of Islamic banks, cannot be dealt with as harshly as were Islamic investment companies, for those banks have international credibility and linkages and, in any case, comply with all central bank regulations. The Faisal Islamic Bank, which commenced operations in 1977, is the oldest and largest of the three Islamic banks. In addition, eleven private commercial banks and one public sector bank (Bank Misr) have opened Islamic branches over

the past fifteen years. Islamic banks' deposits of LE7.4 billion amounted
to 5 percent of total deposits by 1997, having achieved low but steady
growth rates throughout the decade. The rate of growth of deposits and
lending would probably have been substantially higher in the absence of
governmental efforts to contain such growth. Those efforts have consisted of attempts to tarnish the Islamic legitimacy of the institutions, as
well as the placing of legal obstacles in the path of their operations. The
three major Islamic banks, for example, have been forbidden from
opening new branches. The country's official Islamic establishment,
which is under direct governmental control, has conducted a campaign
against the banks. Sheikh al Azhar Muhammad Sayid Tantawi has
issued a string of *fatwas* favoring conventional banks. In 1997 he
contributed a series of articles to *Akhbar al Yawm* in which he argued
against the religious credentials of "so-called Islamic institutions." He
referred to those who do not set fixed interest rates as "thieves" and
banks that have Islamic branches as "ignorant and hypocritical," causing
one of his al Azhar colleagues to observe that his statements may be
"politically rather than divinely inspired" (Mostafa 1997a: 52–58).
Paradoxically the state itself, as another tactic to contain Islamic
banking, opened its own Islamic branches operated by the state-owned
Bank Misr; free to organize throughout the country, they succeeded by
1998 in attracting more deposits than any of the fully-fledged Islamic
banks (Galloux 1999: 494–496).

Potential or actual manifestations of autonomous political behavior by
business elites are strongly discouraged. Leadership of the principal
business associations is exercised by businessmen with close ties to the
political elite or, in the case of the high-profile Egyptian Center for
Economic Studies, by the younger son of the president. Informal
political "red lines" are made evident to businesspersons less they cross
them and earn the government's ire. One such red line is support for
opposition political parties, which is widely known to invite problems
with the authorities for those businessmen who do provide it. All of the
many businessmen elected to parliament in 1995 were either members
of the ruling National Democratic Party or "independents" affiliated
with it. Private capital is indeed accumulating as the economy is
gradually liberalized, but the power of that capital obviously remains too
limited to be exercised independently of the state. A study of the
behavior of deputies in the 1995–2000 parliament revealed that those
who were businessmen "performed poorly," lagging behind their colleagues in attendance and submission of legislation. Significantly, they
did not take unified stands on key economic issues.

Prospects for bully praetorian republics

Because globalization unleashes forces that reduce the control of states over their national economies, it poses a particular threat in the MENA, where virtually all states are, by global standards, overgrown. Paradoxically, bunker praetorian republics appear to have greater latitude than their "bully" counterparts to formulate policies in response to globalization. This is because those bunker states are less constrained by their civil societies and the power of capital, a freedom which comes at the price of effectiveness of any economic policy these states adopt. The policy choices of regimes in bully praetorian republics are more constrained by civil society and the structural power of capital, but the probable effectiveness of their policies is greater. They at least have the possibility of renegotiating state–society relations to make them more conducive to sustainable, broad-based economic growth. The line between ruler and ruled in the bully praetorian republics is drawn only by their respective relations to the state, not, as is the case in bunker praetorian republics, also by their membership in clans, tribes, or other social formations. Thus redrawing those lines does not necessarily involve a complete reconfiguration of the political community, possibly as a result of civil war.

A renegotiation of state–society relations will ultimately be required if bully praetorian republics are to respond effectively to the threats and opportunities of globalization. The analogy of the colonial dialectic suggests, however, that time is required before the balance of power between them becomes more equal, hence propitious for either negotiations or a breakthrough into power by a new social force. At present the rulers of Egypt seem to be operating on the premise of business as usual. They appear to believe they can reconcile globalization with a political regime based almost exclusively on state institutions, with all the costs such a regime imposes on capitalist development. The one noticeable change is the expansion of the role of crony capitalists over the past quarter of a century, but at an accelerating pace in the decade of the 1990s, a phenomenon which itself reflects the pressure of globalization. Thus far crony capitalism has enabled the regime to have its cake and eat it too – to retain state control while giving the appearance of adopting the Washington Consensus. But this crony capitalism is economically non-sustainable, based as it is largely on rent seeking in protected markets. The worsening balance of trade figures and resultant pressure on the currency are early warning signs of the bigger economic problems yet to come in the early part of the new century. While Egypt's continuing geo-strategic importance will garner it more international rents, it is unlikely that those rents will be sufficient to cushion an economy of 70 million people from the ever harder blows of economic globalization.

For Egypt and the other bully praetorian republics, however, crony capitalism does not have to be the end of the line. It could be a way station on the road to a more genuine, effective capitalism. Although the present number of crony capitalists is not large, their successes do serve as models to be imitated by others. As competition increases it could stimulate efforts to enhance returns through both rents *and* productivity improvements. The calculation of their own economic interests might ultimately cause even crony capitalists to support the creation of "level playing fields" as more profitable alternatives to sharing rents with political elites. This desire might in turn dictate a strategy of support for alternative political actors, including those who speak directly on behalf of this emerging and transforming capitalism.

International pressures of various sorts that impinge on the domestic economy may also enhance domestic competition and provide opportunities for new entrants to the system. Even limited privatization will ultimately erode some of the economic power base of the state. Economic success and political stability could in turn feed the confidence of incumbent political elites, who might then respond by permitting steadily greater latitude for investors. Rent-seeking mentalities would, in this scenario, steadily give way to the understanding that broadly based economic growth will pay the greatest economic and political benefits. In short, crony capitalism could be a developmental phase in the gradual economic reform of a command political economy in which the political elite is insufficiently confident to suddenly throw open the doors to rapid economic and political change. As such, crony capitalism would play a functional, transitional role for the further development of the political economy.

An alternative, much less benign scenario is also possible. It is that the present state-dependent, crony capitalism is not a way station on the road to a more open, competitive free market system, but is an alternative and hindrance to other, more productive forms of capitalism. The nexus between the political elite and successful businesspeople is, in this view, too central to the system, too institutionalized, and too remunerative to both sides for it easily to be broken. Neither side would ever have an interest in modifying rent-seeking arrangements, and outsiders, whether Egyptians or foreigners, will have insufficient leverage to do so. Entrenched in power and protected by purposeful lack of transparency, cronies and their guardian "mamelukes" in the state will ensure that competitors do not arise. They will succeed, for example, in perpetuating tariff barriers to protect monopolized domestic markets secured through rent-seeking arrangements, and will successfully lobby to retain an over-valued currency in order to continue to access imports at lower prices, again in order to service protected markets. According to this scenario, crony capitalism will retain monopolistic and oligopolistic control over domestic markets and will continue to try to isolate that market from globalization, thereby perpetuating both itself and underdevelopment until the strategy ultimately fails as a result of undeniable economic calamity.

Reference to the possibly analogous case of the colonial dialectic might help resolve whether or not the benign or malignant scenario is the more likely of the two. The globalization dialectic has created a first generation of aspiring capitalist imitators – cronies – equivalent in both substantive and sequential terms to the Westernized "compromisers" of the colonial dialectic. Were the door to power to be opened to them now, presumably they would consolidate an imitative system in the shadow of the Washington Consensus – a successful conversion of crony capitalism into a more dynamic, outward-oriented version, à la our first scenario.

But the globalization dialectic has already thrown up a second generation of moralizers, most of whom are searching for radical, non-compromising, nativist solutions of which Islamist ones are far and away the most prevalent. As the globalization dialectic is proceeding at a faster pace than its colonial predecessor, this generation of moralizers has been on the scene for about as long as the capitalist accommodators, with whom they are in competition. But their very radicalism, which has alienated large portions of the population, and the relatively greater power of national as opposed to colonial states, seems to have undermined their chances of a breakthrough. The way may thus have been paved for a third generation antithesis to the thesis of globalization – that is, unless an extreme economic crisis swamps these systems in the meantime.

This third generation is also that of moralizers, but one that is relatively moderate and seeks a synthesis between nativist Islam, on the one hand, and the globalist Washington Consensus of free markets and (implied) secular polities, on the other. With regard to the economy, mention was made in chapters 1 and 2 of the role of Islamic financial institutions, which are growing throughout the region. On the political level the most rapidly expanding sector of civil society, including political parties, appears to be moderate Islamism, a movement which eschews the radicalism of underground terrorist groups and seeks political office, where possible, through the ballot box and an Islamicized, yet modernized society through voluntaristic activities. But neither the economic, the social, nor the political manifestations of this third generation of synthesizers has yet matured sufficiently to assume major financial or political responsibility. The current contest is defined by the incumbent elites and tends to minimize their importance, associate them with more radical Islamist oppositions, and marginalize them in Egypt, for instance, by supporting public sector competitors. But Islamic finance and the capitalists it may spawn, who might in time bring about a qualitative change to the political economy, are probably the best defense against other, radical/revolutionary Islamists.

For both Egypt and Tunisia the scenario of a renegotiation of power between state and society, with the nascent, as yet largely crony capitalism steadily assuming more power and gradually being transformed into a more robust, more independent capitalism, seems possible. The constant economic pressure resulting from globalization may push toward a renegotiation. In Egypt and Tunisia, both the state and society have considerable strengths, suggesting that Islamist radicals are unlikely to prevail. The state has its well-articulated structure, its tradition of rule by law if not of law, its sheer size, and history of centrality to the country. But society can also draw on a long tradition of structured political participation, of some independence of civil society and of capital, and on the resources and impacts of globalization itself. The justification for military or police rule, even indirect, has long passed and the transition back to civilian government is the central issue in current speculation over the next presidential succession, especially in Egypt. The temptation for both countries' nascent capitalists to seek to play more independent and important roles in shaping public policy for both the economy and the polity must likewise be accelerating. In sum, the balance of power between state and society is becoming more equal, thus suggesting that a renegotiation of the relationship could occur. Whether that would precede an overhaul of the constitutional/legal/regulatory structure and the institutionalization of some forms of accountability and transparency, including control of the military, or be a byproduct of those changes, would depend on the historical circumstances.

Tunisia's response to globalization has been somewhat more effective than Egypt's, largely because it garners fewer international rents, has a greater need to export, and has a tighter embrace of Europe, both historically and contemporaneously. But Tunisia's comparatively rapid growth may have already plateaued. Net foreign inflows of capital declined through the mid-1990s and, in any case, during that decade three-quarters of that investment was limited to the oil and gas sector. Only 2.5 percent was in manufacturing industry (Dillman 1999: 5), though in 1998 Tunisia did manage temporarily to increase FDI to $650 million by selling off a couple of cement plants to the European cartel. The Tunis stock exchange fails to attract foreign investment not only because of its small size, but also for lack of transparency compared with Morocco's. As in Egypt, the major banks remain under state control, so as to preserve confidentiality and to cover the non-performing loans of cronies as well as state enterprises. Non-performing loans still amounted to 22 percent of GDP at the end of 1998, after six years of efforts to consolidate and restructure the financing of the public enterprises (IMF 2000: 9, 35–37). Some public sector shares in banks, notably the Banque du Sud, were sold off, but control over management still remains with the government. Total assets derived from privatization from 1990 to 1997 amounted to a minuscule $150 million, placing it almost at the bottom of the MENA privatization table (Dillman 1999: 8–9). The total cost of subsidizing public enterprises from 1993 to 1998 amounted to 2.1 billion dinars, with the annual cost being higher in 1998 than it had been five years earlier. Between 1990 and 1997 the private sector's contribution to GDP dropped from almost 20 percent to about 12 percent, whereas the public sector's share rose (Economic Research Forum 2000: 8–9).

Tunisia's police state is as averse to the free flow of information as is Libya's or Iraq's, whose diplomats it joined in May 2000 in breaking relations with Qatar in protest against the little principality's protection of a satellite TV station, Al-Jazira. The broadcasts from Qatar of controversial debates and discussions have attracted viewers throughout the Arab world, yet Tunisia, like the bunker states, cannot tolerate criticism of its abhorrent human rights record or archaic single-party politics. President Ben Ali, after years of hesitation, finally permitted public access to the Internet in late 1997, and then only through companies controlled by his daughter and other close associates. Any public entity mounting a web page must seek clearance from the local censor. Even faxes are monitored, and under such conditions some international businesspeople have simply left the country for more congenial climates.

Without a more transparent business-friendly climate, advances to higher production technologies are unlikely to happen. Continued production at that level necessarily results in declining national wealth, as competition at the bottom ends of global commodity chains, where most of Tunisia's exports are situated, leads remorselessly to ever lower wages and profits. Changes to the international trading order following the Uruguay Round and the Barcelona Declaration may also have particularly severe consequences for the "Mediterranean tiger," dependent as it is on European markets and threatened as it is by European imports. The first MENA country to have its partnership agreement with the EU ratified, it has received more aid and credits per capita to upgrade its manufacturing than any other southern Mediterranean country. In fact between 1995 and 1999 the EU actually disbursed more funds to Tunisia than to any other southern Mediterranean "partner" (European Commission 2000: 5). But however efficiently its economic diplomacy works, the Tunisian state is predicted to lose over 24 percent of its total revenue, or 6 percent of its GDP, by 2010 as a result of tariff reductions scheduled over twelve years. During that period it is antici-pated that, despite EU support for "restructuring" of Tunisian industry, only 15 percent of private firms will certainly survive the dismantling of import barriers, 70 percent will come under serious threat, and the remainder will go bankrupt (Mahroug 1996: 91). Whatever the outcome, the increasingly intense globalization dialectic is rendering the political economy of Tunisia, like Egypt's, sustainable only if the polity can contain ever increasing pressure resulting from economic stagna-tion. That containment could ultimately cause these bully states to engage in war with their societies, thus coming to imitate the bunker praetorian republics.

The future of Palestine is so heavily dependent upon external assis-tance and the outcome of negotiations with Israel that its domestic political economy will probably have less impact than does that of Egypt or Tunisia on their respective futures. Nevertheless, the trajectories of those two countries probably are indicative of what is likely to happen to Palestine. The Palestinian Authority is in developmental terms at about the radical nationalist phase reached in Egypt under Nasser and in Tunisia in the early 1960s under Planning Minister Ben Salah, although it is not by any means so avowedly or operationally socialist. As part of a strategy to "conquer" society, major components of which remain antagonistic to the ruling elite – especially a large and vociferous "second-moment" Islamist movement – the PA has vastly expanded the size of its governing apparatus and patronage networks. These "state-building" efforts are being financed in large measure by the international donor community, which cares less about democracy and development in Palestine than it does about peace between Palestinians and Israelis and the security of the latter. Moreover, the geographic borders and regional alliances of the mini-Palestine will remain undecided for some time to come. In these circumstances of domestic and regional uncer-tainty, and in the face of an insecure political elite, Palestinian capital will possess neither the means nor the will to make substantial contribu-tions to the economy or polity. Thus the prospective Palestinian state looks set to develop in a bully praetorian direction.

Suggestions for further reading

Galal Amin (1995, 2000) is always stimulating in his observations of Egypt's political economy. Handy (1998), Harik and Sullivan (1992), and Sadowski (1991) also focus on Egypt, while Waterbury (1993) compares its public sector with those of Turkey, India, and Mexico. Hamidi (1998) offers the perspective of a disappointed sympathizer on Tunisia's Islamist opposition, while Murphy (1999) and Zartman (1991) present its political economy. Rocard (1999) critically analyzes the Palestine National Authority, while Brand (1998) and Brown (1997) offer comparative analyses of political liberalization and the rule of law.

The monarchies in the region seem better positioned than praetorian republics to take advantage of the opportunities of the globalizing economies. They have more active private sectors, some of which have joint ventures and other constructive relationships with multinational companies, in petroleum-related industries for the most part. Many of them also have concentrated financial systems, discussed in chapter 3, that enable them to engage in a controlled liberalization that fits some of the commandments of the Washington Consensus. However, the monarchies are also politically more vulnerable than the praetorians because they did not undergo the full political transformation of a colonial dialectic. Yet they depend just as much as the other regimes discussed so far in this book on their military and police forces to stay in power – rather than on any deeply rooted traditional legitimacy to which their official propaganda machines lay claim.

Most of them are relics of British imperialism. Britain generally preferred to intervene as little as possible in the internal affairs of its possessions because their prime importance lay in their geographical positions, astride passages to India, not in any intrinsic worth. It was easier to deal with ruling families by anointing them as monarchs than to reorganize their territories as crown colonies. Borders were matters of chance and political opportunity. As colonial secretary in 1921, for instance, Winston Churchill invented Jordan for the sake of one of the sons of the Sharif Hussein of Mecca. The father was owed favors for sponsoring T.E. Lawrence's Arab Revolt against the Turks in World War I. Abdullah, the son in question, had been promised Iraq, but the British gave this plum instead to his younger and more cosmopolitan brother Faisal, whom the French had expelled from Syria in 1920. The British protected other ruling families, the Sabahs of Kuwait, the Khalifas of Bahrain, the Thanis of Qatar, and the Qabbous of Oman, and other tribal notables along the Arabian coastline of the Persian Gulf, helping them assume the trappings of monarchy. Only Morocco's ruling dynasty has roots in the precolonial past, while Saudi Arabia, defined by the conquests of its ruling family, only fully emerged with defined borders in the early 1930s. Despite receiving British subsidies, the Saud family retained its independence first by winning the holy lands of Mecca and Medina in 1926 and then by offering oil concessions to the Americans.

With the exception of Morocco, the monarchies surviving independence enjoyed relatively superficial and positive colonial encounters, barely touched by nationalist movements. They consequently retain close business links with their old colonial mentors and new American advisors, while encouraging local private entrepreneurs to benefit from the overseas connections. Unlike bunker or bully capitalist regimes, they rarely nationalize foreign or indigenous assets. Even the nationalizations of the American, British, and French oil companies came late, gradually, and reluctantly. In Bahrain and the United Arab Emirates the foreign companies retain minority shareholdings. Aramco, a consortium of American oil companies, managed the Saudi oil business until 1990 and still provides key technical assistance.

Although private capitalists may be perceived as a threat to a secretive and unaccountable regime, they offer most monarchies strategic depth. An active private sector can help such a regime to attract the international and national capital needed to be more competitive in the global economy. In the monarchies the local business elites act as part of a big extended family, for the ruler retains the ability to alter the pecking orders of power, privilege, and wealth. There is no true distinction between public and private property. What a wealthy ruler gives away may be taken back; he may manipulate the private sector resources of his more or less vibrant civil society and the NGOs that formally reflect it. The semblance of civil society buffers political opposition and may facilitate crafty strategies of cooptation for economic development and globalization. It enables the monarchies to project more open business environments than those of the bunker or bully capitalist regimes. They remain wedded to the international order that founded them and facilitated their development.

Indeed, unlike the military regimes with their state enterprises, the monarchies and their principal businesses are relatively well integrated into the global economy through joint ventures. They are consequently more exposed to potential populist backlashes against globalization. Since the structural power of local capital is greater, the rulers cannot bully it. They instead negotiate with their business notables so as to discourage them from making alliances with populist Islamists. Their economic strategies are more constrained by the interests of local capital, which may sometimes be expressed in civil society, than are those of the bully or bunker regimes.

Within these parameters the monarchies display considerable variation. Morocco, with almost 30 million inhabitants, has about three times the indigenous population of Saudi Arabia, ten times Jordan's, over thirty times Kuwait's, and 300 times Qatar's. Morocco's ruling dynasty, the Alawis, achieved power and spiritual hegemony in 1666, centuries before the Saudis and the Hashemites of Jordan and Iraq. The monarchies vary not only with respect to their legitimacy and longevity but also in the degree of sophistication of their civil societies. Morocco, Kuwait, and Jordan have highly articulated party systems (although informal in Kuwait's case), more or less regular elections, and a relatively free press. Morocco and Jordan do not have the mineral wealth of Saudi Arabia or the other GCC states and perhaps compensate by according somewhat greater political freedom to their citizens. But Kuwait, with huge oil wealth, does not need to compensate its citizens with political liberties for diminished economic privileges. Its government supports social services, including sinecures in Kuwait's vast bureaucracy and public sector, at least as extensive as those of the other petrostates, but the sophistication of its merchant class and the shadow of Iraq have also influenced its politics since the 1930s, generally toward a semblance of democracy. The Kuwaiti parliament has a unique if discontinuous history. The other rich monarchies of the GCC keep a tighter lid on their respective oppositions, but Bahrain's new emir pardoned hundreds of detainees and exiles and then held a referendum in February 2001 to endorse plans for an elected parliament. Saudi King Fahd finally appointed a consultative council in 1993 – but only after suffering the traumas of Desert Storm and local petitions against arbitrary government (Gause 1993: 94–98).

Morocco and Saudi Arabia are not only the most populous and influential of the monarchies. They also mark extremes in the continua of longevity, wealth, and civil sophistication. In one respect Morocco is unique among Arab monarchies. It alone weathered a relatively intensive and protracted colonial situation without either, as in Tunisia, being superseded by a mass nationalist movement or, as in Egypt or Iraq, being overthrown by radical military officers. As already mentioned in chapter 1, the French colonial authorities unintentionally transformed Mohammed V, their reclusive, protected sultan, into a national hero by exiling him and his family to Madagascar in 1953. His son, the late Hassan II (1929–1999), then repressed and subdued Morocco's second- and third-moment elites. After physically eliminating his most intransigent opponents in the 1960s, he coopted much of Morocco's political class into a parliamentary system that reserves most significant powers for the monarch. Thus Morocco is not only the oldest but also the most experienced and effective of the Arab monarchies in coping with contemporary nationalist and Islamist oppositions. Jordan, by incorporating the West Bank and receiving hundreds of thousands of Palestinians expelled from Israel in 1948, is the only other surviving Arab monarchy facing comparable internal opposition. The monarchies of the GCC, of interest primarily for their oil, were not colonized extensively; and Western education came much later than to Iran, Iraq, and the Mediterranean states of the region. Consequently "the new middle class" is weaker, so that Saudi Arabia and the other GCC monarchies deal with less articulated civil societies and have less experience coping with organized oppositions than do their northern neighbors. But all of the monarchies are experiencing major social problems that may render them vulnerable to the challenges of traditionalist and radical oppositions.

Morocco

The king's royal household, the *makhzan*, not the official government, dominated economic policy-making, until recently. In precolonial times this *makhzan*, or magazine, stored the grain collected as taxes that the sultan then redistributed in hard times to favored tribes. It remains the central source of patronage in Moroccan politics. The French Protectorate preserved the venerable institution but deprived it of its ruling functions. With independence, however, the king acquired new authority and power, and, with the departure of many colonial landholders and businesspeople, substantial properties as well. By the time Hassan II succeeded his father, in 1961, the royal household included some of the most fertile lands and a variety of businesses purchased from departing settlers. The monarchy also effected an alliance with rural notables, many of whom were Berber, with the intention of curbing the political ambitions of urban nationalists. The notables came in large part from the very families that France had mobilized in the final years of the Protectorate against the sultan and his nationalist allies. The monarchy consolidated its power by distributing ex-settler land and other benefits to the client notables and to military officers, many of whom were also of the same Berber families as the notables. Hassan completed his father's work and confounded most political observers by surviving in power for thirty-eight years rather than the six months they had predicted.

Whereas the Algerians had anarchically grabbed the spoils of their departing settlers, most of whom vanished when independence was proclaimed, the Moroccan monarchy very gradually appropriated much smaller spoils without precipitating any rapid departures of the settlers. The colonial properties were carefully allocated to supporters of the monarchy. By 1973, when much of the land had been quietly redistributed, it was time to Moroccanize commerce, especially after two attempted military coups, in 1971 and 1972, had almost eliminated King Hassan. The law promulgated in 1973 encouraged private Moroccans to gain majority shares in French businesses and also in practice empowered the *makhzan* with greater patronage. Senior administrators could be shuffled off to the private sector, opening the way to government promotions for a new generation of king's men (Leveau 1985: 255). In the mid-1970s positions in ministries and public sector enterprises were multiplied with the help of record revenues from phosphates, Morocco's principal export. While Moroccan phosphate rents pale in comparison with Gulf oil, Morocco enjoyed a modest boom until 1976, when phosphate prices collapsed. It then experienced fiscal deficits comparable to those that affected the Gulf states with the collapse of oil prices. Its balance of payments deficits were far more serious, however, and Morocco was impelled into a series of agreements with the IMF to reduce government expenditures and curb credit. Royal opportunities to dispense patronage were consequently diminished. After 1983, freezes on government employment, tariff reductions and freer trade, the elimination of most price controls and some state trading monopolies, and various other measures of economic liberalization required by either the IMF or the World Bank tended to erode the *makhzan*'s traditional patronage resources. These were, after all, derived from the allocation of official posts and selective implementation of government regulations. The monarchy gained considerable legitimacy in 1975 by orchestrating the Green March to take over the former Spanish Sahara, but it still needed tangible as well as psychic resources to balance the political parties and elite factions and maintain political control. It gained them in the private sector by buying into a final icon of the French Protectorate.

In 1980 the *makhzan* acquired a major interest in the Omnium Nord Africain (ONA). This holding company, founded in 1934, exemplified "German" capitalism under the auspices of the French Protectorate. By gaining control and putting his son-in-law in charge of it, King Hassan, who was already Morocco's leading landowner, gained a dominant position in private sector industry and finance. The industrial conglomerate's gross revenues account for over 5 percent of Morocco's GDP. The ONA acquired major stakes in Morocco's leading commercial banks and thereby enabled the *makhzan* to dominate the economy indirectly behind the scenes. In other words, the king regained in the private sector the influence that policies of economic liberalization were progressively eroding in government and the public sector. He could ardently engage his country in globalization without risking any serious defections in the business community. The Confédération Générale des Entreprises Marocaines (CGEM), official mouthpiece of Morocco's business leaders, is quite naturally "in a symbiotic partnership with the state" (Patton 1999).

The commercial banking system serves as a principal instrument of control. As in the German model, a small number of Moroccan banks operate a tight oligopoly. Reinforced in 1976 by the imposition of credit ceilings, these banks selectively control credit allocation and can make or break most businesses. In 1987 ONA acquired a major stake in the Banque Commerciale Marocaine (BCM), the leading privately owned one, as well as in other banks. Other Moroccan conglomerates close to the palace, the Kittani and Lamrani groups, controlled two of the remaining five privately owned banks. Consequently the king could promote further economic liberalization, including the lifting in 1991 of credit ceilings and formal controls on interest rates. Unlike the Tunisians or Egyptians, he could also afford to privatize Morocco's two public sector banks, holding half of Morocco's domestic deposits, without losing control over the allocation of credit and patronage. In 1995 Othman Benjelloun acquired a core stake in the Banque Marocaine du Commerce Extérieur (BMCE). Although internal management problems have delayed the privatization of the Banque du Crédit Populaire (BCP), the Moroccan banks were in better shape with fewer non-performing loans than their Tunisian or Egyptian counterparts.

Privatization in Morocco poses neither the political nor technical problems experienced by the bully capitalists. The Moroccan owners and principal managers form a tight and exclusive circle, for the most part of Fassi origin like the Benjelloun family. Outsiders such as Miloud Chabbi, who had bid for control of the BMCE, are clearly unacceptable. Benjelloun's winning offer for the BMCE was priced so high that he may have received special encouragement to join the select circle and to keep Chabbi out of it. Chabbi was not even allowed to acquire Shell Oil's downstream operations because the Ministry of Privatization disqualified him, though he has extensive investments in Tunisia and Egypt. But the bankers are the major gatekeepers. Coordinated by the Groupement Professionelle des Banques Marocaines (GPRM), the banking system insures the loyalty of Morocco's capitalist class.

Economic liberalization resulted in ever greater concentrations of market power in the hands of the seven large banks. In the face of globalization the leaders have reinforced their presence in Europe, attracted more minority participation in their capital from major European and Japanese banking consortia, and taken over some of their weaker Moroccan sisters. Consequently the field for royal patronage has expanded rather than contracted. Privatization has offered it further scope. A politically reliable financial system enabled Morocco to privatize substantially more of its public enterprises from 1994 to 1997 than any other MENA state (see Table 3.3), even though its public sector was never as large as Tunisia's or Egypt's. Morocco's "German" model, however, faces a major challenge. The Casablanca stock exchange, reinvigorated to facilitate the privatization efforts, offers an alternative source of financing for enterprises beholden to the banks. It also represents an alien Anglo-American variety of capitalism that insists upon the full public disclosure of the sorts of information that commercial banks deem to be confidential.

During King Hassan's final years the political system became sufficiently liberal to tolerate the required flows of information. The contrast with Tunisia could not be more striking. Four of Morocco's thirteen approved brokerage houses issue periodic bulletins analyzing not only the traded companies but their respective industries, market shares, and competitive strategies. Analysts fresh out of business school present case studies worthy of being taught in the classroom. Behind them, too, are a young generation of journalists specialized in economic affairs. L'Economiste fields some thirty investigative reporters and analysts. Founded in 1991 as a weekly to compete with a prestigious journal left over from the time of the Protectorate, this paper owned by a Moroccan political scientist and a prominent economic analyst is a sign of the times. It expanded to become a daily in 1998 and, supported in part by ONA and other prominent groups, generates sufficient revenues from publicity to finance its presence online and organize its archives on CD-ROM. Such an enterprise, though specializing in economic affairs, could not flourish in an illiberal environment. It retains its credibility, in fact, by being staunchly independent. In 1996, for instance, it left its editorial page blank (February 8, 1996) rather than toe the official line that all was going well with Interior Minister Basri's crackdown against corruption in the port of Casablanca. The crackdown was actually so clumsy and draconian that businesses stopped importing, but at least L'Economiste was not sanctioned for preserving its professional reputation within the business community. In July 1998 it broke a taboo when it reported news taken from a brokerage firm's information sheet that DGAS (Direction Générale des Affaires Sociales of the Royal Armed Forces), which manages officers' pension funds, had taken a major position in a rather poorly performing bank stock. Normally, as in praetorian republics, no civil, political, or economic action of the military is open to independent reporting.

King Mohammed VI has inherited a monarchy that presents some signs of being on the verge of becoming genuinely constitutional. King Hassan handed most economic decision-making over in 1998 to a government headed by a leader of Morocco's once radical secular opposition. The *makhzan* retains control over foreign affairs, defense, internal security, and religious affairs, but an alliance of seven opposition parties holds the rest of the ministries. The young king, however, has much less rapport with the military than his father enjoyed when he acceded to the throne in 1961. King Hassan's political longevity may be due in part to his having served as chief of staff of the Royal Armed Forces when he was crown prince. Similarly young King Abdullah of Jordan may be better prepared for his new post after heading Jordan's Special Forces than will be his more intellectual Moroccan counterpart. Mohammed VI may prefer a more constitutional, less politically engaged role than his father, but he will need protection if his role model is Juan Carlos, the king of Spain who defended his country against military coups as he reigned over the transition from Franco's authoritarian regime to constitutional democracy.

It is not obvious, however, that the new king will be able to play his father's complex game of "coded signals" (Tozy 1999: 74) that implied a national pact permitting the opposition to share power. Any Moroccan transition is fraught with peril. Elections in Morocco have never been fair and free, and the constitution gives the king ample room for maneuver against the parliament, part of which he appoints. An Islamist opposition waits in the wings for the current government to fail to deliver adequate economic growth, employment, or social services. Military officers may also be waiting for the opportunity to "protect" their monarch, should he try, having removed his father's strong man, Driss Basri, from the Ministry of the Interior, to divest the security forces of more prerogatives and power. A selective crackdown on the press in April 2000, for instance, though modest by regional standards, apparently reflects rising military influence (*Middle East International* May 5, 2000: 6–8).

Morocco's traditional political parties have been weakened over the years by cooptation and collusion with the monarchy. King Hassan gave his coalition government of "opposition" parties headed by Prime Minister Abderahman Youssoufi of the Union Socialiste des Forces Populaires (USFP) full responsibility for economic policies, so that the royal cabinet relaxed its supervision of the ministries. Like similar experiments in the past (such as the Abdallah Ibrahim government of

1958–1960), however, the Youssoufi government is weak and divided, with limited means to carry out economic reforms. It must contend with the trade unions, which compete for attention, as well as the CGEM and the powerful oligopolies behind it. Critics accuse the USFP ministers of carrying out the very programs of the IMF and the World Bank that they had criticized earlier, in opposition.

The economic challenges remain daunting. Although poverty may be diminishing, 13 percent of the population lived below the official poverty line in 1991; 63 percent of the rural population is without water, 87 percent without electricity, 93 percent without proper sanitation, and 67 percent illiterate, with 54 percent of the male children and 73 percent of the females not attending school (*Vie économique*, January 15, 1999, cited by Daoud 1999: 29). In 1997 Morocco ranked below Tunisia, Algeria, Egypt, and even the Sudan on the Human Poverty Index, by which the United Nations Development Program measures a combination of unhealthy living conditions, illiteracy, and low life expectancies. Unemployment may average about 23 percent and is greatest among the young, including some 100,000 secondary school and university graduates. The World Bank estimates that it will worsen unless Morocco radically increases its growth rates, up to at least 6 or 7 percent from the current average of less than 4 percent. To this end the government is expected to keep its budget deficits low, to woo foreign direct investment, and to accelerate privatization of public sector enterprises, which still in 1997 accounted for 20 percent of Morocco's GDP. The spectacle of traditionally leftist politicians carrying out Washington Consensus reforms further weakens their parties while strengthening various Islamist organizations. Significantly the Ministry of *Habous* (religious foundations) is among those reserved, along with the interior, foreign affairs, and justice, for royal appointees.

Ironically, however, a thorough application of structural reforms might also undermine the *makhzan*'s economic domination. The Casablanca stock exchange already features a minority of brokerage houses and investment banks that are independent of the commercial banks and can offer alternative sources of financing for medium to large firms. The traditional banks will also face growing competition from foreign banks as liberalization proceeds. While the holding companies close to the palace will doubtless survive growing European and Asian competition, many firms could fail despite the efforts of the European Commission and the Moroccan government to stimulate their "mise à niveau" or upgrading to face the competition. Efforts across all of North Africa have been inadequate, and massive bankruptcies loom on the horizon despite government efforts to encourage commercial lending to small and medium enterprises. The *makhzan*'s oligopolies may continue to grow and become more concentrated, but in an ever more constricted and vulnerable domestic marketplace.

Morocco, however, retains a civil society that seems better articulated than those of its praetorian counterparts and more effective in absorbing Islamist organizations. Many more Moroccan than Algerian or Tunisian non-government organizations (NGOs) were represented at the Beijing Women's Congress in 1995, for instance, although Ben Ali also carefully cultivates women's organizations for his political purposes. While the opposition parties have weakened in Morocco, the palace has tolerated if not actively encouraged networks of NGOs, orchestrated and sustained by policies of political decentralization. Some Islamist cultural associations emerged, and a tame Islamist political party won ten seats in parliament in 1997. King Hassan seemed better able to divide and dominate his Islamists than Hosni Mubarak, Ben Ali, or the faceless Algerian "deciders." As "Commander of the Faithful," he actively dominated the field of religious discourse ever since his rise to power in the 1960s. One measure of his success is the virtual elimination of alternative discourses, but these have also included potentially useful tools such as Islamic banking and finance as well as radical political oppositions.

Islamic finance was apparently rejected in Morocco because it carries the implication that current financial practices are not in compliance with Islam and therefore that the Commander of the Faithful is neglecting his duty. Islamic banking found a warmer reception in post-revolutionary Algeria than in the conservative kingdom. Under Chadli in Algeria the economic reformers permitted the transnational al-Baraka group to establish a joint venture with one of their public sector banks in 1988, and after 1992 other private sector Islamic banks received their permissions. In Morocco, by contrast, the closest al-Baraka ever came to the financial sector was to establish a leasing company well outside the purview of Morocco's central bank. Part of the resistance to Islamic banking, indeed, may lie within the conventional banking system, headed by a central bank that is more autonomous and established than Algeria's. Morocco's first central bank governor, a relative of the king, held office for over two decades, consolidating its relative autonomy, whereas Chadli's economic reformers gave away Islamic banking licenses before reinforcing Algeria's central bank and reforming the ossified state banking system. The Algerians hoped that new blood could inject life into the reform process, whereas the Moroccans preferred to work within the existing structure.

Since there is no official Islamic banking sector in Morocco, however,

King Mohammed VI is deprived of a useful instrument for engineering a Spanish-style transition. An Islamic business sector could help buffer the country from the shocks of further liberalization and foreign competition and attract Islamist youth and university students back into the system. As matters stand, the Islamist political opposition may amplify any economic failures even as policy-makers hesitate to accelerate structural reform for fear of Islamist backlashes. In May 2000 the authorities released Sheikh Abdeslam Yassine, Morocco's Islamist political leader, from house arrest but warned him to be cautious when making any public statements (*Maghreb Weekly Monitor* no. 83, May 21, 2000).

Were Islamists more involved in the country's economic reforms, they could conceivably help to bridge the growing gap between young, largely unemployed generations and ageing political leaderships. Like their counterparts in Algeria, they could support economic liberalization as an Islamic initiative, on a more favorable political terrain than Algeria had offered in 1989. Much will depend upon how the new monarch intends to fulfill his constitutional role as "Commander of the Faithful." As Rémy Leveau observes, King Hassan had consistently opposed "a coalition bringing together young unemployed graduates, ideologists producing a discourse on Islamic modernity, and new currents of the liberal bourgeoisie, [for] it could offer a credible alternative if the present [governing] coalition experiences difficulties" (Leveau 1999: 14–15). Much earlier in Hassan's reign, in 1965, Moroccan agents had kidnapped Mehdi Ben Barka in Paris – in effect eliminating the "third moment" of Morocco's colonial dialectic. Perhaps the old king feared that the new dialectic of globalization could complete Ben Barka's revolutionary project, were Islamist moralizers to develop a practical synthesis. His son may have different ideas.

Saudi Arabia

Saudi Arabia has neither the elaborate infrastructure of parties and associations nor even the degree of ethnic and regional pluralism that favors the role of a patrimonial arbitrator in Morocco. Saudi politics are even less transparent than Morocco's, where oligopolies veil royal influence in the private sector. While less tightly organized than the Moroccan *makhzan*, the monarchy probably exercises more direct influence on the economy, deciding on oil prices and OPEC quotas and grappling with issues such as privatization and other economic reforms, than King Hassan ever did. Since Fahd's illness, Crown Prince Abdullah has apparently taken control of economic decision-making. A recent

Saudi decision to limit ministerial tenure to four years insures a periodic renewal of the government and probably therefore strengthens the hand of the monarch over his ministers. The Higher Economic Council, established in 1999 under the chairmanship of Crown Prince Abdullah, appears to have executive powers (*MEED* September 10, 1999: 26). It includes a consultative committee of ten private sector representatives as well as the key economic ministers and the governor of the central bank.

Without much fanfare the kingdom partially adapted to the economic reality of lower oil prices in the 1990s. After incurring budget deficits from 1984 to 1993 annually averaging over 17 percent of GDP, the government reduced them to 3 percent by 1997 and, after widely fluctuating oil prices, to about 6 percent in 1999 and a projected 5 percent in 2000 (*MEED* March 24, 2000: 10). A Saudi economist could justifiably claim "a degree of resiliency by the Saudi state that was much greater than could be expected for rentier states" (Krimly 1999: 267). On the revenue side the Saudis reached an understanding with Iran and other major producers in 1999 whereby they restricted production to increase oil prices. Non-oil revenues also increased slightly as subsidies were reduced for oil products, electricity, water and telephone services. On the expenditures side, cuts in wheat subsidies led to a dramatic and salutary reduction of water-wasting wheat production. The most significant cuts were in defense expenditures, notably after 1993, while investments in productive infrastructure were also reduced. Fiscal prudence perhaps also helped the Saudi Monetary Agency prevent a run on the riyal in the summer of 1998, when oil prices were reaching record lows. Despite the expenditure cuts, however, spending on "human development" – education and health – steadily increased in the 1980s and 1990s. For Saudi Arabia, despite its oil wealth, faces the same problem that Morocco and other MENA countries confront, namely, the specter of legions of unemployed graduates. A Ministry of Planning study estimated the male unemployment rate to be 46 percent in 1990 (Chaudhry 1997: 297). Spending programs on human development may employ some of them and perhaps in time produce graduates more suited to employment in the private sector.

Saudi Arabia has accumulated a heavy debt burden from financing chronic budgetary deficits since the mid-1980s. Apart from some borrowings on its behalf by Saudi Aramco and the Saudi Arabia Basic Industries Corporation (SABIC), the kingdom shied away from international creditors in favor of local borrowing. Domestic debt, however, rose after the 1998 oil price collapse up to 115 percent of GDP in 1999 (*MEED* August 25, 2000: 20). Roughly one-third of it is owed directly by the government, but the private financing of the government's "contractor bonds" further squeezes financial markets. Reformers appointed to the Economic Higher Council are therefore attempting to make the Saudi stock exchange more attractive, especially to Gulf nationals, who are estimated to own some $500 billion of relatively liquid assets abroad. Despite the stock market's high capitalization, turnover, as was noted in chapter 3, remains low, with relatively few companies listed and limited prospects for new listings. Foreign investors were only permitted to invest in a single fund until 2000, when new ones were planned.

To stimulate economic growth, however, Saudi Arabia is less in need of foreign direct and portfolio investment than is Morocco. The Saudis already have joint ventures in the petroleum and petrochemical industries and require structural adjustment mainly to attract local Saudi capital to generate new employment opportunities. Much of the existing private sector has been financed by the state, which recycled its petroleum revenues through specialized lending agencies. Though these public funds have not been replenished, the specialized agencies continue to make loans with repayments from past borrowers. Current lending collectively amounts to almost half the total credit allocated by the Saudi banking system to the private sector (SAMA 1999: 46, 83). A more market-driven form of credit allocation might expand employment opportunities by opening credit lines based on expected cash flows rather than on family connections. As Fandy (1999: 246) observes, much of the oil revenues have tended to benefit prominent old families and thus reinforce the family-kinship system. Chaudhry (1997: 161–162, 170–172) notes that the loans went disproportionately to prominent Najdi families but that Saudi strategies may be changing in favor of alternative business elites (1997: 298–299). The monarch clearly retains vast patronage at his disposal, but he has to distribute much of it to his siblings, their children, and various other relatives – many thousands of greedy rentiers – to maintain royal family harmony. *The Economist* reports that $4 billion of the $7 billion windfall of unexpected oil revenues in 1999 disappeared in a "bonanza of unbudgeted expenditure" (April 22, 2000: 47).

Prince Abdullah is reputed to be a more careful manager of state funds than his half-brother Fahd or the latter's full brother, Defense Minister Sultan (who is also a member of the Economic Higher Council). He may reduce some of the family corruption in the same quiet and gradual way in which wheat subsidies were reduced. In time, too, the funds allocated by the specialized lending agencies may dry up, leading to a more competitive climate for investment. Meanwhile, however, the priority given to "human development" is to train Saudis to replace at least the half of the country's expatriate labor force of 4.5 million that is not engaged in personal or household services. In 1994 the Saudi labor force totaled 2 to 2.4 million, 1 million of whom were employed by the government. Although Saudi expenditures are not as constrained as Morocco's, neither country can afford to further inflate its bureaucracy. Any new jobs must come from the private sector, which, with only a 20 percent "Saudization" rate, is overwhelmingly staffed by expatriates. Private enterprises are reluctant to hire Saudis. A frequent complaint is their "'mudir syndrome' – the peculiar concept of honor in employment which dictates that nothing less than a position of authority, status, and respect is acceptable" (Champion 1998: 6–7). Universities have tended to expand religious studies at the expense of disciplines more suited to the needs of the private sector. Current efforts to restructure the educational system by channeling Saudis away from the universities into technical training institutes seem unlikely to achieve greater success than comparable Egyptian restructuring efforts in the 1960s. Saudi TV programs try to promote technical jobs and trades to the youth. "Cleverly, whilst actually aiming to ease young Saudis out of the 'mudir syndrome,' the television programs tend to emphasize the supervisory role in factories" (Champion 1998: 7).

Since the early 1980s the kingdom has been attempting "Saudization" with little impact, to date, on private sector recruitment preferences. Favored private entrepreneurs limit government intervention, and too much administrative pressure might dry up businesses or send them offshore to Bahrain or further afield. Meanwhile Islamist oppositions have grown more visible if not necessarily more menacing or effective. An important base has been the Saudi educational system, notably its burgeoning religious faculties. In the mid-1990s the opposition Committee for the Defense of Legitimate Rights, a moderate group based in London advocating a shake-up within the royal family rather than its elimination, estimated that some three hundred political prisoners languished in Saudi jails. In Saudi Arabia some of the Islamist opposition has taken more violent forms, however. Saudi dissidents seem to have been primarily responsible for car bomb explosions in Riyad in 1997 and in El-Khobar in 1998 that were aimed primarily at American military installations and personnel. The Saudi government, in turn, has become more repressive. In March 2000 Amnesty International reported on the prevailing "climate of fear and secrecy" in a scathing report documenting the persecution of political opponents and religious minorities. Of course these are not the only victims of Saudi justice; worse for foreign investors, the report begins by relating how a Syrian businessman was framed by a Saudi superior, tortured by the police, forced into signing a confession, and executed (*A Secret State of Suffering*; Amnesty International 2000a). Amnesty followed up in May with a further report on "A Justice System Without Justice" (Amnesty International 2000b).

Since Saudi Arabia has neither political parties nor most other recognized forms of association, it may be more difficult than in Morocco to tame Islamist opposition forces by bringing them selectively into government. But Islam remains the regime's prime source of legitimacy, incarnated by a conservative religious establishment. Just as the Al-Saud joined forces with Mohammed Ibn Abdul Wahhab in the mid-eighteenth century to found the original dynasty, so Abdul Wahhab's descendants of the Al-Shaikh family usually occupy ministries – currently as many as three under Crown Prince Abdullah. The official Islamic establishment probably limits the kingdom's political options in dealing with the anti-establishment Islamists, who accuse it of betraying the true Islam. Certainly parties cannot be tolerated but the Saudi banking system appears to be more liberal, displaying a greater structural power of private capital than that of Morocco, Jordan, or even Kuwait (see Table 3.6). Might Islamists enter into the establishment through the back door of official Islamic businesses?

Like Morocco, Saudi Arabia has been reluctant to permit Islamic banks to operate in the kingdom despite the Saudi origins of its principal business groups. The one exception, Al-Rajhi, was originally an exchange dealer. Its branch network was too big for the firm not to be licensed when – as the result of the collapse of a smaller dealer in the Rajhi family – exchange dealers were forbidden from taking deposits or making loans. Rajhi shrewdly insisted on becoming an "Islamic" bank, although the official legislation accepted by the religious authorities considered all Saudi banks to be operating on Islamic principles. Al-Rajhi Banking and Investment Corporation, like Islamic banks elsewhere, does not pay interest on deposits. Unlike others outside Saudi Arabia, however, it does not share any of its profits with depositors either. It routinely posts the highest returns on assets of any Saudi bank and has gradually gained in market share since its founding in 1988. It is the kingdom's fourth largest bank, and its net income in 1999 exceeded that of larger ones, Saudi American Bank and Riyad Bank, and possibly of Saudi Arabia's troubled giant, National Commercial Bank (*MEED* May 12, 2000: 12, 16). The latter was too encumbered with bad debts of royal and other privileged clients to issue an income statement on time. Despite repeated efforts, however, neither the Faisal nor Al-Baraka transnational group of Islamic banks has received permission to open commercial banking operations inside Saudi Arabia. The former group is headed by Prince Mohammed Al-Faisal, a visionary son of the late King Faisal who once planned to tow icebergs from Antarctica to make Saudi deserts bloom. The latter group is headed by a serious, self-made Saudi businessman, Sheikh Saleh Al-Kamel, whose holding company is based in Jiddah. Although most conservative religious scholars reject interest on loans or deposits, the Saudi establishment not only accepts it but prevents the presence of these transnational alternatives to interest-based banking inside the kingdom.

Possibly pressures from other commercial banks better explain the paradox of discouraging Islamic financial institutions in an avowedly Islamic state than the legal concerns of conservative religious scholars or worries in the family about the kingdom's legitimacy. Certainly more Islamic banking would cut into the markets and profits of prominent families with stakes in interest-based banking. Other Islamic banks might also take deposits away from Al-Rajhi by offering depositors a share of their profits. Conventional banks also benefit from the cost-free funds of depositors who refuse to take interest. Possibly the interests that would be most adversely affected are those of Prince Walid al-Talal, who has recently propelled a major Saudi bank merger and has a major interest in the Saudi American Bank (Kingdom Holding 2000: 1–2, 16). This dynamic bank, still under a technical management agreement with Citigroup, has actively developed Islamic finance windows in efforts to capture Saudi deposits without going through the pain of converting to be a full-fledged Islamic bank, restricted in its action by a religious advisory council. Such a bank would severely challenge its strategy. Some of the more senior, established members of the royal family may, however, wish to retaliate against Prince Walid since he has already purchased independent media in order publicly to compete with them.

Judging from the periodic rumors in Saudi Arabia that the Faisal and Al-Baraka groups are about to receive licenses, the royal family seems divided over a political and economic strategy. Some may reason that it is more opportune for the monarchy not to encourage an officially Islamist coalition of merchants and bankers within the regime as it might acquire some of the functions of a political party, including an appetite for power. Just as King Hassan was determined to prevent the building of such a coalition in Morocco, some Saudis may also calculate that its emergence would limit their ability to divide and rule their business establishment.

Just "offshore" in Bahrain (which has been attached to Saudi Arabia by a causeway since 1986), however, Islamic banking flourishes. The Bahrain Monetary Agency has granted operating licenses to at least sixteen Islamic banks and other financial institutions (*MEED* August

20, 1999: 4). The oldest, the Bahrain Islamic Bank, has operated in the local market for two decades and was joined in the mid-1980s by Masraf Faisal al-Islami, established as the regional headquarters for the Faisal group but renamed the Shamil Bank of Bahrain E.C. (Islamic Bankers) in 2000, and by Albaraka Islamic Investment Bank, representing Islamic finance's other major transnational. Recent arrivals include investment banks and Islamic subsidiaries of large conventional banks. The Bahrain Monetary Agency introduced Al-Salam (Islamic) bonds to serve as treasury bills, backed by commodities such as oil or aluminum, to help Islamic banks resolve their chronic liquidity problems (*MEED* February 9, 2001:9). Through such initiatives and other private ones, Islamic finance may be acquiring the necessary scale to be able to compete more effectively with conventional banks in the region.

Even more significant may be the public support Islamic banking and finance receives in Kuwait. Technically the Kuwait Finance House (KFH) is not a bank at all; it is regulated by the commerce ministry, not the Central Bank of Kuwait. However, it is in fact among the largest and oldest of Islamic commercial banks in the region, second only to Saudi Arabia's Al-Rajhi in total assets, and it performs retail as well as other functions, serving notably as the repository for the salaries of employees of various government agencies. It is Kuwait's third largest bank in total deposits, and it enjoys strong political support among Islamists. In 1998 the Central Bank of Kuwait drafted a law for Islamic banking that was intended to integrate the KFH and any other Islamic "bank" seeking "investment" (deposits) from the public with the other commercial banks. The KFH argued, however, that some of the draft provisions would force it out of business. A Kuwaiti consultant sympathetic to the bank observed that "KFH has the backing of the National Assembly" (*MEED* March 5, 1999: 10). In Kuwait's relatively pluralistic system Islamist politicians and financiers joined hands to defeat passage of the law, whereas similar displays of solidarity in any praetorian regime would doom the bankers.

For the time being Islamic finance, like its conventional equivalents, is principally a vehicle for investing private fortunes abroad in "Islamic" mutual funds. Dow Jones has set up an Islamic index as a benchmark for Islamic investors. The index excludes firms dealing with pork or alcohol and also excludes firms that have conventional interest-based debt in excess of one-third of their total assets (*MEED* September 10, 1999: 15). Additional economic reforms are needed if much of the private wealth is ever to be reinvested back into the region. Islamic banks are in fact in greater need of such reform, if they are to invest in the region, than are conventional banks. They are currently at a disadvantage because they are not permitted to invest their funds in many ways open to conventional commercial banks, though they may enjoy a competitive edge in their ability to attract deposits. At present the bulk of Islamic financing takes the form of leasing, installment sales, or simple deferred payment sales. Expansion of Islam's distinctive equity-like financing presupposes more transparency, accountability, and regulatory authority than any Middle Eastern business environment yet promises. As two leading authorities on Islamic banking explain, "If, in addition to risks of the investment projects, the investor has to be concerned with the credibility of government policies, or arbitrary government decisions or distortions that threaten long-term price stability in the economy, he/she would be reluctant to invest in contracts that do not provide fixed nominal payoffs" (Iqbal and Mirakhor 1999: 402). In other words, in unreformed business environments investors will prefer interest-bearing bonds or notes over any Islamic profit-sharing instrument.

Islamic finance would become more viable if it were accompanied by an active stock market and other reforms implementing the guidelines of the Washington Consensus and notably the Tenth Commandment – property rights guaranteed by accountable institutions and transparent practices. If Saudi Arabia surmounts its current succession crisis, a Kuwaiti style of pluralism could conceivably be on the horizon to facilitate such developments. Saudi Arabia presents a style of capitalism that already resembles the Anglo-American variety in important respects. An articulate Islamist business community reflected in leading Islamic banks could further promote a more competitive and transparent economy. If it remains offshore, gaining strength in Kuwait, Bahrain, Qatar, and the United Arab Emirates, it will also continue to attract Saudi capital.

Saudi Arabia, however, faces a major dilemma. With or without Islamic financing it may accelerate economic reforms, open up its economy, and enter the World Trade Organization; or it may persist in its habit of moving cautiously with low rates of economic growth dictated largely by unpredictable oil and petrochemical markets. If the rise of oil prices in 1999–2000 is used as an excuse to diminish the pace of reform, the kingdom risks social unrest and economic disaster. Central government debt, already over 100 percent of GDP (Champion 1999: 6), will increase with the next oil price downturn, and the economy will stagnate. Saudi Arabia risks being caught in a debt trap like Lebanon's, with debt servicing, which amounted to 17 percent of the 1999 budget, contributing to a self-perpetuating budget deficit, but without any cushioning of a resilient private sector like Lebanon's (*MEED* March 24, 1999: 13). Saudi Arabia will face an unemployment problem for its youth at least as serious as Algeria's, but without a possible means of escape across the Mediterranean. Primary and vocational school dropouts may constitute up to a quarter of the youths entering the job market each year (Champion 1999). Of greater concern, however, are the ill-trained college graduates, many of them from religious faculties whose most articulate teachers were locked up in the early 1990s for opposing the pro-American religious establishment. Saudi Arabia needs rapid economic growth to mop up unemployment.

Reforms for rapid growth have other political costs, however. A larger and more competitive private sector could sweep away the Najdi bureaucratic and merchant support upon which the regime has relied since the 1970s, without generating any new sources of support. Were the big Saudi public sector to be further privatized in ways that transferred real control from the bureaucrats to new core managers, the likeliest victors would be princes such as Walid al-Talal, perhaps in association with foreign investors, whose entry is facilitated by new legislation. The royals would dominate the stock market and the commercial banking system, but without the same implications for political control as in Morocco. The Saudi royal family is too big and pampered, although its internal deliberations have so far remained confidential. Its leaders would not wish to compete in public, yet the reforms being introduced are not compatible with a closed extended family. The banking system could become more concentrated, but the stock market is a counterweight that would be heavily dominated by the royals and foreigners, dissipating any lingering myth of a tacit division of political and economic labor between the royals and other merchant families. The division of labor has gradually unraveled, amid much talk of corruption (Aburish 1995) since the early 1980s. Full-scale economic liberalization would make the breakdown a matter of public controversy, further upset any tacit understandings (Seznek 2000), and possibly consolidate the holdings of royal family factions in the stock market. In the prevailing political climate "there is no predictability in the behavior of some princes . . . and no assurance that investors will maintain control over their investments" (Okruhlik 1999: 308). The major winners of the economic reform would be royal entrepreneurs such as Prince Walid, but their strength could further unbalance the squabbling family. Dissension in the family might provoke more intense Islamist opposition. It is no wonder that the Saudi government "is still lacking . . . the will to face the politically difficult decisions about economic restructuring . . . [and therefore] must rely on higher oil prices to keep the government budget and the economy afloat." (Gause 2000: 87). In October 2000 soaring oil prices encouraged Saudi Arabia to harden its negotiation stance with the World Trade Organization and delay opening up its telecommunications and financial markets and enforcing intellectual property rights.

The bellwether monarchies: Kuwait and Jordan

Most of the monarchies permit a greater degree of political and economic competition than do the praetorian republics. Their long-term prospects may depend, however, on an ability to absorb Islamist opposition movements into their political mainstreams. They survived the colonial dialectic, which overturned the most powerful of the region's monarchies, in part because they were so peripheral to the Arab world where the rising tides of nationalism were centered in Cairo and the Levant. Globalization, however, is less escapable, and it incites moralizing oppositions to reform. Countries having never experienced a revolutionary third moment may be more vulnerable to new forms of political radicalism than countries where old ruling classes had already been displaced. But monarchies are not necessarily fated to be over-thrown. They may be better able than praetorian republics to develop institutions within which to absorb political oppositions. Praetorian republics, by contrast, currently display tendencies to destroy institutions and keep dictatorship in the family, like the Asads of Syria.

The process of absorbing Islamist oppositions has proceeded further in Jordan and Kuwait than in Morocco or Saudi Arabia. Each of the smaller countries displays a wide spectrum of Islamists with varying degrees of loyalty to their respective monarchies. Each has also tried to move on the economic front, pursuing market reforms while tolerating various oppositions in their respective parliaments. Their very size, of course, differentiates them from the larger monarchies. They are more heavily dependent on outside powers, for aid as well as trade. Kuwait, for instance, is so much in need of the protection of the international community that it is inviting all of the permanent members of the Security Council, including China, to take positions in the development of its petroleum resources. The Saudis, by contrast, reject any foreign upstream investment and refused in 1999 even to renew a Japanese offshore concession, just when Kuwait was positively soliciting foreign involvement upstream. The Kuwaiti government is determined for strategic reasons, pending approval by parliament, to include an American company in the development of its northern oil fields bordering Iraq. During the war between Iran and Iraq (1980–1988) it persuaded both the Soviets and the Americans (catalyzed by Soviet competition) to reflag its oil tanker fleet.

Jordan, sandwiched between Syria, Iraq, and Israel, is almost as vulnerable as Kuwait but enjoys strategic rents based on geographic location. Of course it is also far more dependent than Kuwait on economic assistance and international loans. Consequently it also needs to stay in the good graces of the international financial community. Generally, indeed, small countries may be quicker than bigger ones to adapt to international circumstances. They may undertake reforms to globalize their economies more easily than bigger countries because their domestic oppositions are as aware as their governments of their inherent vulnerability. With very few exceptions, the oppositions in Jordan and Kuwait do not wish to lose their respective countries to some wider scheme, be it a Greater Israel, Greater Palestine, Greater Syria, Greater Iraq, an extension of Saudi Arabia, or a United States of the Arab Gulf. Governments and oppositions in Morocco and Saudi Arabia do not share analogous fears of possible extinction.

Perceptions of external threats may dull the moralizing zeal of opponents of economic reform, rendering comparisons with bigger states problematic. In Jordan and Kuwait, however, the principal opposition to reform seems to come from within their respective regimes, not from their Islamist oppositions. Positively, the experiences of these states suggest that economic reform may run in parallel with political reform that partially opens the door to Islamist oppositions. Islamists have offered the globalizing monarchies useful political cover. They have been involved as official parties in politics for many years, with leaders even serving as ministers and cabinet members in Jordan and Kuwait and sharing in some of the patronage. It may also not be coincidental that these states have been in the forefront of Arab states hosting Islamic banking.

In addition to the Kuwait Finance House, Kuwait is already host to powerful Islamic investment banks that have funded Islamic commercial banks in Bahrain and elsewhere in the Arab world. Although the Kuwait Finance House is presently Kuwait's sole Islamic commercial bank, at least twenty-five others applied to the Central Bank of Kuwait for licenses to set up Islamic banks, pending passage of a new banking law (*MEED* October 9, 1998: 14). Kuwait also hosts among the most active stock markets in the Middle East (see Table 3.8) and a relatively concentrated but apparently competitive conventional commercial banking system. While the National Bank of Kuwait alone has about 30 percent of the deposits, the commercial banks do not appear to be exercising monopoly power upon their clients: the "spreads," or differences between what a bank charges a customer for a loan and what it pays out in interest to depositors, are consistently low, having never exceeded 2 percent in the past decade. Were Islamic banks, including the Kuwait Finance House, to be integrated into the commercial banking system, competition would be even keener. The KFH holds some 35 percent of the private Kuwaiti savings kept in the country.

Jordan, too, is host to Islamic as well as conventional commercial banks and has already integrated them into a single system under the control of the Central Bank of Jordan. The Jordan Islamic Bank for Finance and Investment, partly owned by the Dallah Al-Baraka Holding Company, attracts close to 10 percent of the deposits of Jordan's private sector. To capture some of this market and expand it, the Arab Bank established a separate Arab International Islamic Bank in 1998. Founded in Palestine in 1930, the Arab Bank is the most respected and one of the largest of banks in the Arab world, and its new venture seems also to be testimony to the rising tide of Islamic banking in Kuwait, Bahrain, and Qatar. It is not known whether the Jordanian Islamic banks are as closely linked to Islamist politicians as their Kuwaiti counterparts (Ghabra 1997: 60), but Jordan seems, like Kuwait, to offer sufficient political and economic space for coalitions to develop. Like Morocco and Kuwait, its conventional commercial banking system is relatively concentrated. Its spreads between deposit and lending rates are also low, suggesting a reasonably competitive market place.

Jordan, however, also features a local stock market that, while equally capitalized, has much less turnover than Kuwait's. The somnolent market in Amman reflects the economic activities of an elite of royalty and family retainers brought to Amman by Emir Abdullah, the great-grandfather of King Abdullah II, in the 1920s. Many of the listed companies are run, in effect, by the government. The royal family and leading political families of ministers and higher civil servants have buttressed their political power with economic holdings in land, commerce, and industry (Piro 1998: 81–83, 96–97). In Kuwait the Sabah family is also engaged in commerce, and some of its leading members lost millions in the crash of Kuwait's informal Souk al-Manakh in 1982. Indeed it took the central bank until 1993 finally to clear the rickety Kuwaiti banking structure of bad debts because some of the princes were so recalcitrant to any settlement that might diminish their fortunes. Competition in Kuwait seems more open and freewheeling than in Jordan, and big declines in 1998 and 1999 seem to have only slightly dampened its hyperactive stock market. Kuwait is among the first, along with Egypt, Israel, and Turkey, to have opened up its stock exchange to foreign investors.

Both of the bellwethers have moved ahead with economic reform, but they also illustrate some of the dilemmas the other monarchies will face.

Kuwait's prospects may be brighter than Jordan's because it can afford to move ahead more slowly, modulating reforms to the wishes of parliament rather than imposing them from above. The rise of oil prices in 1999 and windfall current account surpluses take the urgency out of painful structural reforms, though Kuwaiti public sector employment is not sustainable. A huge government bureaucracy and public sector enterprises dwarf the private sector and stifle local initiative, but privatization raises the fear that some Kuwaitis, virtually all of whom are employed by government and the public sector, might lose their jobs. Very few Kuwaitis work in the private sector, which is less well paid and more demanding. But in the face of chronic government deficits, even when oil prices are high, an endless multiplication of cushy public sector jobs seems unrealistic. Flush with oil revenues, the government employed 5,543 young nationals entering the labor market in the first six months of 1999, but efforts to recruit more of them into the private sector have not been successful. The government proposed a tax on private sector employers to establish a fund for increasing the percentage of Kuwaitis in the private sector labor force from 1.5 percent to 5 percent (UN–ESCWA 1999: 12–13). Kuwait's parliament refused to approve the government decree.

Among the GCC principalities, indeed, Kuwait displays the greatest degree of political as well as economic competition. Its elected parliament is hardly docile. The Ninth National Assembly, elected on July 3, 1999, contains only ten pro-government deputies out of fifty. They are clearly outnumbered by thirteen Sunni Islamist and thirteen Liberal opposition deputies. Although divided on various issues, the thirteen Islamists still have significant leverage on economic issues. As already noted, their predecessors in the Eighth National Assembly mobilized parliamentary opposition to legislation viewed by the Kuwait Finance House as unfavorable to Islamic banking. Although the new parliament was thought to be more "liberal," it rejected the government decree granting women the vote. It has delayed other proposed government decrees calling for privatization of Kuwait Airways and the Kuwait Oil Tanker Company, $7 billion upstream investment by international oil companies, and a new system of corporate taxation designed to encourage private sector investment. The parliament did agree, however, to open the stock market to foreign investors and to render it more transparent by requiring everyone, including princes, to declare holdings in excess of 5 percent of a company. Kuwait can perhaps afford to stall a bit longer on reforms – until oil prices, which guarantee budget surpluses for 2000 and 2001, decline again.

Jordan, by contrast, cannot wait. Inheriting a stagnant economy in the summer of 1999 in which one-third of the population is estimated to live below the poverty line (*MEED* June 9, 2000: 21), King Abdullah concentrated almost exclusively on economic reform during the first year of his reign. He appointed Abdel Raouf Rawabdeh, a hard-line member of Jordan's ruling club, as prime minister, but also, perhaps taking a leaf out of Saudi Crown Prince Abdullah's book (see above), established a Higher National Economic Consultative Council under his personal chairmanship including private sector figures alongside ministers. Jordan entered the WTO, and the new king followed up a US Agency for International Development report on the promising job and export earnings potential of this sector by meeting with world business leaders at the World Economic Forum in Davos, Switzerland, in February 2000. Subsequently he invited Bill Gates and others to develop Jordan's information technology sector. He has vigorously marketed Qualifying Industrial Zones (which qualify goods partly made in Israel and Jordan to enter the United States duty- and quota-free) to potential foreign investors while pushing further packages of reforms on privatization, landlord–tenant relations, and taxation. Evidently his priority is to improve Jordan's anemic economic growth rates by finding new sources of capital to supplement the dwindling supplies of Palestinian capital repatriated from Kuwait that kept Jordan going until the mid-1990s. However, he has antagonized some of Jordan's most ardent globalizers by governing with a traditional unreformed power structure, needed to keep nationalist and Islamist opposition to the reforms at bay. Prime Minister Rawabdeh did not hesitate to expel the Jordanian Palestinian leadership of Hamas to Qatar in January 2000, and he has also cracked down on the press. Academic institutions were not spared. Mustafa Hamarneh, an outspoken Georgetown University PhD, temporarily lost the directorship of Jordan University's Center for Strategic Studies for organizing and reporting on polls indicating declines in the government's popularity (Andoni 2000: 86). The irony is evident: not crackdowns but greater transparency lies at the heart of any effective reform program, especially one stressing information technology as part of the solution to Jordan's economic needs.

Jordan was already very exposed to nationalist and Islamist backlashes by virtue of its treaty with Israel in 1994. King Hussein stepped ahead of Yasseir Arafat and Hafez al-Asad in the peace process and then found himself isolated. He still carefully nurtured domestic support and survived a variety of economic and political crises. His response to the bread riots of 1989 had been to open the country up to more democracy. Initial successes were due in part to the close ties established with the Muslim Brotherhood, which Hussein had used in the 1950s and 1960s as a counterweight to Gamal Abdel Nasser. Elections in 1989 brought it substantial representation in the Jordanian parliament, and some Islamists were even admitted into the government. The government rearranged the electoral law in 1993, however, so as to reduce their representation (by increasing tribal representation at the expense of more organized urban constituencies). In response to more IMF reforms and bread riots in 1996, the government cracked down on the demonstrators rather than further liberalize the regime. King Hussein visibly backed his prime minister and the IMF reforms (Ryan 1998: 58). Subsequent elections in 1997 appeared so rigged, in fact, that the National Islamic Front officially called for a boycott, although in the end a reduced number of Islamists were elected anyway. In February 1999 King Abdullah inherited a deliberalizing monarchy (Wiktorowicz 1999).

Advised by his military friends, he continued to crack down on potential centers of opposition. Not only were the leaders of Hamas expelled, but the security forces also conducted a widespread dragnet – perhaps for American consumption (Andoni 2000: 87) – for Islamist terrorists reputed to be followers of Osama Bin Laden. Despite this atmosphere of intimidation, however, some dialogue with the Muslim Brotherhood continues. Possibly a variety of Muslim Brothers and other Islamists connected with business and financial circles can still provide the young king with some cover as he persists in efforts to globalize Jordan's economy and consolidate the peace process with Israel. The reforms have been enacted, however, without their participation except on the fringes of the banking sector. In Jordan's far from transparent atmosphere the old families of the traditional power structure seem more likely to benefit from the reforms than do new entrepreneurs, whether Islamist or not.

Conclusion

Like the praetorian republics, the monarchies, too, need to open their economies and confront the challenges of globalization yet they are peculiarly vulnerable to backlashes by radical nationalist or Islamist oppositions because they never experienced the full play of the colonial dialectic. Kuwait has progressed furthest in defending itself from backlashes by admitting political Islamists into ruling coalitions and deriving some legitimacy from them for their reforms. But the reforms have been more limited and gradual than poorer monarchies such as Jordan and Morocco can afford. Jordan's young king has pushed ahead with reforms without the Islamists. If he seeks more political cover, however, to be insulated from his military coalition and to give himself greater autonomy as an indispensable arbitrator, he may have to turn again, like his father in 1989, to the Muslim Brotherhood. In Amman and elsewhere, coalitions between the Islamic financiers and Islamist political oppositions could be useful safety valves for incumbent regimes. They offer kings and governments greater strategic depth and margins for maneuver. Not only can Islamic finance moderate Islamist political oppositions, by giving them stakes in the economic system, but it can also legitimate government efforts to reform their respective economies. In Kuwait Islamists joined other deputies in parliament to adopt government laws for regulating the stock market to make its operations more transparent and to encourage foreign investment. Islamic finance has the potential to transform the ostrich-like second moment, comprising those rejecting globalization, into an Islamization of the Washington Consensus. The political cost to the monarchies, however, may be new Islamic institutions that render their political economies more transparent and their governments more accountable than the old generation of monarchs could ever have accepted.

The monarchies, like praetorian republics, still tend to be information averse. The exceptions are Kuwait, Bahrain, and even tinier Qatar, whose new ruler, Hamad bin Khalifa al-Thani, enabled a controversial satellite TV station, Al-Jezira, to broadcast throughout the Arab world, as mentioned in the preceding chapter. Little Qatar stood firm despite the decision of three information-averse praetorians, Tunisia, Libya, and Iraq, to withdraw their ambassadors in May 2000. The new generation of monarchs may be ready to accept greater transparency and accountability, although both King Mohammed VI of Morocco and King Abdullah II of Jordan deferred to their military hard-liners and cracked down selectively on the press during the first year of their respective reigns.

Suggestions for further reading

Hammoudi (1997) updates the picture of the Moroccan monarchy depicted by Waterbury (1970). On Saudi Arabia see Aburish (1995), Chaudhry (1997), Fandy (1999), and Gause (1993), who deals with the other GCC monarchies, as do Crystal (1990) and Kostiner (2000). Piro (1998) discusses Jordan's political economy.

7 Fragmented democracies

This category of democracies is too diverse for an exemplar to be useful, and therefore we will deal separately in this chapter with Iran, Israel, Lebanon, and Turkey. The fact that these countries are so diverse, however, raises the question of whether the category of "democratic" is a meaningful one and, if so, which of these countries really deserves to be included in it.

Real democracies in the MENA?

The conventional view is that only Israel really qualifies. Indeed, only Israel has consistently managed to change its government through free and fair elections, the single best indicator of democracy. So by that single measure, Israel is the only established democracy in the MENA. This definition is too restrictive, however, and overlooks the similarities of these states. Iran, Lebanon, and Turkey have all had elections resulting in significant changes in their governments, although such elections are either ultimately indecisive (in the case of Iran), punctuated by military interventions (in the case of Turkey), or subject to considerable external influence, as in Lebanon, especially during the 1990s. So these are at least "one-time" democracies, if not established ones. The transfer of governmental power through elections, even if uncommon, nevertheless sets these states apart from both the praetorian republics and the monarchies.

As the existence of free and fair elections resulting in governmental change suggests, the MENA democracies have all managed to institutionalize more effectively than praetorian republics or monarchies peaceful means for political competition over incumbency and formulation of public policy. This is not because social forces in these countries are fundamentally any less antagonistic than they are elsewhere in the region, including in the bunker states. The examples of Arabs and Jews in Israel, Christians and Muslims in Lebanon, Kurds and Turks in Turkey, and multiple linguistic groups in Iran suggest that the level of primordial hostility may be just as great between social forces in these democracies as it is in Iraq or Yemen. Indeed, when political order has broken down in the democracies, the bloodletting has been of a magnitude that, by this measure, would qualify them as bunker states. But what differentiates the democracies from the other states is that at least intermittently they have managed to integrate those social forces into national political institutions, where they have contested for power peacefully, if not equally. The democracies, in other words, may appear at a cursory glance to have weaker states than do republics or monarchies but in fact are stronger – better able to integrate social forces into the body politic and give them the experience, at least once, of changing their rulers through the ballot box.

Magnitude of information flow, which is a correlate of democracy, tends to group these four countries at the top of the MENA tables. As Figure 3.3 revealed, Israel towers over every other country except Kuwait in newspaper readership – and also, indeed, in such correlates as radio and TV ownership and Internet hosts and subscribers. Of the Arab states other than the mini-GCC states of the Gulf, Lebanon ranks highest on newspaper circulation, together with Turkey. Iran tends to outperform the praetorian republics, but falls behind the monarchies and other democracies on this and other measures of information flow. The MENA countries with the most Internet hosts per capita are, in descending order, Israel, the UAE, Kuwait, Lebanon, and Turkey. As regards freedom of information flow, which is highly correlated with the magnitude of flow, the "Triangle Index" combines and weights "the economic, social and information exchange foundations on which each country rests." In 1997 that index's ranking of thirty-five developing economies ranked Israel 4th, Turkey 24th, Tunisia 26th, Egypt 30th, and Morocco 31st (USAID 1997: 151–152).

That there is a relationship between the strength and autonomy of political institutions, on the one hand, and economic ones on the other, is suggested by the indicator of institutional credibility presented in Figure 3.2, which is the ratio of contract-intensive money to total money supply. The highest performers on this measure, in descending order, were Israel, Lebanon, Kuwait, Turkey, Bahrain, Qatar, the UAE, and Iran. Iran outperformed all of the praetorian republics and all but the smallest, wealthiest monarchies. The citizens of these democracies tend to trust their financial structures more than do citizens in the monarchies and praetorian republics, pointing to the existence of an interaction effect between economic and political institutions and faith in them. Good politics may make for good finance, and vice versa.

The grouping of the democracies on the CIM index cannot be a byproduct of similar financial systems, for their systems are not similar. Israeli banking is run according to the French model, with ubiquitous governmental involvement in the allocation of credit. Turkey's system is a relic of the German model, with concentrated but relatively autonomous banking, while Lebanon's freewheeling financial sector is both deconcentrated and autonomous, more or less along American lines. Iran's banking system is the most heterogeneous, with the French model coexisting with Islamic practices.

As far as stock markets are concerned, Israel's and Turkey's feature the greatest numbers of listed companies, the highest turnovers, and the largest proportions of foreign investment in the MENA. Their combination of size and diversity of economy, access to external investors, amount and reliability of relevant information, rate of return, and general confidence in the political system apparently attracts investors. The Beirut exchange, by contrast, is overshadowed by Lebanon's much more dynamic and aggressive banking industry, while Tehran's exchange is, in relation to the size of the Iranian economy, minuscule.

Democracy in the MENA appears to be compatible with very different systems of banking and levels of development of equities markets, but those differences do not affect the willingness of the citizens of those democracies to entrust their money to financial institutions. That willingness is not due to the fact that those institutions are free from governmental interference. Democracy in the MENA, in fact, is accompanied by a high degree of state involvement in the economy, much more, in fact, than is gospel according to "serious economists." The Heritage Foundation country rankings on its Index of Economic Freedom, for example, are based on ten factors (Beach and O'Driscoll 2000: 71–89), nine of which are essentially surrogates for the Washington Consensus and are averaged in Figure 7.1.[1] The most economically "free" states by this reckoning are the small GCC states, whereas the democracies, even excluding Iran, are only roughly as "free" as the liberal monarchies or bully republics. Although the democracies far outshine the bunker states and appear to have political economies that are relatively credible to their populations, they still have a long way to go before they are well equipped to deal with the challenges and opportunities presented by globalization.

Most MENA political economies are affected by the "drag" factor of intra-regional conflicts, although in varying degrees. Israel, a virtual

[1] The factors concern trade policy, fiscal burden of government, government intervention in the economy, monetary policy, capital flows and foreign investment policy, banking, wages, and prices, property rights, regulation and licensing requirements, and the black market. The fiscal variable was excluded from the averages presented in Figure 7.1.

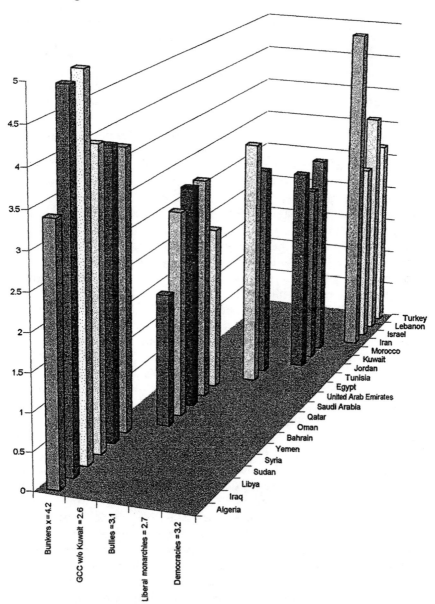

Figure 7.1 Composite indicator of economic openness, 1998–1999
Note: Values range from 1 = highly open, to 5 = closed economy.
Source: 2000 Index of Economic Freedom (O'Driscoll et al. 2000)

garrison state, is among those most affected, while Lebanon, sucked into the vortex of the Arab–Israeli conflict, has all but lost its sovereignty as a result of it. Post-revolutionary Iran was invaded by Iraq, against which it fought an eight-year war from which its economy has yet to fully recover. Turkey maintains the largest standing army in NATO and is in a semi-permanent state of simmering conflict with Iraq and Iran.

Intra-regional conflicts exact a heavy price from these democracies including, but not limited to, spending on their militaries. Regional problems, however, may be less important in structuring their political economies and determining their economic performance than strictly internal factors. Chief among these and common to all four countries is, paradoxically, a problem that is virtually the mirror image of the fundamental defect of state–society relations in praetorian republics. In those republics the state is either overly autonomous from society (i.e. the bully republics), or the prisoner of just one social force within it (i.e. the bunker republics). In the democracies, by contrast, the state has too little autonomy from society to make and implement truly effective economic policies. So while in the praetorian republics ruling elites have to utilize the state to subdue society, and thus cannot grant it sufficient autonomy for effective capitalist development, incumbent elites in the democracies have to make expensive "side payments" to constituencies in order to retain their support. Such side payments include benefits of various sorts, as well as purposeful market distortions and privileged access to state structures. As a consequence, the fiscal and monetary discipline necessary for sustained capitalist development cannot be imposed. Whereas political elites in praetorian republics are in a sense enemies of their societies, in the democracies they are prisoners of them, having to bribe social forces to construct ruling coalitions.

While the need to build coalitions among social forces is not unusual, the excessive fragmentation of political communities and a concomitant fracturing of political institutions inflate the costs of coalition formation in the MENA democracies, none of which is able to host a majoritarian political party. In Israel, Lebanon, and Turkey the formation of government has traditionally been a laborious process of stitching together minority parties, with the glue being side payments to those parties and the social forces they represent. So in Israel, for example, the dominant Labour Party from 1948 to 1977 made a side payment to the National Religious Party to induce it into the governing coalition dominated by Labour secularists. That side payment took various forms, including the portfolio of education, which in turn provided the means for subsidies to be channeled to religious educational institutions. In the Islamic Republic of Iran, where political parties are illegal, virtually the entire governmental apparatus is an elaborate coalition of competitive factions to whom various sinecures and fiefdoms are parceled out.

In all the democracies the primary business of government, as suggested by political rhetoric that focuses largely on ethnicity and religion, is wrestling with the various problems of political identity that beset these fragmented polities. Business in its pure sense is thus a secondary matter, as the raison d'être of the state is not managing the economy to maximize growth, but utilizing resources to contain or resolve identity issues and conflicts. While the costs to economic development of this approach are substantial, they are not as high as the costs incurred by the praetorian republics, where the state seeks to stifle expressions of societal interests.

The conflicting identities that undermine political cohesion in the MENA democracies are in all cases multiple and overlap with material inequalities, further exacerbating conflict. In Israel, the dominant Jewish majority is divided between Ashkenazim (European) and Sephardim ("Oriental"), and between secularists, ultra-Orthodox and Hasidim. The subordinate Arab population is divided between Christians, Druze, and Muslims, differences that have taken on increasing social and political importance in parallel with increasing intra-Jewish tensions. While the two dominant Israeli parties have always been led by Ashkenazim, those parties have had to form coalitions with parties representing either Sephardim or ultra-Orthodox, and occasionally even with Arab parties. These contending social forces have, as payment for their support of the coalition, been allowed to penetrate governmental institutions, including the public sector of the economy, converting these bodies into resource-generating satraps. Downsizing the state in Israel thus involves attacking power bases of contending groups. It could only be achieved through a broadly based compromise or by a very dominant, strong coalition, prospects for either of which recede ever further as ethno-religious identities increase in political salience. Possessing technology, capital, and skilled labor in abundance, Israel's primary economic problem is its inability effectively to deploy those factors of production. The state is preoccupied with maintaining socio-political harmony between competitive ethno-religious groups, to say nothing of national security, so responding to the economic challenges and opportunities of globalization is of less concern.

The Turkish Republic, the other ethno-religious democracy, carries an even heavier burden of identity conflicts, a burden that has intermittently overwhelmed democracy. On three occasions since the establishment of democracy in Turkey in the mid-twentieth century, the military seized direct power, while on a fourth, in 1997, it removed from power a duly elected Islamist government, replacing it with a weak governing coalition dependent upon itself. The self-appointed guardian of the Kemalist legacy of Turkish secularism, the military is necessarily in opposition to all non-secularists and non-Turks, the most numerous and politically important of which are Kurds and Islamists. While the military's chosen instruments to deal with these social forces are coercive ones, the civilian political system, when it is allowed by the military to struggle with identity and other issues, responds much as the Israeli system has. Standard operating procedure is the making of extensive side payments to politicians and the social forces they represent in order to secure their support. For this reason the governmental budget remains in chronic deficit, inflation continues at one of the highest levels in the region, the Turkish lira steadily devalues, the public sector persists as a substantial net drain on national resources, and the state in general remains disproportionately large for the size of the economy. As in Israel, fiscal and monetary discipline have to be subordinated to the demands of forging ruling coalitions out of unruly, competitive, and distrustful social forces, or to the subordination by coercion of one or more of those forces. Although Turkey's factor endowment is not as generous as Israel's, it is much more substantial than its economic performance indicates.

Lebanon's democracy is typically described as "consociational," by which is meant that democracy is achieved in circumstances of societal fragmentation through the coalition building efforts of the leaders of those forces. Because of the centrality of political elites to the viability of the system, Lebanese political institutions are comparatively weak. Personal networks leading up to those elites constitute the main sinews of political, social, and economic life. State institutions in Lebanon, even more than in Israel or Turkey, serve the function of maintaining socio-political tranquillity and ruling coalitions. They do so by virtue of being carved into precisely determined shares for each of the seventeen officially recognized confessions, and by serving as conduits of patronage to them. Socio-political fragmentation in Lebanon is yet more pronounced than in either Israel or Turkey, so that the primary challenge of government is simply keeping the country together.

The only viable political economy in these circumstances is one in which the state does little more than adjust weights in order to maintain sectarian balance, leaving most of the tasks of economic management to others. The reaffirmation of laissez-faire as being the only approach which the fragile political economy can sustain was provided in the wake of the civil war, when an attempt was made to construct a Sunni Muslim dominated, relatively activist state within the shell of the multi-confessional, laissez-faire one. From 1992 to 1998 the government of Prime Minister Rafiq Hariri sought to erect a Saudi-style rentier state, an endeavor that ultimately collapsed because of the lack of economic resources, because of the political counter-mobilization of the other confessions, and because of ever-present regional factors. In this case the Syrians came to believe that Prime Minister Hariri had developed a back channel to Israel, an initiative which, if true, could have seriously compromised the Syrian bargaining position in the peace process with Israel. The paradox of the Hariri effort was that while it presented itself as an aggressive attempt at globalizing Lebanon, in fact it de-globalized what had been the most cosmopolitan of the Arab political economies. Whether a return to laissez-faire is economically viable in the globalized world which has developed since Lebanon essentially collapsed in the mid-1970s is an open question, but its underlying political system essentially precludes any other model.

Iran is an outlier in the category of MENA democracies for two, seemingly contradictory, reasons – it is the least "democratic" and the least fragmented into competitive social forces. The 1997 presidential election was free and fair and brought to power Muhammad Khatami, a liberal cleric whose electoral chances had been erroneously discounted by the powerful conservative clerics who, until that time, had the upper hand in government. Khatemi's ascension to power, made possible by popular reactions against the conservative clerics, tended to even the balance between the two broad political forces, thereby causing competition between them to intensify. Although it has intermittently turned violent, that competition has been conducted essentially peacefully and within the institutions of the state, although not primarily, as would be the case in an established democracy, in the parliament. As is the case in the other MENA democracies, intense political contestation cannot be confined within the legislative branch, but spills over into all state structures, which are in turn subordinated to the interests of the competitive forces. Like the other three democracies, the Iranian political system is unable to make and implement economically rational public policy, for the primary rationale of politics is conflict resolution.

The social forces most in conflict in Iran are not primordial as they are in Israel, Turkey, and Lebanon, although antagonisms do exist between the dominant Farsi-speaking Iranians, on the one hand, and minority Arabs, Azeris, Baluchis, Kurds, and various other social forces, including Baha'is, on the other. Iran is in a post-revolutionary condition, in which the transition from revolution to an established order has not yet been completed. Contending political actors, anchored in different social forces, conflict over the very nature of the political system and, most importantly, the role to be played in it by Islam and the clerics who represent it. Ayatollah Khomeini created an Islamic democracy that has very usefully prevented the competition over Iran's post-revolutionary future from dissolving into chaos, but it has been inadequate as a system for economic management, as the country's low growth and high inflation rates, depreciating currency, and escalating foreign debt attest.

Most forms of government, including democracy, have both costs and benefits. The primary benefit of democracy in these four countries is that it has been comparatively successful in facilitating peaceful resolution of conflicts between competitive social forces. Only in Lebanon has a sustained bloodletting occurred, but that was when the democracy broke down. In Turkey, the counter-insurgency campaign against Kurds has been run by a military that is not under civilian control. These partial exceptions, when compared with much more devastating and protracted violence in Algeria, Iraq, Sudan, Syria, and Yemen, for example, suggest what a benefit societal peace truly is. On the other hand, that benefit comes at the very substantial cost of these countries' abilities to respond effectively to globalization. Their governments are concerned primarily with resolving problems that arise from conflicting identities, not with imposing the economic discipline necessary for improved international competitiveness. Indeed, those two objectives are for the most part contradictory. Overgrown state structures, including large public sectors – with the partial exception of Lebanon – are retained precisely because those structures help to alleviate conflicts between competitive social forces. These social forces hinder economic performance by penetrating the state, but the economic damage seems less than that caused by the bunker or bully states that war against them. In the brief sections that follow we will identify some of the economic costs that each of the four countries has had to bear as a result of its democratic political system.

Israel

Israel's endowment of factors of production suggests that it should be the most successful MENA country in meeting globalization's challenges. Its human resources are the envy of the region. Life expectancy, at 77.5 years, is the highest in the MENA. It is one of the few MENA countries that outperforms its level of income on the Human Development Index, as presented in Table 1.1. Perhaps most relevant to globalization is the fact that Israel has the highest percentage of scientists in its population of any country in the world, with 135 for every 10,000 citizens, compared, for example, with 85 in the USA (Dunn 1998: 11).

Israel, although having no oil, is almost as well endowed with capital as the MENA's wealthiest oil exporters. On a per capita basis its GDP is higher than that of all but the minuscule GCC oil producers – Kuwait, the UAE, Bahrain, and Qatar. If foreign public and private capital transfers are included, capital available per capita in Israel is the most in the MENA. FDI amounted to some $7.4 billion between 1993 and 1997 (see Figure 2.6), compared with the next highest MENA performer, Egypt, at $3.9 billion. Israel receives more public foreign assistance per capita than any other country in the world if military assistance is included.

A superficial overview of Israel's economic performance might suggest that it is cashing in on its rich factor endowment. Its manufactured exports rose from $7.2 billion in 1987 to $20.7 billion a decade later, making them the region's most valuable, just ahead of Turkey's at $19.7 billion (see Table 3.1). Of these exports, high-tech goods and services accounted in 1997 for almost one-third, or some $6.2 billion, which are far and away the highest proportional and absolute amounts in the MENA (Dunn 1998: 11). Its intra-industry trade index rating of 0.584, the highest in the MENA, suggests that Israel is the most integrated into global commodity production chains (see Table 2.2). That Israel succeeded in bringing its import duties down from 4.9 percent of total tax revenues in 1987 to only 2.1 percent five years later and 0.5 percent by 1997, the lowest in the MENA, suggests a commitment to become globally competitive, as does the fact that its effective duty rate of 0.7 percent in 1997 was also the lowest in the MENA (see Table 3.1). Outstanding economic performance, if that is what it in fact is, would be consistent with Israel's relative political capacities, which, as shown on Figure 3.4, are on all three dimensions – extraction, credibility, and transparency – the highest in the region.

A more detailed examination of the economic data, however, reveals that Israel's economic performance has been uneven. Among the first MENA countries to undergo economic stabilization, which it did in the mid-1980s, Israel has since then been unable to bring its inflation rate down even to the level of such MENA competitors as Jordan, Morocco, and Tunisia, to say nothing of the GCC countries, whose inflation rates are the lowest in the region (see Table 3.2). Israel continues to experience difficulties in maintaining its stabilization measures. Its average per capita GNP growth rate, which at 4.5 percent for the period 1965–1975 was the highest in the MENA, deteriorated in the following decade to 1.2 percent, making it among the lowest in the MENA. It recovered in the decade after 1985 to again become one of the region's leaders, but after 1995 fell off rapidly, dropping by 1997 to a negative 0.8 (see Figure

1.2). As has been the case virtually since the state's foundation, Israel continues to run a significant balance of trade deficit. Israel's economic performance has thus been mixed, suggesting that it is not utilizing its factor endowment as well as it could.

The explanation of Israel's economic underachievement lies primarily with the nature of the state and society and the relationship between the two, which may in fact be too close from the perspective of economic competitiveness. Civil society in Israel has from the outset been closely tied to the state, the Zionist enterprise being a centrally organized one with capital provided through the organizations that ultimately became integrated into the state itself. Capital in Israel has traditionally been concentrated and lacking autonomy from the government. The close association with different elements of the Zionist movement of three of the four largest commercial banks illustrates the nexus between state and capital. Bank Leumi was founded shortly after the turn of the century by the Zionist movement, which continued to own it until, like the other big banks, it came under direct government ownership in 1983. Bank Ha'Poalim was controlled by the Histadrut, the Israeli Labor Federation, and Bank Ha'Mizrahi was owned by a movement of Orthodox Jews that constitutes one of the country's political parties. What amounted to the nationalization of these banks in 1983 resulted from a financial crisis brought on by them having utilized their depositors' funds to speculate in their own shares. The ensuing crash caused the stock exchange to be closed for two weeks as the government put together a rescue package that transferred to it controlling interest in the banks, where it remained until Ha'Poalim was privatized in 1997–2000.

Other indications of the "French" nature of the Israeli banking system are the lack of autonomy of the central bank and its requirement that commercial banks place on deposit with it a substantial percentage of their time deposits. This latter measure provides the government cheap money at the expense of depositors, increases the spread in interest rates between deposits and loans, keeps interest rates at high levels, and in general provides a disincentive for competitive banking. Having structured much of Israeli manufacturing and commerce into cartels, the government then utilized the banks to ration credit to them, something which the banks preferred as "it provided a guarantee in the sense of diminution of the risk incurred by the lending bank" (Plessner 1994: 170).

Mirroring the non-autonomous, concentrated banking system, the Israeli economy until very recently was under tight governmental control. The cartels just referred to, which were founded during the 1930s and strongly supported by the chief business lobby, the Manufacturers' Association, dominated the large-scale private sector until the late 1980s and still play a major role. These cartels were supported not only by the allocation of credit through the banks, but by high tariffs and extensive export subsidies that were subsequently reduced or eliminated. The companies within the cartels were and, in some cases, still are owned by the leading banks. The legal framework within which they operated typically provided monopolies and some, such as those regarding the importation, shipping, and sale of oil, still do (Plessner 1994: 146). Alongside the nominally private cartels, the public sector provided for direct governmental involvement in the economy. As late as the mid-1980s it accounted for about a quarter of the ownership of the country's largest fifty enterprises, and very much more if the Histadrut-controlled companies are thought of as being in the public sector, which for all intents and purposes they are. Histadrut-controlled companies accounted in the 1980s for about one fifth of all employment and an equal share of the GNP, bringing the public sector's total share of ownership of large companies to more than half, its employment to more than one-third of the country's total, and its contribution to GNP to just less than one-half (Plessner 1994: 115). The legacy of such direct state control and involvement in the economy is reflected by the continuing absence of large, truly private companies. None makes it on to the list of the world's largest 500 corporations. On the list of the MENA's fifty largest ones, Israel contributes a handful, proportionately fewer than the relative size of its economy and fewer in absolute numbers than Turkey and several GCC countries.

Civil society's search for material resources thus inevitably led it to the state, with the politicians acting as doorkeepers. For the secular left the dominant role of the state, manifested especially as it was for them in the Histadrut, was ideologically acceptable while being sound tactically, for the left controlled that state without interruption from its formation until 1977. What is harder to understand is why the right, as represented by the Likud Party and its allies since 1977, has accepted more or less the same formula of quasi-socialism, ostensibly committed as they are – or at least as election sloganeering would have it – to a free market economy.

That paradox is resolved with reference to two considerations – the primary objective and political base of the right. That objective has been to maximize the size of the country, not economic growth. Committed to Greater Israel, Likud and its allies have needed the state to fulfill their Zionist dream. Business, if left to its own devices, might well decide that a smaller Israel and peace with its neighbors would be better for business than an aggressive, expansionist state. Likud, in other words, has never really trusted the large-scale, cosmopolitan private sector, nor been trusted by it. So a natural alliance between business and the political right has never eventuated, leaving the Labor Party to develop ties with the private sector. So Labor has been the principal architect of Israel's most effective responses to globalization, including the original stabilization program, but there are real limits on how far the Labor Party, given its heritage and continued linkages to labor, can go in fostering capitalism.

The political base of the right also impedes its embrace of capitalism. Increasingly that base has become Sephardim, the poorest, most marginal component of Jewish society. Constituents of the right are thus yet more demanding of social transfers and services than those of the nominal left, whose ideology and long-established expectations also support such expenditures, even though their income levels and ties to the private sector may not. For coalitions of the right or left, therefore, reining in the budget is politically difficult to the point of being impossible, so deficits, inflation, and pervasive governmental involvement in the economy continue to hobble Israel's growth. The manner in which the budget has had to be trimmed reflects the political calculations of both left and right. Since stabilization commenced, public expenditure has fallen from 75–80 percent of GNP to about 55 percent. Those categories of expenditure favorable to business, including debt service, export and other subsidies, and domestic defense procurement, have fallen most rapidly, while social transfers and services have actually grown in both absolute and percentage terms (Shalev 1998: 31–33). Although the public sector has been reduced, most notably through the sale of the Koor conglomerate and other Histadrut-owned enterprises, some components of it that are large employers, including electricity and telecommunications, have been expanded.

Israel thus has an extremely brainy economy, but one in which the brain power is not as effectively deployed as it would be were the two principal competitive political forces (Labor and Likud) not both looking to the state for material resources in their efforts to gain and exercise power. The primary role of the state is to provide the services to integrate highly disparate social forces, as the politicians may all agree, but compounding the problem of its functional overload is Israel's minimal capitalist legacy. It is, in comparison to the size and robustness of the economy, extremely poor, because the state led development from the outset, imposing a French model on the financial sector. Israel's real capitalist tradition is barely a generation old, if by tradition is meant the high-tech private sector that is becoming the backbone of Israel's attempts at export-led growth. The entrepreneurs behind this drive typically emerged from the state itself, especially its military-industrial wing. So, for example, former computer engineers from the Israeli army established Checkpoint, a company that now commands 40 percent of the global market for network firewall systems, which protect corporations from hackers. In 1997 Checkpoint exported $86 million worth of such products. Companies similar to this account for a very large proportion of the 109 Israeli firms listed on US stock markets, which have a total value of $29 billion. Israel has more than 3,000 high-tech start-ups annually, more than any other country except the USA (Dunn 1998: 11).

Israeli capitalism is thus "spinning off" from the state, a development that presumably will continue, but may or may not gather more pace. A resolution of conflicts with its Arab neighbors and final definition of the borders and nature of the state may well be preconditions for export-led growth of East Asian proportions, the empirical preconditions for which Israel certainly already possesses. But as long as the Revisionist Zionist agenda preoccupies the political right and as long as both major political forces remain finely balanced and unwilling to take the risk of leaving their moorings in the state to forge new coalitions with the private sector, the high-tech and other components of that private sector will remain hobbled by a state that is consumed primarily with resolving Israeli's identity conflicts, rather that fostering more rapid growth.

Turkey

Turkey's economic performance, like Israel's, has been uneven, not realizing the potential inherent in its factor endowment, and considerably less than "serious economists" have hoped it would achieve. In the early 1980s, Turkey became a prize pupil of the IMF and World Bank, hence the recipient of massive infusions of public foreign assistance in support of stabilization and structural adjustment programs. By the end of the decade, however, when stabilization had achieved only mixed results and the prize pupil still balked at implementing much of the structural adjustment program, the purveyors of the Washington Consensus lost interest in their one-time protégé. Turkey's stabilizing role in the Arab–Israeli conflict, by which is meant its tacit support for the latter, combined with its renewed geo-strategic importance in the wake of the collapse of the Soviet Union, nevertheless ensured continuing external public support for its economy, albeit at reduced levels.

Residues of what was touted in the early 1980s as the Turkish economic miracle are still reflected in the data. GNP growth per capita (see Figure 1.2) was higher in the decade after 1985 than in the decade before, and achieved almost 7 percent in 1997, after Tunisia the best performance in the region. Manufactured exports as a percentage of GDP rose appreciably in the decade after 1987 (see Table 3.1), resulting in Turkey ranking fourth in the MENA on this measure by 1998, after Israel, Jordan, and Tunisia, but second in absolute amount, just behind Israel. Its growing integration into global commodity production chains is reflected in its score on the intra-industry trade index, which jumped from 0.159 to 0.284 between 1984–1986 and 1992–1994, placing it behind only Israel, Oman, and Tunisia, and at about the same level achieved by the Andean Pact countries. Despite shaky financial management and turbulent politics, Turkey during the 1990s continued to attract large amounts of foreign private capital, receiving more FDI than any other Muslim country in the region except Egypt (virtually all of whose FDI was concentrated in the oil industry). Among these countries, Turkey attracted the most private equity investment to its stock market (see Figure 2.6). Contributing to Turkey's appeal to investors has been its financial system, which boasts a comparatively large and active stock market (its value traded as a percentage of GDP and turnover ratios being the highest in the region in 1998; see Table 3.5), and a deconcentrated, private sector led, competitive banking system. More remittances pour into Turkey than any other country in the MENA. It ranks fourth in the region on the CIM ratio measure of institutional credibility, sixth on the transparency index, and sixth on the extraction index (see Figure 3.4).

Uneven economic performance, however, is suggested in the first instance by measures of financial stability, which reveal extremely weak governmental discipline over the budget, given Turkey's level of overall economic development. Turkey's inflation rate, which vexed the serious economists throughout the 1980s, in fact increased in the 1990s, reaching the region's highest level of almost 85 percent per annum in 1998, as compared with an average of 51 percent in the 1985–1989 period (Table 3.2). Driving this almost runaway inflation are large budget deficits, which have grown from 3.5 percent to 8.4 percent of GDP during the same period (Table 3.2). Its debt service ratio has in the 1990s remained within the range of the region's worst offenders, Algeria, Iran, and Morocco (Table 2.3). Fiscal laxity appears to be due in considerable measure to the public sector's drag on the economy. Despite extensive privatization in the 1990s that dropped its share of employment from 3.7 percent in the late 1980s to 2.9 percent in the 1990s, the public sector sucked up substantially more capital from the government in this latter period. Its deficit almost doubled as a percentage of GDP over those years (see Table 3.3). Reflecting the surprising persistence of the public sector in this "prize pupil" economy is the fact that in the mid-1990s its private sector received less credit, as a percentage of GDP, than any others in the MENA countries except Algeria, Iran, Sudan, Syria, and Yemen (Table 3.4).

Incurable governmental profligacy stems from political weakness, a malady which the IMF and World Bank thought would be overcome by military rule in the early 1980s. That intervention was, however, a relatively brief interlude, for Turkish civil society is too developed for unveiled military rule to persist. The fragmentation of political parties is such that the largest of them does not obtain much more than a fifth of the votes in parliamentary elections. Underlying that fragmentation are rifts between competitive social forces that threaten and indeed have resulted in extensive violence over the past twenty years. The major task of Turkish democracy is thus attempting to resolve such conflicts as peacefully as possible, a task which requires much more liberal distributions of governmental resources than neo-liberal textbooks prescribe.

The utilization of governmental largesse for the political objectives of sustaining coalition governments and dampening societal conflicts dates to the commencement of competitive democratic politics at mid century. At that time the primary political divide was between the urban-based elite whose power stemmed from the state, and rural social forces who felt and indeed were disadvantaged by the workings of that state. This divide continues to be a central one, but the political expression of the interests of those rural social forces that were first mobilized into politics against the then ruling Republican People's Party by the Democratic and then Justice parties, has changed. Most notably that expression is now largely, although not entirely, within an Islamist framework. The thesis of a secular, state-based civilian elite backed ultimately by an ardently secular military establishment has over the past quarter of a century stimulated an Islamist antithesis that appeals to those who resent what they see as the privileges of that elite. Both sides have drawn liberally upon the state's resources when they have been in power. Indeed the secular elite may perceive the Turkish–Kurdish ethnic conflict, a civil war that has dragged on throughout the decade of the 1990s, as less politically threatening than Islamism. The Kurds could not actually displace that elite from power, but the Islamists could and nearly did.

It was that fear that led the military to dismiss the Islamist Welfare Party from government in 1997, although it had won more votes in the December 1995 elections than any other party. Following the dismissal the National Security Council, the organization through which military control over civilian government is exercised, instigated a purge of

Islamists that resulted in the dissolution of the Welfare Party and the banning from politics of its leadership. Yet constraints on arbitrary rule are considerably greater in Turkey than in the Arab praetorian republics. The military could not "eradicate" Islamists as in Syria, for example. A new, successor Islamist party, the Party of Virtue, was permitted to form and contest the April 1999 elections, in which, despite considerable harassment by the authorities, including threats to close it down, it managed to finish third in the balloting. Moreover, the Virtue Party has attracted yet more young, urban elements into its ranks, while further moderating some of the planks of the former Welfare Party's platform, including disavowal of its opposition to entry into the EU.

The tenacity of Turkish Islamism reflects the strength of the thesis against which it is reacting, and the relative autonomy and power of the capital base upon which it rests. As for the thesis, it is the nexus of military–bureaucratic–entrepreneurial elites who have been the primary beneficiaries and wielders of state power under the Republic, first created in 1923. The ideological component of that thesis has been Turkish secularism, while its economic content was, until the 1980s, state-led, import substitution industrialization (ISI). When ISI had clearly run its course and the World Bank and IMF stepped in to help shoulder the financial burden at the outset of the 1980s, the state-based elite rapidly shifted gears, presenting themselves as advocates of export-led growth within the framework of a free market economy. But the nexus between those in the state and the large, cosmopolitan, primarily Istanbul-based capitalists it had spawned remained intact, although the latter came in the 1990s to advocate a more open economy and polity than the military and its civilian bureaucratic and political partners were willing to tolerate. The economy thus came to be a much more sophisticated and successful version of the crony capitalism that also emerged in Egypt at about this time. Intensification of conflict between the secular, state-based elite, on the one hand, and Islamists and Kurds on the other, narrowed the space for the crony-entrepreneurs, whose clamorings for more economic and political freedom subsided when the threat to their own interests became more apparent (Bugra 1998: 521–539).

That Islamism has been able to withstand the state's heavy blows attests to the resources at its disposal. Its political leadership is comparatively sophisticated, at the highest levels having been active in Turkish democratic and even parliamentary politics for a quarter of a century. Necmettin Erbakan, the leader of the Welfare Party, for example, had served as a cabinet member in the 1970s. A host of the party's members cut their political teeth as mayors of Turkish towns and cities, including

Istanbul itself. Islamist political leadership can draw on a dense network of Islamist social organizations that provide both human and material resources for political contestation. That Turkish Islamism has eschewed violence has also reinforced its position, for it has been hard to present it as being "beyond the pale." Its non-violent approach results at least in part from Turkish democracy, which has offered that movement a path to power, albeit one strewn with obstacles.

But political talent, Islamist voluntarism, and a democratic system would, by themselves, be insufficient to sustain Islamism as the country's largest and most effective political movement, were it not for the material resources upon which it can draw. Those resources include the large-scale, formal financial system, a more informal adjunct of it, and the plethora of small and medium business enterprises owned and operated by provincial capitalists, especially those in the country's heartland of Anatolia. Their cultural roots are Islamic, and they resent the secularism and governmental privileges bestowed upon the big capitalist cronies of the military-political elite. Islamic banks in Turkey date to the early 1980s, when the then prime minister, Turgut Özal, was seeking to develop economic linkages to the oil-producing Arab states and a domestic political counterbalance to the secular left, which he was seeking to destroy to help pave the way for structural adjustment. The Islamic banks have prospered and provided a source of capital to a steadily growing small to medium Islamist business sector. Joining these banks have been numerous investment companies which, like their Egyptian counterparts, have specialized in serving the financial needs of Turkish workers abroad, especially those in Europe, and which, precisely because they pose both economic and political threats to the state, have become the target of its retribution. As far as "Islamist capitalists" are concerned, their growing material and organizational capacities are reflected in MUSIAD, the Association of Independent Industrialists and Businessmen, which was founded in 1990 and has come to aggregate their interests and speak on behalf of them.

The globalization dialectic in Turkey has thus proceeded much further than elsewhere in the region, a consequence of the country's more open polity and developed economy. Globalization spawned a first generation of state-linked capitalists, who, had they not been outflanked by a second generation of moralizers and hemmed in by them on one side and by the state on the other, might have been able to engineer a more thoroughgoing liberalization of the polity and economy. But their economic links to the state and fears of the Islamist challenge have led them to backpedal on earlier demands for reform (Bugra 1998: 521–539). This has, in turn, cleared the way for an Islamist antithesis, which is seeking a synthesis between the globalist challenge and an Islamist response. It is worth highlighting some of its key elements, because Turkey could be a model that other countries in the region might emulate – just as Nasser, for example, was apparently much influenced by Atatürk and his state-centered approach.

The economic response is an effort to reconcile globalism and Islam, not use the latter in an attempt to combat the former. That reconciliation, or synthesis, includes several dimensions. One is an embrace of the world capitalist economy and even the instruments of the Washington Consensus. The Welfare Party, for example, nurtured strong ties to the IMF and World Bank. A second is an embrace of the Washington Consensus itself. Indeed, having been less favored by the state than their secularist competitors, Islamist capitalists in Turkey are ardent free marketers, wanting the state to be dramatically downsized. The Welfare Party, for example, privatized at a faster pace than any other government in Turkish history. But the embrace of globalism is not uncritical nor without qualifications. For one thing it requires recognition and utilization of Islamic methods of finance. For another it seeks implementation of some elements of an Islamic moral economy, in which competition is tempered by ethical and moral concerns. This particular element of the synthesis appears to grow out of the very nature of Islamist capitalist enterprise in Turkey, which tends to be small and medium scale and family based. It is, therefore, stridently anti-labor union, arguing that commonality of interests of owners and workers, with recognition of their mutual and shared objectives, should provide the guidelines for any model of labor–management relations. Finally, the Islamist synthesis prioritizes the Islamic world as a source for capital and markets and general economic interaction.

The globalization dialectic has, however, been at least temporarily arrested in Turkey by a government intent on limiting, if not destroying, the capacity of Islamism to formulate and enact its synthesis. Whether the synthesizers are able to withstand this pressure and return to the fray, or will succumb to the pressure and be superseded by either the first-moment secularists or much more radical moralizers, remains to be seen. In the meantime the Turkish state and economy are held hostage to these and other political struggles that limit the freedom of both political and economic markets.

Iran

The Islamic Republic of Iran has contributed much less to a viable synthesis between globalization and Islam than has secular Turkey. This paradox results from the fact that in post-revolutionary Iran there has been no sustained dialogue between globalizers and moralizers. The revolution swept away the secular, pro-Western elite and delivered the state to Islamists, thus removing the thesis against which an Islamist antithesis could react. Instead of becoming a tool with which to forge a synthesis with globalization, the Islamic state turned in on itself, both because of the imposition of sanctions by the USA, and because of the perceived need to consolidate and defend the revolution. Thus it became the exercise of state power, rather than a reaction against it or the use of that power in the international economy, that has preoccupied Iran's moralizers. And as in other MENA democracies, the state has been used more as a distributive tool to alleviate socio-political conflicts, than as an instrument with which to propel more rapid economic development.

To be fair, the regional and global contexts have hardly been propitious. Since the revolution of 1979, the Iranian government has had to contend with an eight-year war with Iraq, an economic embargo imposed by the USA, a massive influx of refugees from Iraq and Afghanistan, and two oil price collapses, one in the mid-1980s and another in 1998–1999. But the instinctive impulse of Iran's Islamist revolutionaries, once in power, was in any case inimical to economic growth or formulating a productive response to the challenges of globalization. That impulse included, as is typically the case in the wake of revolutions, nationalization of the means of production. In 1983–1984, twenty-eight of the country's thirty-six banks, thirteen of which had foreign partners, were nationalized, followed by forced mergers that reduced the number of banks to six commercial and three specialized ones and the number of total branches from some 8,300 to less than 6,600 (Zangeneh 1998: 123).

In order to control private enterprises, including those formerly owned by the shah's Pahlavi Foundation, the mullahs established *bonyad*s, or what a former Iranian minister of finance has referred to as "independent and monopolistic . . . mafia-type religious conglomerates" (Amuzegar 1998: 90). *Bonyad*s co-exist uneasily alongside a directly state-controlled public sector comprising yet other nationalized enterprises, as well as those which the Islamic revolutionaries inherited directly from the shah's large public sector. Of these two "public sectors," the one consisting of *bonyad*s under the direct control of various factions of mullahs is much larger than the one managed by the state itself. The oldest and biggest *bonyad*, the Foundation for the Oppressed, originally formed to take control of the assets of the Pahlavi Foundation, "is second in size only to the central government." It is claimed by its president to be the largest economic enterprise in the Middle East (Akhavi-Pour and Azodanloo 1998: 80). It accounts for a fifth of all textiles and apparel produced in Iran, a quarter of the sugar, and about half the beverages, plus dominant shares of construction materials markets. Conservatives, especially those entrenched in the *bonyads*, bitterly and successfully opposed a home-grown structural adjustment program that President Ali Akbar Hashemi-Rafsanjani had launched shortly after the death of Ayatollah Khomeini. The privatization program ground to a halt by 1994, leaving the state and the *bonyads* in control of four-fifths of the economy, producing some 5,000 different goods and services, employing about a fifth of the labor force, handling about three-quarters of all imports, and achieving total annual sales of $3.5 billion (Amuzegar 1998: 90). The budget of the 404 largest public sector firms amounted to almost 40 percent of GDP by 1997. The share of all public firms' allocations in the general budget increased from 53 percent in 1989 to 67 percent in 1996. Their claim on bank loans during that period rose from 8 to 30 percent (Salehi-Isfahani 1999: 35).

The Iranian revolution has evolved into competing factions within a large government and a massive but politicized and fragmented public sector, ensuring that distribution inexorably would triumph over production as the primary logic driving economic policy, amid a rising level of poverty and unemployment accompanied by political apathy and antipathy. Factions have vied with one another to build and service constituencies by distributing governmental largesse. As a consequence, the usual indicators of fiscal profligacy, including high inflation, budgetary deficits, much seignorage (earned from printing money), and a declining currency, characterize the Iranian economy. Inflation rates have been exceeded only by Turkey and occasionally the Sudan in the 1990s (see Table 3.2), and the Iranian riyal, for which the government has established four exchange rates, trades on parallel markets at about one-third of its nominal value (see Table 3.2). In the late 1990s, Iran's debt servicing as a percentage of its exports peaked at almost one-third of GDP, second only to Algeria (Table 2.3). Tariffs were doubled on "non-essential" imports in 1998 and many items added to the list of prohibited imports. Capital flight intensified as the end of the decade approached and capital available for investment declined, dropping from about one-quarter of GDP in the mid-1970s to 15 percent in the 1990s. As one Iranian economist has noted, "Iran's post-revolution adjustment policy has protected private consumption at the expense of investment" (Salehi-Isfahani 1999: 35).

The election of Muhammad Khatami as president in 1997 resulted in part from a widespread desire for improved economic performance, a desire to which his new government attempted to respond by fusing "development with social justice" as part of a strategy to satisfy both the champions of continued welfare subsidies and reformist technocrats (Amuzegar 1998: 86). But the combination of plummeting oil prices in 1998–1999, division within Khatami's own camp, and, most of all, staunch opposition by the leadership of the conservative faction, entrenched in the *bonyad*s and various parts of the state apparatus, caused the mild reform to be stillborn. Even lukewarm attempts to render more transparent the state's accounts, which include large but unknown transfers and subsidies to the *bonyad*s from the public treasury, ended in failure. In the first year of Khatami's presidency no more than one-quarter of the some 1,200 state enterprises even bothered to submit their annual financial reports. Although the finance minister promised closer supervision of public finances, some of the public sector companies financed by the state transferred money out of Iran and invested abroad without the control authorities' knowledge of the nature and magnitude of these outlays (Amuzegar 1998: 90). Significantly, on our transparency indicator, Iran more closely resembles the bullies and bunkers than the other democracies in the MENA (see Figure 3.3).

The opacity of the Iranian political economy is purposeful, as competitive factions entrenched in the state use its resources to vie for power. As these struggles have intensified, they have polarized the factions, which have coalesced into two basic camps. "Conservatives" – in the sense that they want to conserve what they see as the gains of the revolution – claim the mantle of Ayatollah Khomeini. They seek to maintain the rule of the mullahs, most especially through the supremacy of the post of *velayat-e faqih*, or religious jurist, which is occupied by their leading figure, Ayatollah Khamani'i. The moderates, also known as liberals, reformers, or technocrats, found their champion in President Khatami. They advocate greater respect for the rule of law, a commensurate reduction in revolutionary zeal, and more democracy, including an expanded political role for non-clerics.

The steadily intensifying struggle between these two factions has resulted in the state being carved up between them, such that each controls counterbalancing fiefdoms. The constitutional/legal structure of the Islamic Republic, which is extraordinarily elaborate, is both the result and a continuing cause of this fragmentation. The executive and legislative branches consist not just of a single executive and legislature, but of numerous institutions assigned roles in both domains. The supreme leader, or *faqih*, is counterbalanced by the president, and both have to deal with the Assembly of Experts, the Council of Guardians, and the Council for Discernment of Expediency, to say nothing of the parliament and the various components of the executive branch, almost all of which share numerous executive and legislative functions in Byzantine fashion. Roughly speaking the Conservatives, whose champion is the *faqih*, are entrenched in what might be thought of as those institutions that parallel the normal state structure, within which the Moderates, led by President Khatami, are entrenched. So, for example, the Moderates tend to control the Council of Ministers, the central bank, and mayors, whereas the Conservatives hold sway in the judicial branch, the legislature, and the assembly and councils identified above (Akhavi-Pour and Azodanloo 1998: 70–72). In the economic domain, the major bases for the Conservatives are the *bonyad*s and networks of religious institutions that generate revenues. The Moderates, centered in the executive branch, are responsible for the governmental public sector as well as the treasury, through which taxes, as well as oil and gas revenues, nominally pass. Complicated as this structure is, it is made yet more elaborate and inefficient by competitive jurisdictions between various ministries, such as the three that are responsible for education (Education, Higher Eduction, and Islamic Guidance) or agriculture (Agriculture, Sazandegi, and Cooperatives). The vital means of coercion are also divided between the two major factions, with the Conservatives having much the larger share.

Such governmental complexity precludes transparency and renders personalistic connections vital to the conduct of any business, small or large. Thus the factions rest upon patronage networks that weave down through the state and into society, thereby integrating social forces into the governmental structure itself, which enjoys no autonomy or institutional integrity. Democracy, which in Iran takes the form of different components of the state and quasi-state being penetrated and controlled by competitive political factions roughly representing different social forces, has had obvious costs and maybe some not so obvious benefits.

The costs are borne principally by the economy, which is viewed essentially as a pie to be carved up by the competitive factions, rather than as a cluster of factors of production that need to be integrated by appropriate public policy and actions of private actors. As a leading economist of Iran has noted, its economy resembles that of a centrally planned one but "without the central planning" (Salehi-Isfahani 1999: 35). Iran's non-oil exports slid steadily in the 1990s, making the country yet more dependent upon oil than it was under the shah. The Islamic banks created in the early 1980s, like all other financial institutions, operate in conditions of near-chaos that prevent them from developing any significant capacities to assess risks and utilize their capital accordingly, to say nothing of their inability to forge a new synthesis with secular globalization. The de-globalization of Iran results less from the embargo imposed upon it by the USA than from the nature of its political system. Accordingly, when that embargo is lifted, as by 1998 it began to be, the capacity of Iran to respond is too limited for it to take much advantage of more favorable regional and global contexts.

But the benefit of this fragmented, Islamic democracy is that it probably has helped avert degeneration into serious political violence, even civil war, which might have happened were it a more authoritarian, winner-take-all system. While this prospect cannot be entirely discarded and growing economic pressure may ultimately contribute to its eventuation, the democratic characteristics of the Islamic Republic have given large numbers of Iranians stakes in the system and have prevented a single target of popular wrath from emerging. As presently constituted, however, the political economy is not sustainable for it cannot provide the preconditions for the emergence of a successful Islamic or any other form of capitalism.

The paradox of the Islamic Republic of Iran is that it has contributed less than the secular Republic of Turkey to the development of a synthesis between globalization and Islam. This unexpected outcome results primarily from the fact that Iran has de-globalized since the revolution, a consequence of sanctions being imposed upon it and of the bifurcation of the state between competitive factions, which has caused the economy to be inward- rather than outward-looking.

Lebanon

Lebanon, in which a similar bifurcated state emerged in the 1990s, also has a paradoxical relationship with globalization. The most globalized of Arab countries until the mid-1970s, when civil war essentially removed it from the global and even regional economy for fifteen years, Lebanon embarked on a reconstruction program in the early 1990s that has in fact de-globalized it. Further adding to the paradox is that the reconstruction program, led by Prime Minister Rafiq Hariri between 1992 and 1998, was presented as a plan to restore Lebanon to its role as regional entrepôt, to become once again a twentieth-century version of Phoenician mercantilism. The political economy of Lebanon has thus traced a path that is the obverse of that followed by the praetorian Arab republics. When they were pursuing policies of import substitution industrialization and essentially isolating their economies, Lebanon was their window on the world, a cosmopolitan, essentially free-trade area governed with the light hand of laissez-faire. All that was really required was to stabilize the currency, as Lebanon's vigorous mercantile capitalism did the rest. But when the praetorians commenced their cautious, controlled openings to the global economy in the 1980s and 1990s, Lebanon emerged from its civil war to embrace not global capitalism, but a provincial, *dirigiste* protectionism from which it has yet to emerge.

During the decade of the 1990s Lebanon basically squandered its factor endowment in pursuit of an inappropriate development model that resulted from political, not economic calculations. Lebanon has one of the highest literacy rates in the Arab world and, as revealed in Table 1.1, is one of the Arab countries showing the least divergence between its rank on the Index of Human Development and on real per capita GDP. Comparatively well-developed human resources have matched the nominal availability of capital. Between 1993 and 1997, Lebanon received more than a quarter of a billion dollars of FDI and managed to float externally almost $2 billion in government bonds, more than any MENA country other than Turkey (see Figure 2.6). Our evaluation of relative political capacities, as provided in Figure 3.4, shows that while its extractive capacity places it in about the middle of the range of MENA countries, it ranks second on the credibility index and seventh on transparency, preceded only by Israel, Turkey, and the mini-states of the GCC.

But performance indicators for the economy in the 1990s tell a very different story. Although basic economic information is scarce for Lebanon because it still has not rebuilt its capacity to gather and report it, what is available reveals inadequate performance. As a result of heavy governmental borrowing, its debt service ratio began to balloon out toward the end of the decade, more than doubling in the single year 1996–1997 (see Table 2.3). Central government debt as a percentage of GDP had started to climb some three years earlier, and by 1997 had reached almost 100 percent, the second highest proportion in countries for which data are reported in Figure 2.7. Debt service by 1998 consumed half of all governmental expenditures, which, when combined with civil service salaries, an additional two-fifths of the government's budget, resulted in only 6 percent being available for capital expenditures. This is an exceedingly low proportion and absolute amount for a country nominally in the process of postwar reconstruction. As governmental profligacy was increasing in the 1990s, growth rates were steadily dropping, from 8 percent in 1994 to 1.4 percent four years later. The government's voracious appetite for credit sucked funds away from the private sector as Lebanon's private banks purchased about three-quarters of the treasury bills issued during the decade, which have come to constitute the bulk of the loan portfolios of many if not most of the banks. T-bills were paying in the mid- and late 1990s interest at 18 percent and more, making domestic financing far too expensive for Lebanese businesses (Denoeux and Springborg 1998: 158–174). The banking sector, however, being drip-fed by T-bills, reported record earnings as taxes, in effect, were being converted into bank profits. The downward economic spiral also dragged Lebanon further away from the global economy, as tariff rates had to be increased in desperate efforts to raise revenues to reduce ballooning deficits. By 1997 some 40 percent of those revenues came from tariffs, probably the highest proportion in the MENA. Lebanon's balance of trade had, by 1998, become spectacularly negative, with exports of some $1 billion and imports of $8 billion.

The paradox of Lebanon, the putative inheritor of the Phoenician mercantile tradition, becoming an enclave, inward-looking economy, just as most other MENA economies were beginning cautiously to look outward, results from regional and domestic political factors. Chief among the former is increasing Syrian control of the country, especially after 1990. While Syria may want its own Hong Kong, it has exerted too much control over both the polity and the economy for Lebanon to play that outward-oriented role. Domestic political factors, which are shaped by Syria's presence, can be summed up as efforts to displace the state based on consociational democracy with a more unitarian one, an effort which appears ultimately to have failed, as symbolized by the removal of Prime Minister Hariri in the fall of 1998.

Hariri, the country's merchant prince who had made his fortune in Saudi Arabia, seduced his countrymen with a dream of an entirely new, steel, glass, and concrete Beirut that would be the financial center of the MENA region. The Faustian bargain he was offering was that in return for promises of petro- and other dollars flowing into the country, thereby stabilizing the Lebanese pound, they would award him the right to run the country's affairs. The residual state was placed at the disposal of the warlords who had been recycled as politicians, giving them governmental resources to be doled out to their followers. Having struck this bargain upon coming to power in late 1992, Hariri immediately set about building his own state alongside the decrepit, confessionalized, patronage-based one that he had inherited and which he essentially turned over to the other politicians.

Hariri's state consisted of an opaque mix of public and private institutions. He imposed his confidants on the commanding heights of the state, which were those that channeled the flow of public monies. His former stockbroker at Merrill Lynch became the head of the central bank, for example, whereas the Ministry of Finance was given to the chief financial officer for Hariri's business conglomerate. Solidere, a private company founded and controlled by Hariri, was ceded ownership of central Beirut, whereas the Council for the Development and Reconstruction of Lebanon, nominally a governmental agency but in fact under the direct control of Hariri's team, was awarded a virtual monopoly over governmental construction. The monopoly could be used, among other things, to provide a vast network of infrastructure for Solidere's city center. From this public/private base Hariri reached out to bring the media and banking sectors under his control, buying up the most prestigious newspapers and television stations and taking controlling interests in the country's most profitable banks, yet further enriched by the T-bills that Hariri's central bank auctioned off.

Hariri, in sum, created a business enterprise cum state alongside the rickety old confessionalized state that he had inherited. As the years went on, "his" state came to control a much larger share of the public purse than the nominal state. Lest the mounting opposition crystallize against what was increasingly in the street being referred to as the "theft" of the country, Hariri bought the largest bloc of deputies in parliament.

In the end Hariri could not deliver on his bargain and was sacked by the Syrians, who had come to view him as a liability and possibly a traitor as well. He could not provide the flow of funds he had promised because the public/private state he was constructing, modeled in part on the tribal/merchant states of the Gulf, was inimical to attracting large amounts of external capital. Those rentier states, after all, exist on domestically generated resources and do not attract external investments outside the enclave hydrocarbon sector. The transparency required for such investments, to say nothing of overall political stability and physical infrastructure, were all missing in Hariri's Lebanon. Thus, lacking his own oil rents, he had to beg his Gulf backers for intermittent infusions of capital to keep his sinking ship of state afloat, but more capital than that he could not induce into Lebanon. In the meantime, the confessionalized state had to be fed more patronage to pacify the increasingly discontented politicians and their clienteles, thus draining yet more resources away from redevelopment. Hariri's Lebanon, in sum, was an attempt to build a rentier state without domestic rents, a venture that seems doomed despite Hariri's return to power in 2000.

So Lebanon wasted the decade of the 1990s pursuing a false dream. It is in need of an entirely new model of political, economic, and physical reconstruction that is consistent with its factor endowment and political capacities. Its consociational democracy, which was essentially put on ice during most of the decade as the failed effort at building a rentier state without rents progressed, will ultimately have to forge the new model, or the state will be subsumed by Syria. Like the other MENA democracies, what Lebanon did in the 1990s was to use the state to provide sufficient integration of competitive social forces to reduce the likelihood of violent socio-political conflict. In that it succeeded, but at the cost of provincializing an economy that was ostensibly in a process of post-war reconstruction. As in the case of the other democracies, it is clear that an appropriate model is one that seeks to limit the scope of the state, for the integration of social forces into it causes it to be driven by political, rather than economic, logic. For Lebanon this was in fact the historic role model for the state, a model that many believed is what Hariri was attempting to implement, but in fact he was not. While a return to the laissez-faire state of the pre-civil war era is impractical for many reasons, a more muscular version of that state would be consistent with its historical traditions, the limits imposed by the fragmented society, and with Lebanon's economic factor endowments. But that a state that has been so marginalized by both external and internal actors can regain control of the country's fate remains to be seen.

Conclusion

The MENA democracies govern societies that are sharply fragmented and threatened by the ever present danger of violent political conflict. For the most part they have done a better job in managing this conflict than have the bunker states, where the solution to societal conflict is for one social force to seize the state and seek to impose its will on the others. The democrats probably spend less on side payments to those social forces than either the bunker or bully praetorians spend on control and coercion. And the indirect costs to economic development of side payments are probably on balance less than the costs of obtrusive state control, which in the most dramatic cases have pulverized capitalists and civil society, leaving the state without societal mechanisms to respond to whatever opportunities public policy might provide. Thus the democrats are rather more capable of meeting the challenges of globalization than the praetorians, but, because they govern more fractious societies, are not appreciably better placed than at least some of the monarchies. By and large, however, the democrats are less frightened of information flow, have stronger civil societies, more developed and competitive economic institutions, lower transaction costs, and better established external linkages, and, in general, are more cosmopolitan than either the praetorians or the monarchies. But in all MENA democracies, political systems continue to impede more rapid growth because questions of identity and security take precedence and drain resources.

Suggestions for further reading

On Iran see Amuzegar (1993), Rahnema and Behdad (1995), and Mack (2000). For Israel see Barnett (1996) and Plessner (1994). Denoeux and Springborg (1998) and Picard (1996) discuss Lebanon, while Öniş (1998), Ozbudun (2000) and the Popes (1997) look at the Turkish economy, political system, and recent history, respectively.

8   Conclusion

In the preceding chapters we have sought to demonstrate that MENA economies are not performing at levels commensurate with their factor endowments, and to explain this inadequacy as a result of political factors at the global, regional, and national levels. Globalization, today's equivalent to yesterday's imperialism, at least in many of its impacts on non-Western economies, is the primary external thesis against which MENA countries are reacting. Having formerly been sustained by global rents resulting from geo-political considerations or hydrocarbon extraction, regimes throughout the region are now having to make dramatic adjustments to capture new sources of revenue, most of which are private, hence less susceptible than global rents to political pressures and calculations. These adjustments are having profound domestic consequences. They are bifurcating elites into "globalizers" and "moralizers," the former of which seek to be local apostles for the Washington Consensus, the latter of which are seeking either to reject globalization in its entirety, or to formulate a synthesis between it and nativist, primarily Islamic values and practices. Threatened by both the ardent globalizers and the moralizers, most regimes are cautiously seeking to control the pace and content of globalization, lest they be swept away by it. As yet none of the regimes has succumbed to this fate, nor will they necessarily, as gradual adaptation may enable them to survive, albeit in modified form. But if the analogy to imperialism holds, it suggests that globalization's powerful forces will ultimately prove too much for at least some incumbent elites to contain and will bring to power new political actors representing different social forces.

Just as globalization will be the primary external force impacting MENA political economies in the twenty-first century, so was imperialism such a force in the nineteenth and twentieth centuries. The MENA, more than any other region, was defined by it and continues to struggle with its legacy. At the regional level a central element of this definition has been a high level of intra- and inter-state conflict resulting primarily from contradictions between various nationalisms, primordial sentiments, and state borders. The main economic consequence has been an imbalance between guns and butter in MENA governmental expenditures. While this imbalance is now being reduced, presumably the resolution of the region's major conflict, that which pits Israel against Arabs, is a necessary if not sufficient condition for military expenditures in MENA ultimately to decline to global averages. Less deeply rooted but expensive ones, such as the conflict between Iraq and its Gulf neighbors, would also require political settlement. Reductions in military expenditures might in turn lessen the role of militaries in MENA political systems and open up possibilities for civilian control of them, or reinforce it in those few instances where it is at least partially established.

At the national level, imperialism's impact and legacy may have been yet more profound. A powerful thesis against which nationalists formulated various antitheses, imperialism, more than any other factor, determined the nature of regimes in the post-colonial era. Monarchies and their attendant civil societies tended to survive where imperialism's impact was absent, abbreviated, or weak, whereas praetorians ultimately seized the reins of power in countries where imperialism enervated the very social forces it cultivated. Imperialism can claim much of the credit (or blame, depending on the perspective) for the emergence of an ethno-religious democracy in Israel, while the reaction against its "neo" form is primarily responsible for Iran's Islamic variant of democracy. Turkish democracy is more a home-grown product than any other in the region, while Lebanon's was largely inherited from delicate institutional balances established by the imperialists.

Imperialism and the post-colonial states it gave rise to also shaped civil society, the most important component of which is that which generates the capital to sustain it. In the monarchies, the palace tended to accommodate if not indulge indigenous merchants, manufacturers, and even finance capitalists, thus providing their economies with capacity to respond to the challenges and opportunities of globalization. In the praetorian republics, on the other hand, radical nationalists wreaked their vengeance upon civil society as a whole, and especially its capitalist component, key elements of which frequently were of minority or foreign backgrounds. Taking direct control of the economy, praetorians typically then harnessed the factors of production to ill-fated attempts at state-led import substitution industrialization, thus compounding their economic problems and leaving their states with yet bigger adjustments to make and fewer capitalists to help in making them. Finally, in the "qualified" democracies, the politics of identity have preoccupied states and civil societies, thereby diverting both from the tasks of economic development, tasks for which they are nevertheless better equipped than the praetorian republics or monarchies.

In most MENA countries the very heart of the capitalist component and engine of civil society, the financial sector, was structured first by imperialism, and then modified by the post-colonial elites. The two models characterized by centralized control – a French one involving significant governmental involvement, and a German one predicated on private oligopoly – have tended to prevail, as the Anglo-American model of deconcentrated, private ownership asks both less and more than most MENA states have been able to give. It requires less governmental involvement, on the one hand, and on the other requires governments to provide more effective legal/regulatory environments, including transparency and accountability, something which both the imperialists and their successors have seen as being at least partially inconsistent with their own interests. The French model, predicated as it is on an administrative, rather than market rationale, has tended to hobble development in those countries where it persists, including Israel. The Anglo-American model, which is at the core of the Washington Consensus and which the World Bank and IMF are seeking to propagate globally, has yet to be firmly established anywhere in the region and may not be for a long time, if ever. But in the absence of something approaching an Anglo-American model, with its attendant transparency and accountability, the MENA will continue to forgo its fair share of foreign private investment, while the hemorrhage of flight capital from the region will probably persist.

Various other paradoxes that characterize MENA political economies further underscore the utility of the Hegelian dialectic in understanding historical processes. One is that the political movement of moralizers culturally most distant from the West, that of Islamism, is the one that is also among the most committed to implementing the Washington Consensus. The regimes with which the purveyors of that Consensus must or choose to work are, by comparison, very much less committed to it. So in the conservative Gulf states, for example, and especially in Saudi Arabia, the foundations for an Anglo-American-style banking system are more developed than in ostensibly more modern, quasi-secular countries, such as Egypt or Tunisia. This does reflect the more globalized nature of these hydrocarbon dependent financial sectors, but it also results from demand for more open markets expressed by the comparatively strong capitalists in those countries, many of which are involved in traditional or modern Islamic economic practices and institutions. In Turkey, where Islamists have been granted political space as a result of the partially democratic political system, they have articulated in thought and action Islamist financial institutions that both require and propagate key elements of the Consensus. Islamism in Iran, on the other hand, because it gained control of the state structure within which a post-revolutionary struggle for power is occurring, is too caught up in the exercise of that power for it to generate useful new syntheses of Islam and globalization.

The Turkish and Iranian cases thus raise the question as to whether it is the relation to state power that determines Islamist attitudes toward globalization and the Washington Consensus, rather than anything inherent in Islamist thought and practice. Since implementation of that Consensus tends to further dilute state control over the economy, hence also the polity, it could be that were Islamists to take power in countries other than Iran, their desire to assert political control would take precedence over their commitment to free markets. Thus any creative and viable synthesis of Islamic economics and secular globalization may have to occur while Islamists remain excluded from the state, but that synthesis could, presumably, persist once Islamists were in power.

Another paradox this investigation of the impact of globalization on MENA political economies has revealed is that the nominally "modern" Arab states are less capable of responding to its challenges than are the so-called "traditional" ones. The Arab countries that appeared to constitute the region's vanguard in the post-colonial era, including Algeria, Egypt, Iraq, Syria, and Tunisia, built states that overpowered and ultimately seriously degraded civil societies and capitalist capacities, as the states themselves became overgrown and increasingly committed to societal control. Thus in the praetorian Arab republics neither states nor societies are well equipped to handle the information, management, allocation, and other tasks required by successful globalization, although there are clear and important differences among them. The monarchies, which were predicted some thirty years ago to be on the verge of extinction (Huntington 1968), have persisted. The greater societal pluralism they permitted, including that for their native capitalists and the markets in which they operated, provided space in which skills and other resources could be developed, which are now being deployed in efforts to respond to globalization.

That the MENA constitutes a region of the global political economy and not just a linguistic/cultural area is suggested by yet another paradox, which is that while it is closest geographically to Europe, it has adapted less successfully to globalization than regions more distant. A possible explanation is that geography does not matter, especially as globalization itself results in part from the revolution in communication and transportation technologies. But this view undervalues the lingering importance of the colonial experience, including the displacement of perceptions of yesterday's imperialists on to today's globalizers. In no other region of the world have moralizers constituted such a strong oppositional force to globalization. This opposition, combined with the relative fragility of most MENA regimes, has impeded effective responses to globalization, thereby opening the door to various antitheses, some rejectionist, some accommodationist.

This study has also implied a paradox involving financial sectors that has broader relevance. It is that banking systems established in late and "late, late" industrializers for the purpose of aggregating and allocating scarce capital have, as a result of globalization, become less efficient at both tasks. Implementation of at least some components of the Anglo-American model increasingly appears to be a necessary if not sufficient condition to attract substantial foreign private investment, as those who channel it expect efficient capital markets, coupled with appropriate information and regulations. Similarly, the economically rational allocation of capital in the increasingly competitive, rapidly changing global economy also would appear to require the agility and even ruthlessness of competitive financial markets, rather than the more ponderous, long-range focused, German and French models. The MENA region, dominated by more "administrative" approaches to aggregating and allocating capital, has lagged behind other developing regions in creating both the regulatory/information contexts and the structures/processes of more market-driven methods to capital aggregation and allocation. The relative concentration of capital and the role of governments in its aggregation and allocation have proved not to be an advantage, but a liability for MENA countries, a liability that is likely to intensify as ever greater proportions of global investment flow through equity markets. Many MENA financial systems, which were some of the first modern ones to be developed outside Europe and North America, have been rendered almost obsolete by the actions of post-colonial states and by the impact of globalization.

Another paradox is that the degree of societal heterogeneity does not seem to matter to rates of development and adaptation to globalization *within* the MENA. The democracies, which by and large have performed better, have comparatively high levels of social heterogeneity, even fragmentation. Egypt and Tunisia, among the most socially homogeneous of the countries in the region, are comparatively poor globalizers. Syria and Lebanon have similar degrees of societal complexity, yet Lebanon has developed much more sophisticated capitalist capacities. The evidence suggests that it is political structures and processes, rather than underlying social systems, that account for variations in economic development. Comparatively heterogeneous societies in the MENA have been made to "work" economically by political systems that balance the needs of conflict resolution with those of capital accumulation and investment. But it remains the case that social heterogeneity in the MENA region complicates the task of governance, hence of economic development, thereby underscoring the advantage of social homogeneity enjoyed by many East Asian countries.

A final paradox that also summarizes much of the foregoing is that instead of preparing the MENA to respond effectively to globalization, imperialism militated against effective responses. It did so primarily because it resulted in the establishment of brittle regimes that are unable to respond flexibly and dynamically to rapidly changing economic threats and opportunities. East Asia, generally less penetrated by imperialism than the MENA, and responding more effectively to globalization, further underscores the fact that globalization can be a positive or negative force, depending upon the responses to it by states and civil societies.

In conclusion, this study has suggested that the response to globalization in the MENA has been defensive, as political elites have sought to temper in varying degrees its potential political impacts. No MENA country has eagerly embraced all or even most of the Ten Commandments of the Washington Consensus, as all have been willing to pay substantial economic costs to preserve the political status quo. But the forces of globalization cannot be entirely contained or channeled by ruling elites, for they impact on political economies as a whole, stimulating widely varying responses. In virtually all MENA countries there are eager globalizers, typically businesspersons who want to accelerate the pace of economic reform by adopting most or all of the tenets of the Washington Consensus. These "first-moment" elites have varying degrees of capacity and influence. In no country in the region, however, does it appear that they are on the verge of supplanting incumbent defensive globalizers and establishing sustainable, liberalized political economies that would terminate the dialectic with globalization. That dialectic, therefore, looks set to continue, stimulating second- and third-moment antithetical responses, one radical and the other synthetic. The likelihood of the former displacing incumbent elites appears to vary in direct proportion to the rigidity of political systems. The praetorian republics have either essentially destroyed their civil societies and the capitalist components thereof, or subdued them such that the only real capitalists extant are of the crony variety. Islamist radicals challenge them by riding a wave of nativist reaction against the perceived secular forces of globalization. In the more flexible political systems that are monarchies or qualified democracies, on the other hand, civil societies are generating synthetic responses that incorporate both the tenets of globalization and nativist, primarily Islamic principles. The contest for power between incumbent elites and these first-, second-, and third-moment counter elites will be the central feature of most if not all of the region's political economies in the twenty-first century. Its outcome will determine their economic futures, and hence that of the MENA region in general.

References

Abdel-Razek, Sherine, 2000, "Market Poised for Recovery," *Al-Ahram Weekly*, May 4–10, 6

Abu Amer, Muhamed Zaki, 1998, cited in *The Egyptian Gazette*, 5 December, 2

Aburish, Saïd K., 1995, *The Rise, Corruption and Coming Fall of the House of Saud*, London, Bloomsbury

Addi, Lahouari, 1991, "Les réformes économiques et leurs limites," *Les cahiers de l'Orient*, 23, 3, 115–122

    1999, "L'armée algérienne se divise," *Le monde diplomatique*, March

Akhavi-Pour, Hossein and Azodanloo, Heidar, 1998, "Economic Bases of Political Factions in Iran," *Critique: Journal for Critical Studies of the Middle East*, 13, Fall

Al-Ahnaf, M., Botiveau, Bernard, and Frégosi, Frank, 1991, *L'Algérie par ses islamistes*, Paris, Karthala

Al-Hindi, Adnan, 1998, cited by Agence France Press, April 21

Al-Kikhia, Mansour O., 1997, *Libya's Qaddafi: The Politics of Contradiction*, Gainesville, FL, University Press of Florida

Alonso-Gamo, Patricia, Fennell, Susan, and Sakr, Khaled, 1997, "Adjusting to New Realities: MENA, the Uruguay Round, and the EU–Mediterranean Initiative," IMF Working Paper WP/97/5, *http://www.imf.org/external/pubs/ft/wp/wp9705.pdf*

American–Egyptian Chamber of Commerce, 1998, *Potential and Uncertainty*, Cairo, Report of the Business Studies and Analysis Center, July

Amin, Galal A., 1995, *Egypt's Economic Predicament: A Study in the Interaction of External Pressure, Political Folly, and Social Tension in Egypt, 1960–1990*, New York, E.J. Brill

    2000, *Whatever Happened to the Egyptians? Changes in Egyptian Society from 1950 to the Present*, Cairo, American University in Cairo Press

Amnesty International, 2000a, *Saudi Arabia: A Secret State of Suffering*, London, Amnesty International, 28 March

    2000b, *Saudi Arabia: A Justice System Without Justice*, London, Amnesty International, 10 May

Amuzegar, Jahangir, 1993, *Iran's Economy Under the Islamic Republic*, London, I.B. Tauris

    1998, "Khatami's Iran, One Year Later," *Middle East Policy*, 6, 2 (October), 76–94

Andoni, Lamis, 2000, "King Abdullah: In His Father's Footsteps?" *Journal of Palestinian Studies*, 29, 3 (spring), 77–89

Ayubi, Nazih N., 1995, *Over-stating the Arab State: Politics and Society in the Middle East*, London, I.B. Tauris

Banque du Liban (BDL), 1999, *Quarterly Bulletin*, 80, March

Barnett, Michael N., ed., 1996, *Israel in Comparative Perspective: Challenging the Conventional Wisdom*, Albany, State University of New York Press

Batatu, Hanna, 1999, *Syria's Peasantry, the Descendants of its Lesser Rural Notables, and their Politics*, Princeton, Princeton University Press

Beach, William W., and O'Driscoll, Gerald P. Jr., 2000, "Methodology: Factors of the Index of Economic Freedom," in O'Driscoll, Gerald P., Jr., Holmes, Kim R., and Kirkpatrick, Melanie, *2000 Index of Economic Freedom*, Washington, DC, The Heritage Foundation, 71–89

Beau, Nicolas, and Tuquoi, Jean-Pierre, 1999, *Notre ami Ben Ali: l'envers du "miracle tunisien,"* Paris, Editions La Découverte

Belkhodja, Tahar, 1998, *Les trois décennies Bourguiba*, Paris, Publisud

Bellin, Eva, 2000, "Contingent Democrats: Industrialists, Labor and Democratization in Late-Developing Countries," *World Politics*, 52, January, 175–205

Bennoune, Mahfoud and El-Kenz, Ali, 1990, *Le hasard et l'histoire: entretiens avec Belaid Abdesselam*, 2 vols., Algiers, ENAG

Bentley, John, 1994, *Egyptian Legal and Judicial Sector Assessment*, 2 vols., Cairo, USAID

Berger, Sharon, 2000, "Gov't to Raise up to NIS 2.6b. from Sale of Bank Hapoalim Today," *Jerusalem Post*, June 6, 11

Berger, Suzanne, and Dore, Ronald, eds., 1996, *National Diversity and Global Capitalism*, Ithaca, Cornell University Press

Bill, James A., and Springborg, Robert, 2000, *Politics in the Middle East*, 5th edn., New York, Addison-Wesley

Bolbol, Ali A., 1999, "Arab Trade and Free Trade: A Preliminary Analysis," *International Journal of Middle East Studies*, 31, 1 (February), 3–17

Boogaerde, Pierre van den, 1991, *Financial Assistance from Arab Countries and Arab Regional Institutions*, Washington, DC, IMF, September

BP Amoco, 2000, *Statistical Review of World Energy 1999*, available online at *http://www.bp.com/worldenergy/* (22 September)

Brahimi, Abdelhamid, 1991, *L'économie algérienne: défis et enjeux*, 2nd edn., Algiers, Dahlab

Brand, Laurie A., 1998, *Women, the State and Political Liberalization: Middle Eastern and North African Experiences*, New York, Columbia University Press

Brown, L. Carl, 1984, *International Politics and the Middle East: Old Rules, Dangerous Game*, Princeton, Princeton University Press

Brown, Nathan, 1997, *The Rule of Law in the Arab World*, Cambridge, Cambridge University Press

Bugra, Ayse, 1998, "Class Culture and State: An Analysis of Interest Representation by Two Turkish Business Associations," *International Journal of Middle East Studies*, 30, 4 (November), 521–539

Caprio, Gerard and Claessens, Stijn, 1997, *The Importance of the Financial*

System for Development: Implications for Egypt, Cairo, Egyptian Center for Economic Studies (April)

Carapico, Sheila, 1998, *Civil Society in Yemen: The Political Economy of Activism in Modern Arabia*, Cambridge, Cambridge University Press

Cassarino, Jean-Pierre, 1999, "The EU–Tunisian Association Agreement and Tunisia's Structural Reform Program," *The Middle East Journal*, 53, 1 (Winter), 69–72

Central Bank of Egypt, 1998/99, *Economic Review*, 39, 34

Central Bank of the Republic of Turkey (CBRT), 2000, *Quarterly Bulletin*, 2000/ 1 (January–March), available online at *http://www.tcmb.gov.tr/yeni/ucaylik/ 3aymenuing.html* (September 2)

Champion, Daryl, 1998, "The Kingdom of Saudi Arabia: Elements of Instability Within Stability", Paper presented to the Australasian Middle East Studies Association, September 18–19. Online version published by *Middle East Review of International Affairs*, 3, 4 (December 1999), *http:// www.biu.ac.il/SOC/besa/meria/journal/1999/issue4/jv3n4a4.html#Author*

  1999, "Saudi Arabia on the Edge of Globalisation: 'asabiyya capitalism' and socioeconomic change at the end of the boom era," *Journal of Arabic, Islamic & Middle Eastern Studies*, 5, 2, 1–24

Charef, Abed, 1995, *Algérie: le grand dérapage*, Le Château, France, Editions de l'Aube

Chaudhry, Kiren Aziz, 1992, "Economic Liberalization in Oil-Exporting Countries," in Harik, Ilya, and Sullivan, Denis J., eds., *Privatization and Liberalization in the Middle East*, Bloomington, Indiana University Press, 145–166

  1997, *The Price of Wealth: Economies and Institutions in the Middle East*, Ithaca, Cornell University Press

Corm, Georges, 1993, "La réforme économique algérienne: une réforme mal aimée?" *Maghreb-Machrek*, 139 (January–March), 9–27

  1998, "Reconstructing Lebanon's Economy," in Shafik, Nemat, ed., *Economic Challenges Facing Middle Eastern and North African Countries*, New York, St. Martin's Press

Crystal, Jill, 1990, *Oil and Politics in the Gulf: Rulers and Merchants in Kuwait and Qatar*, Cambridge, Cambridge University Press

Daoud, Zakya, 1999, "L'alternance à l'épreuve des faits," *Le monde diplomatique*, April, 29

Denoeux, Guilain, and Springborg, Robert, 1998, "Hariri's Lebanon: Singapore of the Middle East or Sanaa of the Levant?" *Middle East Policy*, 6, 2 (October), 158–174

Dillman, Bradford, 1997, "Reassessing the Algerian Economy: Development and Reform Through the Eyes of Five Policy-Makers," *Journal of Modern African Studies*, 35, 1, 153–174

  1999, "Facing the Market in North Africa," article under review at *The Middle East Journal*

  2000, *State and Private Sector in Algeria: The Politics of Rent-Seeking and Failed Development*, Boulder, CO, Westview

Doron, Gideon, 1996, "Two Civil Societies and One State," in Norton, Augustus Richard, ed., *Civil Society in the Middle East*, II, Leiden, Brill, 193–220

Dunn, Ross, 1998, "High-Tech Success Beats Toil in the Soil," *Sydney Morning Herald*, 29 April, 11

Economic Research Forum, 2000, *Economic Trends in the MENA Region*, Economic Research Forum, Cairo

Economic and Social Commission for Western Asia (ESCWA): see United Nations

Eken, Sera, Helbling, Thomas, and Mazarei, Adnan, 1997, *Fiscal Policy and Growth in the Middle East and North African Region*, IMF Working Paper 97/101 (August)

El-Erian, Mohammed A., 1996, "Middle Eastern Economies' External Environment: What Lies Ahead?" *Middle East Policy*, 53 (March), 137–146

El-Ghonemy, M. Riad, 1998, *Affluence and Poverty in the Middle East*, London, Routledge,

El Kadi, Ihsan, 1998, "L'administration, éternel butin de guerre," *Pouvoirs: Revue française d'études constitutionelles et politiques*, 86, 57–66

El-Kenz, Ali, 1991, *Algerian Reflections on Arab Crises*, Center for Middle Eastern Studies, Austin TX, University of Texas at Austin

El-Mikawy, Noha, 2000, Summary of paper presented to Economic Research Forum conference on Economic and Institutional Change, Cairo, April 25–26

Entelis, John P., 1986, *Algeria: The Revolution Institutionalized*, Boulder, CO, Westview

Entelis, John P., and Arone, Lisa J., 1992, "Algeria in Turmoil: Islam, Democracy and the State," *Middle East Policy*, 40, 2nd quarter, 23–35

EPIC, 2000, "The Transformation of the Egyptian Labor Market: 1988–1998," *EPIC Newsletter*, Cairo (January), 1–4

Essam El-Din, Gamal, 1999, "Privatisation Strapped for Cash," *al Ahram Weekly*, September 2–8

European Commission, 2000, "Reinvigorating the Barcelona Process," Working document of the European Commission services for the "think tank" meeting of Euro-Mediterranean Foreign Ministers, Lisbon, May 25–26

Fandy, Mamoun, 1999, *Saudi Arabia and the Politics of Dissent*, New York, St. Martin's Press

Feld, Lowell and MacIntyre, Douglas, 1998, "OPEC Nations Grappling with Plunge in Oil Export Revenues," *Oil and Gas Journal*, September 21, 29–35

Galloux, Michel, 1999, "The State's Responses to Private Islamic Finance Experiments in Egypt," *Thunderbird International Business Review*, 41, 4–5 (July–October), 481–500

Garçon, José and Affuzi, Pierre, 1998, "L'armée algérienne: le pouvoir de l'ombre," *Pouvoirs: Revue française d'études constitutionelles et politiques*, 86, 45–56

Gause, F. Gregory III, 1993, *Oil Monarchies: Domestic and Seccurity Challenges in the Arab Gulf States*, New York, Council on Foreign Relations
    2000, "Saudi Arabia Over a Barrel," *Foreign Affairs*, May–June, 80–94

Gereffi, Gary, and Korzeniewicz, Miguel, 1994, *Commodity Chains and Global Capitalism*, Westport, CT, Praeger

Gerstenfeld, Dan, 2000, "Arison Seeks to Sell Holdings in Housing & Construction," *Jerusalem Post*, May 31

Ghabra, Shafeeq N., 1997, "The Islamic Movement in Kuwait," *Middle East Policy*, 5, 2 (May), 58–72

Ghilès, Francis, 1998, "L'armée a-t-elle une politique économique?" *Pouvoirs: Revue française d'études constitutionelles et politiques*, 86, 85–106

Glain, Stephen J., 2000, "Stronghold Can Backfire: Iraqi Tribes Are Key Source of Loyalty, Rebellion," *Wall Street Journal*, May 23

Goddard, C. Roe, Passe-Smith, John T., and Conklin, John G., 1996, *International Political Economy: State–Market Relations in the Changing Global Order*, Boulder, CO, Lynne Rienner

Gray, John, 1998, *False Dawn: The Delusions of Global Capitalism*, New York, The New Press

Hadj-Nacer, Abderrahmane Roustoumi, ed., 1989, *Les cahiers de la réforme*, Algiers, ENAG

Haggard, Stephan, and Kaufman, Robert R., eds., 1992, *The Politics of Economic Adjustment*, Princeton, Princeton University Press

eds., 1995, *The Political Economy of Democratic Transitions*, Princeton, Princeton University Press

Haggard, Stephan, and Lee, Chung H., 1993, "The Political Dimension of Finance in Economic Development," in Haggard, Stephan, Lee, Chung H., and Maxfield, Sylvia, eds., *The Politics of Finance in Developing Countries*, Ithaca, Cornell University Press, 3–20

Haggard, Stephan, Lee, Chung H., and Maxfield, Sylvia, eds., 1993, *The Politics of Finance in Developing Countries*, Ithaca, Cornell University Press

Hamidi, Muhammad al-Hashimi, 1998, *The Politicization of Islam: A Case Study of Tunisia*, Boulder, CO, Westview Press

Hammoudi, Abdellah, 1997, *Master and Disciple: The Cultural Foundations of Moroccan Authoritarianism*, Chicago, University of Chicago Press

Handy, Howard, 1998, *Egypt: Beyond Stabilization, Toward a Dynamic Market Economy*, IMF occasional paper no. 163, Washington, DC, International Monetary Fund (May)

Harik, Iliya, and Sullivan, Denis, eds., 1992, *Privatization and Liberalization in the Middle East*, Bloomington, Indiana University Press

Havrylyshyn, Oleh, and Kunzel, Peter, 1997, "Intra-Industry Trade of Arab Countries: An Indicator of Potential Competitiveness," IMF Working Paper WP/97/47

Henry, Clement M., 1996, *The Mediterranean Debt Crescent: Money and Power in Algeria, Egypt, Morocco, Tunisia, and Turkey*, Gainesville, FL, University Press of Florida

Heston, Alan, and Summers, Robert, 1999, *Data on Real GDP Per Capita (PPP)*, Philadelphia, University of Pennsylvania, Department of Economics (March)

Hidouci, Ghazi, 1995, *Algérie: la libération inachevée*, Paris, Editions de la Découverte

Hilal, Rida, 1987, *The Construction of Dependency* (in Arabic), Cairo, Dar Al-Mustaqbal Al-Arabi

Hilferding, Rudolph [1910] 1981, *Finance Capital: A Study of the Latest Phase of Capitalist Development*, London, Routledge

Hirst, David, 1997, "Behind the Veil of Sudan's Theocracy," *The Guardian*, May 27

Hoogvelt, Ankie, 1997, *Globalization and the Postcolonial World: The New Political Economy of Development*, Baltimore, The Johns Hopkins University Press

Hudson, Michael, 1977, *Arab Politics*, New Haven, CT, Yale University Press

Huntington, Samuel, P., 1968, *Political Order in Changing Societies*, New Haven, CT, Yale University Press

IMF (International Monetary Fund), 1998, *Algeria: Special Issues and Statistical Appendix*, Staff Country Report No. 98/87 (September)

    2000, *Tunisia: Recent Economic Developments*, Staff Country Report No. 00/37 (March)

International Institute for Strategic Studies (IISS), 1998, *The Military Balance 1998/1999*, London

    2000, *The Military Balance 2000/2001*, online at *http://www.iiss.org/pub/mbglobal.asp* (December 4, 2000)

Iqbal, Zamir, and Mirakhor, Abbas, 1999, "Progress and Challenges of Islamic Banking," *Thunderbird International Business Review*, 41, 4–5 (July)

Istanbul Stock Exchange (ISE), 1999, *Annual Factbook 1999*, online at *http://www.ise.org/data.htm* (September 2)

    2000, *Quarterly Bulletin*, January–June 2000, online at *http://www.ise.org/data.htm* (September 2)

Jabar, Faleh A., 2000, "Shaykhs and Ideologues: Detribalization and Retribalization in Iraq, 1968–1998, *Middle East Report*, 215, summer, 28–31, 48

Karl, Terry Lynn, 1997, *The Paradox of Plenty: Oil Booms and Petro-States*, Berkeley, University of California Press

Kheir-El-Din, Hanaa, and El-Sayed, Hoda, 1997, *Potential Impact of a Free Trade Agreement with the EU on Egypt's Textile Industry*, Cairo, Eyptian Center For Economic Studies (September)

Kingdom Holding, 2000, *Twentieth Anniversary*, special publication of *Middle East Economic Digest*, April

Kostiner, Joseph, ed., 2000, *Middle East Monarchies: The Challenge of Modernity*, Boulder, CO, Lynne Rienner

Krimly, Rayed, 1999, "The Political Economy of Adjusted Priorities: Declining Oil Revenues and Saudi Fiscal Policies," *The Middle East Journal*, 53, 2 (Spring), 254–267

Lawson, Fred, 1992, "Divergent Modes of Economic Liberalization in Syria and Iraq," in Harik, Ilya, and Sullivan, Denis J. eds., *Privatization and Liberalization in the Middle East*, Bloomington, Indiana University Press, 123–144

Lesch, Ann Mosely, 1996, "The Destruction of Civil Society in the Sudan," in Norton, A. Richard, ed., *Civil Society in the Middle East*, Leiden, E.J. Brill

Leveau, Rémy, 1985, *Le fellah marocain défenseur du trône*, 2nd edn., Paris, Fondation Nationale des Sciences Politiques

    1998, "Acteurs et Champs de Force," *Pouvoirs: Revue française d'études constitutionelles et politiques*, 86, 29–43

    1999, "Réussir la transition démocratique au Maroc," *Le monde diplomatique*, April, 14–15

Linz, Juan J., and Steppan, Alfred, 1996, *Problems of Democratic Transition and Consolidation: Southern Europe, South America, and Post-Communist Europe*, Baltimore, The Johns Hopkins University Press

Loriaux, Michael, ed., 1997, *Capital Ungoverned: Liberalizing Finance in Interventionist States*, Ithaca, Cornell University Press

Lustick, Ian S., 1999, "Hegemony and the Riddle of Nationalism," in Binder, Leonard, ed., *Ethnic Conflict and International Politics in the Middle East*, Gainesville, FL, University Press of Florida

Mack, Arien, ed., 2000, *Iran Since the Revolution, Social Research: An International Quarterly*, 67, 2 (Summer), 285–640

Mahdavy, Hussein, 1970, "The Patterns and Problems of Economic Development in Rentier States: The Case of Iran," in Cook, M., ed., *Studies in Economic History of the Middle East*, London, Oxford University Press

Mahroug, Moncef, 1996, "Champions, menaces et condammés," *Jeune Afrique* 1853, July

Maxfield, Sylvia, 1997, *Gatekeepers of Growth: The International Political Economy of Central Banking in Developing Countries*, Princeton, Princeton University Press

Maxfield, Sylvia, and Schneider, Ben Ross, eds., 1997, *Business and the State in Developing Countries*, Ithaca, Cornell University Press

Ministry of International Trade and Supply, 1998, *The International Competitiveness of Egypt in Perspective, First Report, 1998*, Cairo, Research Information Sector

Mittelman, James H., 1996, *Globalization: Critical Reflections*, Boulder CO, Lynne Rienner

Mohieldin, Mahmoud, 1995, *Causes, Measures and Impact of State Intervention in the Financial Sector; The Egyptian Example*, Cairo, Working Papers of the Economic Research Forum for the Arab Countries, Iran and Turkey, no. 9507

Monroe, Elizabeth 1981, *Britain's Moment in the Middle East, 1914–1971*, rev. edn, Baltimore, The Johns Hopkins University Press

Montety, Henri de [1940] 1973, "Old Families and New Elites in Tunisia," in Zartman, I. William, ed., *Man, State, and Society in the Contemporary Maghrib*, New York, Praeger, 171–180

Mostafa, Hadia, 1997a, "Pennies from Heaven," *Business Today*, June, 52–58 1997b, "One in a Hundred," *Reuters*, 15 September

Murphy, Emma C., 1999, *Economic and Political Change in Tunisia: From Bourguiba to Ben Ali*, New York, St. Martin's Press

Myntti, Cynthia, 1999, *Paris along the Nile: Architecture in Cairo from the Belle Epoque*, Cairo, American University in Cairo Press

Naim, Moises, 2000, "Washington Consensus or Washington Confusion?" *Foreign Policy*, Spring, pp. 87–103

Nashashibi, Karim, Alonso-Gamo, Patricia, Bazzoni, Stefania, Féler, Alain, Laframboise, Nicole and Horvitz, Sebastian Paris, 1998, *Algeria: Stabilization and Transition to the Market*, IMF occasional paper 165, Washington, DC

Nathan Associates, 1997, *Egypt: A Comparative Study of Foreign Direct Investment Climates*, Cairo, Submitted to USAID, August 20

O'Driscoll, Gerald P., Jr., Holmes, Kim R., and Kirkpatrick, Melanie, 2000, *2000 Index of Economic Freedom*, Washington, DC, The Heritage Foundation

Okruhlik, Gwenn, 1999, "Rentier Wealth, Unruly Law, and the Rise of Opposition: The Political Economy of Oil States," *Comparative Politics*, Spring, 295–315

Öniş, Ziya, 1998, *State and Market: The Political Economy of Turkey in Comparative Perspective*, Bebek/Istanbul, Bogazici University Press

Owen, Roger, 1992, *State, Power and Politics in the Making of the Modern Middle East*, London, Routledge

Owen, Roger and Pamuk, Sevket, 1998, *A History of Middle East Economics in the Twentieth Century*, London, I.B. Tauris

Ozbudun, Ergun, 2000, *Contemporary Turkish Politics: Challenges to Democratic Consolidation*, Boulder, CO, Lynne Rienner

Page, John, 1999, "The Impact of Lower Oil Prices on the Economies of Gulf States," *Middle East Policy*, 6, 4 (June), 59–67

Patton, Marcie J., 1999, "Open for Business: Capitalists and Globalization in Turkey and Morocco," CEMOTI (Cahiers d'études sur la Mediterranée Orientale et le monde Turco-Iranien), 27, January–June, 195–212

Perthes, Volker, 1997, *The Political Economy of Syria under Asad*, London, I.B. Tauris

Picard, Elizabeth, 1996, *Lebanon, a Shattered Country: Myths and Realities of the Wars in Lebanon*, New York, Holmes & Meier

Piro, Timothy J., 1998, *The Political Economy of Market Reform in Jordan*, London, Rowman & Littlefield

Plessner, Yakir, 1994, *The Political Economy of Israel: From Ideology to Stagnation*, Albany, State University of New York Press

Pope, Nicole and Pope, Hugh, 1997, *Turkey Unveiled: Atatürk and After*, London, John Murray

Posusney, Marsha Pripstein, 1997, *Labor and the State in Egypt: Workers, Unions and Economic Restructuring*, New York, Columbia University Press

Przeworksi, Adam, 1991, *Democracy and the Market: Political and Economic Reforms in Eastern Europe and Latin America*, Cambridge, Cambridge University Press

Quandt, William B., 1998, *Between Ballots and Bullets: Algeria's Transition from Authoritarianism*, Washington, DC, Brookings Institution

Radwan, Samir, 1997, *Towards Full Employment: Egypt into the 21st Century*, Cairo, Egyptian Center for Economic Studies (December)

Rahnema, Saeed, and Behdad, Sohrab, eds., 1995, *Iran after the Revolution: Crisis of an Islamic State*, New York, St. Martin's Press

Richards, Alan, 1999, "The Global Financial Crisis and the Middle East," *Middle East Policy*, 6, 3 (February), 62–71

Richards, Alan, and Waterbury, John, 1996, *A Political Economy of the Middle East*, 2nd edn., Boulder, CO, Westview

Rivlin, Paul, 2000, "Trade Potential in the Middle East: Some Optimistic Findings," *Middle East Review of International Affairs*, 4, 1 (March); *http:// www.biu.ac.il/SOC/besa/meria/journal/2000/issue1/jv4n1a6.html* (July 26)

Roberts, Hugh, 1994, "Doctrinaire Economics and Political Opportunism in

238   References

the Strategy of Algerian Islamism," in Ruedy, John, ed., *Islam and Secularism in North Africa*, New York, St. Martin's Press, 123–147

Rocard, Michel, ed., 1999, *Strengthening Palestinian Institutions*, Washington, DC, Brookings Institution

Rodrik, Dani, 1997, *Has Globalization Gone Too Far?*, Washington, DC, Institute for International Economics

Rogowski, Ronald, 1989, *Commerce and Coalitions: How Trade Affects Domestic Political Alignments*, Princeton, Princeton University Press

Ross, Michael L., 1999, "The Political Economy of the Resource Curse," *World Politics*, 51, 2 (January), 297–322

Roy, Sara, 1999, "De-development Revisited: Palestinian Economy and Society Since Olso," *Journal of Palestine Studies*, 28, 3 (Spring), 64–82

Ryan, Curtis R., 1998, "Peace, Bread and Riots: Jordan and the IMF," *Middle East Policy*, 60 (October), 54–66

Sachs, Jeffrey, 1998, "International Economics: Unlocking the Mysteries of Globalization," *Foreign Policy*, Spring, 97–111

Sachs, Jeffrey, and Warner, Andrew, 1995, "Economic Reform and the Process of Global Integration," in Brainard, William C., and Perry, George L., *Brookings Papers on Economic Activity*, I, Washington, DC, Brookings Institution, 1–117

Sadowski, Yahia M., 1991, *Political Vegetables? Buisnessman and Bureaucrat in the Development of Egyptian Agriculture*, Washington, DC, Brookings Institution

Salamé, Ghassan, 1990, "'Strong' and 'Weak' States: A Qualified Return to the Muqaddimah," in Luciani, Giacomo, ed. *The Arab State*, Berkeley, University of California Press, 29–64

Salehi-Isfahani, Djavid, 1999, "Labor and the Challenge of Economic Restructuring in Iran," *Middle East Report* Spring, 34–37

Salem, Eli, 1973, *Modernization without Revolution*, Bloomington, University of Indiana Press

Saudi American Bank, 1999, *Lebanon: A Resilient Economy, an Investment Opportunity*, November

Saudi Arabian Monetary Agency (SAMA), 1998, *Thirty-Fouirth Annual Report 1419H (1998G)*, Riyadh, Research and Statistics Department

   1999, *Thirty-Fifth Annual Report 1420H (1999G)*, Riyadh, Research and Statistics Department

Saul, Samir, 1997, *La France et l'Egypte de 1882 à 1914– intérêts économiques et implications politiques*, Paris, Ministère de l'Economie, des Finances, et de l'Industrie

Seznek, Jean-François, 2000, "Redefining Economics and the Markets," unpublished manuscript, May

Shafik, Nemat, ed., 1997, *Economic Challenges Facing Middle Eastern and North African Countries: Alternative Futures*, New York, St. Martin's Press

   ed., 1998, *Prospects for Middle Eastern and North African Economies: From Boom to Bust and Back?*, New York, St. Martin's Press

Shalev, Michal, 1998, "The Israeli Political Economy," *Middle East Report*, Summer, 31–33

Snider, Lewis W., 1996, *Growth, Debt, and Politics: Economic Adjustment and the Political Performance of Developing Countries*, Boulder, CO, Westview

Sorsa, Piritta, 1999, "Algeria – The Real Exchange Rate, Export Diversification, and Trade Protection," IMF Working Paper WP/99/49, April

Souaïdia, Habib, 2001, *La sale guerre*, Paris, La Découverte.

Stallings, Barbara, ed., 1995, *Global Change, Regional Response: The New International Context of Development*, Cambridge, Cambridge University Press

Stockholm International Peace Research Institute (SIPRI), 1999, *Yearbook 1999*, Stockholm SIPRI

Stone, Martin, 1998, *The Agony of Algeria*, New York, Columbia University Press

Subramanian, Arvind, 1997, *The Egyptian Stabilization Experience*, Cairo, Egyptian Center for Economic Studies (October)

Terterov, Marat, 2000, draft of thesis submitted to St. Antony's College, Oxford, in partial fulfillment of requirements for PhD (February)

Tozy, Mohamed, 1999, "Réformes politiques et transition démocratique," *Maghreb-Machrek*, 164, April–June, 67–84

Union of Arab Banks, 1998, *Arab Banks*, No. 215 (November)

United Nations Children's Fund (UNICEF), 1999, *The State of the World's Children 1999*, New York, Oxford University Press

United Nations, Educational, Scientific and Cultural Organization (UNESCO), 1997, *Correspondence on Cross Enrolment Ratios*, Paris, UNESCO (November)

United Nations Economic and Social Commission for Western Asia (UN-ESCWA), 1999, *Preliminary Overview of Economic Developments in the ESCWA Region in 1999*, New York, United Nations

US Agency for International Development (USAID), 1993a, *Assessment of the Legislative Sector*, Cairo

   1993b, *Assessment of the Potential for Liberalization and Privatization of the Egyptian Cotton Subsector*, Cairo, USAID (July)

   1997, *Egypt: A Comparative Study of Foreign Direct Investment Climates*, Cairo, Office of Economic Analysis and Policy (August 20)

US Department of State, 2000, Daily Press Briefing No. 61, Monday, June 19, 12:15 p.m.

Vandewalle, Dirk, ed., 1996, *North Africa: Development and Reform in a Changing Global Economy*, New York, St. Martin's Press

   1998, *Libya since Independence: Oil and State-Building*, Ithaca, Cornell University Press

Vitalis, Robert, 1999, Review of Chaudhry 1997, *International Journal of Middle East Studies*, 31, 659–661

Vogel, Frank, and Hayes, Samuel L. III, 1998, *Islamic Law and Finance: Religion, Risk and Return*, Boston, Kluwer Law International

Waldner, David, 1999, *State Building and Late Development*, Ithaca, Cornell University Press

Warde, Ibrahim, 1997, "Rating Agencies the New Superpowers?" at *http:// www.idrel.com.lb/shufimafi/archives/docs/iwarde1.htm* (September 1, 2000)

Waterbury, John, 1970, *Commander of the Faithful: The Moroccan Political Elite – A Study in Segmented Politics*, New York, Columbia University Press

   1993, *Exposed to Innumerable Delusions: Public Enterprise and State Power in Egypt, India, Mexico, and Turkey*, Cambridge, Cambridge University Press

1997, "From Social Contracts to Extraction Contracts: The Political Economy of Authoritarianism and Democracy," in Entelis, John P., ed., *Islam, Democracy, and the State in North Africa*, Bloomington, Indiana University Press, 141–176

Weiss, Dieter and Wurzel, Ulrich, 1998, *The Economics and Politics of Transition to an Open Market Economy: Egypt*, Paris, Development Centre of the Organisation for Economic Co-operation and Development

Westley, John, 1998, "Change in the Egyptian Economy, 1977–1997," unpublished ms, Cairo, January

Wiktorowicz, Quintan, 1999, "The Limits of Democracy in the Middle East: The Case of Jordan," *The Middle East Journal*, 53, 4 (Autumn), 606–620

Williamson, John, ed., 1994, *The Political Economy of Reform*, Washington, DC, Institute for International Economics

Willis, Michael, 1996, *The Islamist Challenge in Algeria: A Political History*, Reading, Ithaca Press

Winters, Jeffrey A., 1994, "Power and the Control of Capital," *World Politics*, 46, 3 (April), 419–452

World Bank, 1991, *Arab Republic of Egypt Cotton and Textile Sector Study*, Washington, DC, World Bank

  1995, *Claiming the Future: Choosing Prosperity in the MENA*, Washington, DC, World Bank

  1997, *World Development Report 1997: The State in a Changing World*, Washington, DC, Oxford University Press

  various years, *World Development Indicators*, CD-ROM database, Washington DC

Yeşilada, Birol, 1998, "The Mediterranean Challenge," in Redmond, John, and Rosenthal, Glenda G., eds., *The Expanding European Union Past, Present, and Future*, Boulder CO, Lynne Rienner, 177–193

Yousef, Tarik M., 1998, *Demography, Capital Dependency and Growth in MENA*, Cairo, Economic Research forum (January)

Zangeneh, Hamid, 1998, "The Post-Revolutionary Iranian Economy: A Policy Appraisal," *Middle East Policy*, 6, 2 (October)

Zartman, W., ed., 1991, *Tunisia: The Political Economy of Reform*, Boulder, CO, Lynne Rienner

Zghal, Abdelkader, 1991, "The New Strategy of the Movement of the Islamic Way: Manipulation or Expression of Political Culture?" in Zartman, I.W., ed., *Tunisia: The Political Economy of Reform*, Boulder, CO, Lynne Rienner, 205–217

Zoubir, Yahia, ed., 1999, *North Africa in Transition: State, Society, and Economic Transformation in the 1990s*, Gainesville, FL, University Press of Florida

Zysman, John, 1983, *Governments, Markets, and Growth: Financial Systems and the Politics of Industrial Change*, Ithaca, Cornell University Press

Index

Abd al Aziz, Mahmud 157
Abdel-Razak, Sherine 159
Abdesselam, Belaid 105–109, 111, 117
Abdullah II of Jordan 168, 175, 189,
    191–193
Abdullah bin Abdulaziz, Crown Prince
    of Saudi Arabia 178–179, 180, 182,
    191
Abu Amer, Muhammed Zaki 150
Aburish, Saïd 186, 193
accountability 74–75, 78–83, 225
    and banking system 28, 94, 98, 185
    in bully states 150, 164
    in bunker states 126, 130
    and colonialism 8, 10
    in monarchies 185, 193
    and taxation 76, 78
Addi, Lahouari 112, 114, 120, 131
Aden, and British colonialism 9, 17, 124
adjustment, structural 19, 26, 28–29, 48,
    51–52, 61, 62, 67–69
advantage, competitive 12, 42
agriculture, in bunker states 108–109, 116,
    128–129
aid, foreign 11, 49–51, 187–188
    and colonialism 13–14
    and economic reform 35–36, 166
    military 31
    reduction in 12, 31, 32, 33–34
Al Ahram Weekly 148, 157, 158
Al Arabi, Raga 158
Al Ayouti, Alia 158
Al-Asad, Bashar 99, 129, 131
Al-Asad, Hafez 18, 24, 99, 122, 125, 127,
    130–131, 191
Al-Hindi, Adnan 97
Al-Kamel, Sheikh Saleh 183
Al-Kikhia, Mansour O. 124, 133
Alawi sect (Syria) 99, 125–126, 129–130
Algeria
    and banking system 79, 86, 88–89, 88,
        109, 113–114, 177

and budget deficits 118–119, 132
as bunker state 20, 63, 99–100,
    102–121, 123–125, 133, 226
and business class 24, 124, 126
and capital flows 50, 58, 95–96, 117,
    121
and capitalism 23, 24, 95–96, 112
civil and political rights 65, 123
and debt 53, 53, 58, 114, 117–118,
    120–121, 208, 214
"deciders" 99, 105, 111–112, 113,
    116–117, 121, 126, 177
and economic freedom 197
and economic integration 132–133
and elites 105, 109, 124, 131
and European Union 35, 41
and French colonialism 9, 16, 17, 21, 24,
    99, 102, 171
and Human Development Index 3
and Human Poverty Index 7, 176
and inflation 69, 114, 118
and information flows 82, 83, 112–113
and interest rates 71
and the Internet 81
and Islamist opposition 20, 102, 113,
    115–117, 120–121
and labor migration 36, 95–96, 114, 118
militarization 19, 103, 104, 105–113,
    115–117, 118–121
and oil and gas revenues 39, 40, 53, 69,
    76, 105–111, 117, 120
and political capacity 76, 77, 80, 81, 82,
    83, 84, 226
and political reform 112–117
postwar economy 1
as praetorian republic 20, 63
and private sector 108–19, 118, 121, 209
and privatization 72
and public sector 72, 73, 118–119
and stock exchange 58, 86
and structural adjustment 19, 29, 67–69,
    70, 71, 102, 114, 116–119, 132

Algeria (*cont.*)
  and trade 41, 43, *43*, 67, *68*, 119, 121
  and unemployment 59
  and United States 121
Algérie confidentielle 119, 120, 130
Ali, Mohammed 138
American–Egyptian Chamber of
    Commerce 143
Amin, Galal A. 167
Amnesty International 181
Amuzegar, Jahangir 213–215, 222
Andoni, Lamis 191, 192
Arab Bank 189
Arab–Israeli economic summits 26
Arab–Israeli preace process
  economic effects of 12–13, 129, 132,
    136, 207, 224
  political effects 6, 153, 166, 191–192,
    198, 201
  trade effects 43
  and Turkey 207
  and United States 31, 33–35
Arafat, Yasser 134–135, 191
Aramco 9, 169
arms
  expenditure on 10–11, 13, *104*, 224
  transfers 31–33, *34*, 59
  unconventional 33
Army of National Liberation (Algeria) 103
asabiya (clan solidarity) 131
Asia, and arms transfers 31–33, *34*
assimilation, and dialectic of globalization
    15–16
assistance, official development (ODA) 12,
    44, *45*, 46, 52, 54, 59, 136, 203, 207
Atatürk (Mustafa Kemal) 23–24, 212
autonomy
  in banking systems 22–23, 87, 88–89,
    90–91, 94, 95, 96, 114, 145,
    156–157, 177, 196, 204
  in bully states 150, 155, 156–157, 160,
    206
  in bunker states 99–100, 109–111, 114,
    130, 134
  in democracies 195, 204
Ayubi, Nazih N. 11, 98, 122

Baath party
  Iraq 24, 103, 122, 131, 133
  Syria 24, 103, 122, 125, 133
Bagehot, Walter 22
Bahgat, Ahmad 154
Bahrain
  and banking system *86*, *88*, 91, 183–184,
    188, 189
  and civil and political rights *65*

and economic freedom *197*
and Human Development Index 2, *3*
and Human Poverty Index *7*
and information flows *82*
and the Internet 81
military expenditure *104*
as monarchy 20, 64, 168–169
and oil industries 8, *40*, 169
and political capacity 76, *77*, *80*, 81, *82*,
    84, 195
and stock market *86*, 91
and structural adjustment *70*
and trade 43, *43*, *68*
Bakr, Hassan 18
balance of payments
  Algeria 117–118
  Egypt 145, 155
  Morocco 172
balance of trade
  Egypt 155, 161
  Israel 204
  Lebanon 219
  and oil prices 39, 52
banks and banking *86*, *88*, 97, 100, *101*,
    227
  and capitalist legacies 21–23, 27, 62, 85,
    94–95
  central banks 49, 145, 156–157, 177,
    204, 219–220
  and debt 52, 54–58
  and interest rates 71
  Islamic 25, 92–93, 96, 116, 159–160,
    177, 182–185, 188–189, 190, 196,
    211, 216–217, 226
  mixed ownership 90–91
  and nationalization 213
  and political capacity 78–79
  and private capital flows 44, 48, 52
  private sector 172–174, 177, 186,
    218–219
    concentrated 22, 91–92, 157, 168,
      186, 188–189, 204
    deconcentrated 92–94, 196, 208
  public sector 87, 88–89, 97–98, 113,
    127, 140–142, 154, 156–158, 177
  privatization 89, 97, 140, 141, 165,
    173
  reforms 52
  types of 87–94
Barcelona Declaration (EC) 35, 41, 137,
    165
Barnett, Michael N. 222
Bashir, Omar 99, 122, 132
Basri, Driss 174, 175
Batatu, Hanna 133
Bayar, Celal 22, 23–24

Bechtine, Mohammed 112, 123
Belkhodja, Tahar 105
Bellin, Eva 21
Ben Ali, Zine al-Abidine 81, 167, 177
Ben Barka, Mehdi 178
Ben Bella, Ahmed 103, 108
Ben Salah, Ahmad 137, 166
Bencherif, Ahmed 106
Benhamouda, Abdelhak 130
Benjedid, Chadli 103, 105, 109–112,
    115–117, 122, 133, 177
Benjelloun, Othman 173
Bentley, John 147–148
Berger, Sharon 89
Bernis, Gérard Destanne de 105
Bin Laden, Osama 192
black market 71, 111, 114, 122, 145
Bolbol, Ali A. 19
bonyads (Iran) 213–214, 215, 216
Boogaerde, Pierre van den 46, 54
Boudiaf, Mohammed 112, 117, 130
Boumédienne, Houari 103, 105, 106–109,
    116, 117, 122, 124, 133
Bourguiba, Habib 16–17, 18, 109
Bouteflika, Abdelaziz 112, 121, 133
BP-Amoco 39
Brahimi, Abdelhamid 105, 109–111, 113
Brand, Laurie A. 167
Britain
    and colonialism 9–10, 17–18, 74, 138,
        168–169
    see also capitalism, types
Brown, Leon Carl 8, 29, 30
Brown, Nathan 148, 167
budget deficits 51, 179, 206, 208, 214
    reduction 69, 70, 118–119, 132, 145,
        176
Bugra, Ayse 210, 211
bully states 20, 66, 79–81, 134–167
    and capitalism 134, 156–160
    and civil society 63, 95, 136, 139, 146,
        161, 163–164, 198, 226, 228
    and information flows 81, 82, 142–143,
        165, 174
    and oppositions 160
    and private sector 135–136, 139,
        141–145, 148, 151, 158, 165
    prospects for 161–166
    and public sector 62, 72–74, 73, 135,
        138, 140–141, 143–145, 149–152,
        155, 157–158, 164–165
bunker states 20, 51, 65–66, 71, 79–81,
    99–133
    and banking 79, 88–89, 90, 100–102,
        101, 109
    and capitalism 100, 131

and civil society 27, 66, 100, 102, 103,
    117, 120–121, 122–125, 130–131,
    133, 161, 198, 226, 228
and control of information 81, 100, 107,
    112–113
and elites 81, 99, 100, 123–125, 130
and informal economy 83, 100
and oil revenues 102
and oppositions 121
and private sector 114, 118–119, 121,
    123–125, 131–132
and public sector 62, 113–115, 118–119,
    124
and structural adjustment 102, 112–117,
    132
    see also Algeria; Iraq; Libya; Sudan;
        Syria; Yemen
bureaucracy 11
    in bully states 149–150, 155
    in monarchies 170, 181, 186, 190
business class, indigenous 9–10, 21, 22–25,
    28, 63, 100, 124

capacity, political 6, 62–83
    and banking systems 78–79, 94–95, 208
    and bully states 63, 66, 226
    in bunker states 63, 66, 100, 226
    compared 84
    in democracies 64, 66, 195, 203, 208,
        218, 220
    extractive 11, 74, 75–78, 83, 84, 100,
        203, 208, 218
    and institutional credibility 79, 80, 83,
        84, 203, 208, 218
    in monarchies 63–64, 66
    and types of capitalism 63
    see also accountability; capital,
        structural power of; information;
        transparency
capita
    flight of 95, 97, 131, 155, 156, 214, 225
    flows 44–52, 45, 47, 50, 133, 204
    global 26, 56, 96–98
    private 12, 44–48, 89, 160, 169, 182
    structural power of 62–63, 83–85
        in bully states 156–160, 161
        in bunker states 123–124, 126–127,
            161
        and types of capitalism 22–23, 27, 87,
            89–95
capitalism
    crony 97, 134, 228
    in Egypt 90, 135, 138–140, 147, 149,
        152–155, 161–164, 210
    in Tunisia 90, 154, 164
    in Turkey 210–211

capitalism (*cont.*)
  and economic reform 26–27
  Islamic 25, 27–28, 177–178, 183–185,
    192–193, 211–212l
  legacies of 83–98
  local 17–21, 26–27, 61, 62, 85, 94–95
  mercantile 217–218
  "national" 138
  state 25, 27, 48, 61, 95, 100
capitalism, types 21, 225
  Anglo-American 24–25, 28, 61, 93–96,
    98, 185
    and competitiveness 87–88, 91,
      92–93
    and laissez-faire economics 21
    and stock markets 21–22, 85, 91, 93,
      158, 174
    and Washington Consensus 27, 227
  French 22–26, 28, 62, 158, 196, 206
    and private sector 21
    and state capitalism 25, 27, 48, 85,
      87–88, 90, 95
    and technocratic control 22–23
  German 22–25, 48, 62, 93, 196
    in monarchies 23, 24–25, 91–92,
      94–95, 97, 172–174
    and private sector 23–24, 27
    and state capitalism 48
    and universal banks 21, 22, 23, 27–28,
      85, 87, 89, 91
Carapico, Sheila 133
Cassarino, Jean-Pierre 156
censorship 123, 127, 146, 165
  see also information; press
Central Bank of Egypt 145
Central Bank of the Republic of Turkey
    (CBRT) 85
Chabbi, Miloud 173
Champion, Daryl 181, 185–186
Charef, Abed 115
Chaudhry, Kiren Aziz 71, 75–76, 124,
    131–132, 133, 179–180, 193
China, and Iraq 30–31
Churchill, Winston S. 9, 168
CIM (contract-intensive money) ratios *80*,
    83, 89
  in bully states 79, 157
  in bunker states 79, 100–102, *101*, 109,
    110, 124, 126–127, 131
  in democracies 79, 195–196, 208
  in monarchies 79
civil society
  in bully states 63, 95, 136, 139, 146,
    161, 163–164, 198, 224, 226, 228
  in bunker states 27, 66, 95, 100, 102,
    103, 117, 120–121, 122–125,

130–131, 133, 161, 198, 224, 226,
    228
  and capitalism 62, 83–84, 89, 95,
    98
  and colonialism 15–16, 224
  in democracies 64, 198, 204, 205,
    209, 221, 224–225, 229
  and economic reform 75
  and Islamism 163, 228–229
  and middle classes 18–19
  in monarchies 64, 66, 93, 169, 170–171,
    177, 224, 229
clans and tribes, in bunker states 18, 99,
    109, 112, 113, 118, 120–121, 123,
    125–126, 130–131, 161
Clinton, Bill 33, 39
Cold War
  and arms transfers 31, 33
  economic effects 2–6, 10–12, 44
  effects of ending 30–31
colonialism
  and civil society 15–16
  dialectics of 15–20, 60, 161, 163, 168,
    178, 187, 192
  internal 59
  regional effects 8–15, 63, 223–228
  and state revenues 74
Committee for the Defense of Legitimate
    Rights (Saudi Arabia) 181
communication, electronic 61, 142–143,
    148–149, 154, 165, 187, 191,
    193
competition
  in banking systems 22, 87, *88*, 91–93,
    95, 96, 188–189, 204, 208, 227
  political 63–64, 66
concentration
  in banking system 22, 87, *88*, 91–93,
    95, 96, 188–189, 208
  in industry 144
conflict
  internal 64, 200–202, 207, 209, 213,
    215, 221, 223–224, 227–228
  intra-regional 2, 6–8, 11, 196–198, 213,
    223–224
contract, social 77, 102
Corm, Georges 79, 112, 113
corruption
  in bully states 157–158
  in bunker-states 105, 112, 117
  in monarchies 174, 180, 186
Cromer, Evelyn Baring, Earl 23
Crystal, Jill 193
currency
  common national 76, 78–79, 102
  devaluation 42, 71, 114, 145, 200

customs duties, revenue from 41–42, 67, 74, 203
Cyprus
  and European Union 35
  and Human Development Index 2, *3*
  and Human Poverty Index *7*

Daoud, Zakya 176
debt 52–58
  in bully states 52, 53–54, *53*, 56, 58, 69, 140, 145, 155, 157
  in bunker states 111, 114, 117–118, 120–121, 132
  in democracies 202, 208
  domestic 54–58, 145, 157, 179–180
  long-term 51, 52
  in monarchies 179–180, 185
  rescheduling 114, 118, 121
  servicing 52–54, *53*, *55*, 58, 69, 117, 120, 185, 206, 208, 214, 218
democracies 20–21, 194–222
  and accountability 79, 83
  and capitalism 25, 63, 66
  and civil society 20, 64, 198, 204, 205, 221, 224–225, 229
  and colonialism 224
  "conscociational" 64, 200, 219, 220
  and economic costs 202–221
  "ethno-religious" 64, 199–200
  fragmentation in 198–201, 206, 209, 214–217, 221, 227
  genuine democracy 194–202
  and information flows 66, 195, 196, 218, 221
  and intra-regional conflict 196–198
  Islamic 64, 202
  and private sector 23–24, 185, 204–207, 208–209, 213, 219–220
  and privatization 72, 204, 208, 212, 214
  and public sector 72–74, *73*, 199, 200, 202, 205–206, 208–209, 213–215
  and rights and liberties 65
  and transparency 81, *82*, 83
  see also Iran; Israel; Lebanon; Turkey
Democratic Party (Turkey) 209
Destour (Constitution) Party (Algeria) 16
devaluation
  and economic reform 42, 114, 145, 200
  and interest rates 71
development
  export-led 11, 67
  import substitution 11, 67, 69
  political obstacles to 15
Dillman, Bradford 112, 114, 118–119, 131, 133, 164–165

Doron, Gideon 89
Dunn, Ross 202–203, 207
Economic Research Forum 6, 78, 142, 165
economics
  as driven by politics 14, 15, 28–29, 48, 52, 61
  Islamic 19
  laissez-faire 21–22, 200–201, 217, 221
The Economist 85, 180
economy
  command 6, 19, 142, 147, 149, 162
  free market 26, 114–115, 148, 205, 210, 212
  globalized 15, 19, 60, 114, 122, 142
  informal 79–81, 83, 89, 95, 100, 131–132, 136
  integration of 132–133
  military 150–152, 155
  planned 106–107, 115, 137, 216
  transition 62, 158
economy, reform 11–14, 19, 24, 26–29, 30, 35–36, 44, 46, 58–61, 66–74, 89, 228
  in bully states 145–148, 154–155, 160
  in bunker states 112–125, 126–127, 129, 132, 177
  in democracies 210–212, 214–215
  in monarchies 172–180, 184–186, 187–192, 193
  and oppositions 121
education
  and colonialism 17–18
  and economic growth 1, 2, 38, 128, 179
  and employment 60, 181, 186
Egypt
  and banking system *86*, 88–89, *88*, 90, 14000142, 156–158, 165, 225
  and budget deficit 145
  as bully state 20, 63, 134–135, 138–146, 226
  and business class 24, 160, 162
  and capital flows 49–51, *50*, 203, 208
  and capitalism 22, 23, 24, 25–26, 28, 90, 96, 135, 138–140, 147, 149, 152–155, 156–160, 161–164, 210
  and civil and political rights *65*
  and colonization 17–18, 138
  constitutional, legal and regulatory structure 139, 147–149, 164
  and de-globalization 142, 227
  and debt 52, 53–54, *53*, 56, 58, 69, 140, 155
  and economic freedom *197*
  and effects of Cold War 2
  and European Union 35–36, 41, 142, 143

Egypt (*cont.*)
  and executive 149–150
  and foreign aid 14
  and guest workers 36
  and Human Development Index *3*
  and Human Poverty Index *7*, 176
  and industry 42, 143–145, 157
  infitah 139
  and inflation 69, 71
  and information flows 81, *82*, 142–143
  and Iraq 52, 140
  and Islamist opposition 20, 146
  and Israel 26, 138–139, 153
  militarization 10, 19, 103, *104*, 137, 147,
     150–152, 153–154, 164
  oil revenues 40, *40*, 140
  and overthrow of monarchy 18
  and political capacity 76–78, *77*, *80*, 81,
     83, *84*
  postwar economy 1, 115
  and private sector 135–136, 139,
     141–145, 148, 151–152, 158
  and privatization 72, 140, 141–142, 144,
     148–149, 152, 157, 158n., 162
  and public sector 62, 72, *73*, 135, 138,
     140–141, 143–145, 149–150, 155,
     157–158, 164–165
  and stock market *86*, 90, 141, 158–159
  and structural adjustment 19, 52, 67–71,
     70, 102, 115, 118, 140, 145–147,
     149, 153
  and trade 41–43, *43*, 67, *68*, 119, 142,
     155
  and United States 33, 90, 139–140
El Kadi, Ishan 119
El Watan 112, 118, 119
El-Erian, Mohammed A. 40, 46
El-Ghonemy, M. Riad 10, 29
El-Kenz, Ali 133
El-Mikawy 160
elites
  in bully states 134–136, 138–139,
     151–155, 160, 162, 164, 166, 198
  in bunker states 100, 105, 109, 118,
     123–125, 129–131, 198
  under colonialism 15–19, 63, 102–103,
     124
  in democracies 198, 200, 209–211, 213
  and economic reform 61, 228–229
  and electronic communication 61
  military 18–19
  in monarchies 63, 169, 170–172, 178,
     180, 189, 192
  and taxation 26
  traditional 17–18, 20, 99, 134, 171, 209
  see also business class

employment 59–60
  private sector 181, 190
  public sector 118–119, 140–141, 190,
     205
EMU Survey 85
emulation, and diaectic of globalization 16
Entelis, John P. 103, 112, 115
enterprise, state-owned (SOE) 59
EPIC 141
Erbakan, Necmettin 210
Essen el-Din, Gamal 159
European Commission 36
European Investment Bank 35
European Union
  Barcelona Declaration 35, 41, 137, 165
  and economic reforms 12, 26, 62, 176,
     210
  and foreign aid 35, 166
  Partnership Initiative 12, 26, 35–36, 166
  and trade 41, 43–44, *43*, 67, 142, 143,
     164, 165–166
exchange rates, and economic reform 54,
     67, *70*, 71, 114, 116, 117–118, 145,
     214
exports
  and debt service ratios 53–54, *53*
  decline in 12, 142, 216
  and economic growth 116, 126,
     135–137, 142–143, 155, 172, 205,
     206–207, 210
  and free trade 42, 66
  increase in 41, 67, 203, 208
  manufactures 67, *68*, 143–145
  non-petroleum 41, 44
  petro-chemical 67, 128

Fahd bin Abdulaziz of Saudi Arabia 178,
     180
Fahmy, Mahmoud 148
Faisal I of Iraq 168
Faisal bin Abdulaziz of Saudi Arabia 93,
     183
Fandy, Mamoun 180, 193
finance, globalization of
  and banking 22
  for development 31
  early stage of 8, 15
  and regional identity 6, 28
Financial Times 159
France
  and colonialism 9–10, 16–18, 21, 24–25,
     74, 102, 170, 171, 178
  and guest workers 35, 36, 95–96
  and Iraq 30–31
  see also capitalism, types
Freedom House 64–65

Front of National Liberation (Algeria) 103,
    112, 115, 117

Galloux, Michel 160
Gates, Bill 191
GATT 143
    Uruguayan Round 36, 41, 43, 165
Gause, F. Gregory III 170, 186, 193
GDP
    and banking systems 79
    and capital flight 156
    and debt 53–56, 55, 58, 185, 208, 214,
        218
    and private sector 165, 172
    and public sector 72, 141, 176, 206, 214
    and taxation 76–78, 83
    and trade 40, 66–67, 208
General Agreement on Trade in Services
    (GATS) 43
General People's Congress (Yemen) 122
Germany
    and colonialism 74
    and guest workers 35
    and Iraq 30–31
    see also capitalism, types
Gerstenfeld, Dan 89
Ghabra, Shafeeq N. 189
Ghannoushi, Rashid 17
Ghillès, Francis 112, 121
Ghozali, Sid Ahmed 117
Glain, Stephen J. 99
globalization
    of capital 6, 8, 15
    and capital flows 44–52
    challenges of 30–61, 95–98, 143, 156,
        161–164, 192, 196, 226
    and de-globalization 142, 201, 217
    and debt problem 52–58
    dialectics of 15–21, 29, 102, 112, 163,
        166, 178, 211–212
    and oil revenues 38–40
    and pressures for reform 58–61, 75
    and strategic rents 30–38
    and trade 40–44
GNP, and debt 56–58, 57
Gramsci, Antonio 15
Gray, John 61
Greece
    effects of Cold War 2
    and Human Development Index 2, 3
    and Human Poverty Index 7
    postwar economy 1
growth, economic
    in bully states 135, 142–143, 149, 153,
        161–162, 164
    in bunker states 118, 126

in democracies 202–205, 207–208
    export-led 116, 126, 135–137, 142–143,
        172, 206–207, 210
    and forms of capitalism 27
    inter-regional comparisons 2–6, 4, 5
    in monarchies 175–176, 180, 186, 191
guest workers, remittances from 35, 36–38,
        37, 46, 95–96, 114, 124, 211
Gulf Cooperation Council (GCC)
    and arms transfers 33
    and economic reform 59
    and inflation 203
    and monarchies 64, 170–171
    and privatization 72
    and trade 41
    and transparency 81, 83

Hachani, Abdelkader 130
Hadj-Nacer, Abderrahmane Roustoumi
    113
Hamad bin Khalifa al-Thani of Qatar 193
Hamarneh, Mustafa 191
Hamidi, Muhammad al-Hashimi 167
Hammoudi, Abdellah 18, 193
Hamrouche, Mouloud 105, 111, 112–113,
        119, 122
Handy, Howard 141, 142, 167
Harb, Talaat 22
Hariri, Rafiq 54, 56, 94, 201, 217,
        219–221
Hashemi-Rafsanjani, Ali Akbar 214
Hassan II of Morocco 170, 171–172,
        174–175, 177–178, 183
hegemony, and nationalist elites 15–17
Herfindahl-Hirschman Index (HHI) 87,
        91–94
Hidouci, Ghazi 105, 106–109, 111,
        112–113, 115–116, 119, 122
Hilal, Rida 14
Hilferding, Rudolph 22
Hirst, David 124
Histadrut (Israeli labor federation) 25, 89,
        204, 205, 206
Hoogvelt, Hankie 61
Hoss, Salim 54
Hudson, Michael 11
Human Development Index, 2, 3, 38, 202,
        218
Human Poverty Index 6, 7, 176
Huntington, Samuel P. 226
Hussein Ibn Ali, Sharif 168
Hussein, Saddam 18, 99, 122, 125
Hussein Talal II of Jordan 191–192

Ibn Khaldun, Abd al-Rahman 74
Ibrahim, Abdallah 175–176

identity, politics of 19, 64, 66, 199–202,
    207, 221, 224–225
Idris al-Mahdi al-Senussi, Mohammed of
    Libya 124
IIT index 42–44, *43*, 46, 49, 62, 128, 203,
    208
import substitution industrialization (ISI)
    11, 67, 69, 143, 210, 224
imports 66–67, 132, 143, 154, 163
    monopolies 100, 109, 116, 119, 124
    see also tariff barriers
independence, and dialectic of
    globalization 15–16
Index of Economic Freedom 196, *197*
Indonesia, and banking system 157
industry
    in bunker states 105–111, 115–116, 119,
        127–128
    in bully states 141, 143–145, 151–152,
        164–166
    in democracies 203
    foreign investment in 44, 49
    in monarchies 172
    see also manufacture; textile industry
inflation
    in bunker states 114, 118
    in democracies 51, 54, 200, 202, 203,
        206, 208, 214
    and economic reform 67–69, *70*, 71
    in monarchies 54
information 26–27, 74–75, 76, 81–83, *82*
    in bully states 81, *82*, 142–143, 165, 174
    in bunker states 100, 107, 112–113, 127
    in democracies 66, 195, 196, 208, 214,
        218, 221
    and investment 11, 46–48, 49, 83, 85,
        98, 227
    in monarchies 26, *82*, 165, 174–175, 193
information technology 191
infrastructure
    and economic reform 75, 179, 220
    foreign investment in 44
    and taxation 74
interest rates
    and economic reform 52, 67, 69–71, *70*,
        145, 173
    levels 54–56, 204
International Institute for Strategic Studies
    (IISS) 31, 33
International Monetary Fund (IMF) 51, 69
    and aid 14
    and Anglo-American capitalism 225
    and banking systems 48
    and bully states 140, 165
    and bunker states 102, 114, 116, 117,
        119, 132

and democracies 207, 209–210, 212
    and free trade 42, 44
    and monarchies 172, 176, 192
Internet 61, 81, 83, 127, 142–143, 165,
    195
investment
    in bunker states 114
    in democracies 196, 208, 214, 218
    foreign direct 12, 25, 44–48, 49–51, 58,
        75, 97, 121, 142, 176, 180,
        190–191, 203, 225, 227
    Islamic 159
    in monarchies 44
    and need for information 11, 46–48, 49,
        83, 85, 227
    portfolio 12, 51, 58, 96, 97, 180, 218
        bond 44–46, 48–49, 51, 56
        equity 44–48, 49
        sovereign bonds 51, 52
    stagnation in 2, 12, 164–165
Iran
    and banking system *86*, *88*, 89, 196, 213
    and budget deficits 214
    and business class 25
    and capital flows *50*, 51, 214
    and capitalism 217
    and civil and political rights 65, *65*
    and coalition-building 198–199
    and debt 53, *53*, 202, 208, 214
    as democracy 20, 64, 194, 201–202,
        212–217, 224
    and economic freedom 196–198, *197*
    and fragmentation 214–217
    and Human Development Index 2, *3*
    and Human Poverty Index *7*
    and inflation 202, 214
    and information flows *82*, 195
    and interest rates 71
    and Islamism 212–216, 224, 226
    and militarization 2, 10, *104*
    and monarchy 18
    and oil revenues 1, 8, 39, *40*, 213, 215,
        216
    and political capacity 76, *77*, 79, *80*, *82*,
        83, *84*, 195
    postwar economy 1–2
    and private sector 209, 213
    and privatization 72, 214
    and public sector 72, *73*, 213–215
    stock market *86*, 89, 196
    and structural adjustment 69, *70*, 71,
        214
    and trade 41, *68*, 214
    and United States 31, 33, 53, 213, 217
Iraq
    and Arab–Israeli peace process 13

and banking system *88*, 89
as bunker state 20, 63, 99–100, 124–125, 133, 226
and business class 24, 125
and capitalism 24, 95
and civil and political rights *65*
and colonialism 10, 18
and economic freedom *197*
and Egypt 36
and elites 131
and Human Development Index *3*
and Human Poverty Index *7*
and information flows *82*, 165, 193
and interest rates 71
and the Internet 81
and middle class 125
and militarization 10, 19, 103, 111, 122
and monarchy 168
and oil revenues 1, 8, 31, 39, *40*
and overthrow of monarchy 18
and political capacity *80*, 81, *82*, 83, *84*, 226
postwar economy 1
and structural adjustment 71, 132
and Syria 128, 133
and trade 41
and UN sanctions 31, 39
and United States 20, 30, 33
Islah Party (Yemen) 122
Islamic Front of Salvation (FIS; Algeria) 113, 115–117, 121–122, 123, 130
Islamism 17, 223, 225–226, 228
    and banking 25, 92–93, 96, 116, 159–160, 177–178, 182–183, 188–189, 190, 196, 211, 216–217, 226
    in bully states 17, 20, 146, 163–164, 166
    in bunker states 99, 102, 112, 115–117, 120–122, 126–126
    and civil society 163, 177, 228–229
    in democracies 196, 209–212, 213–216
    and economics 19–20, 121, 163
    and the military 120, 122
    in monarchies 20, 169, 171, 175–178, 181–182, 186, 187, 190, 191–193
Israel
    and banking system *86*, *88*, 89, 95, 196, 204
    and budget deficits 206
    and capital flows *50*, 51, 203
    and capitalism 25, 89, 205–207, 225
    and civil and political rights *65*
    and coalitions 198–199, 206
    and constitutional, legal and regulatory structure 149
    and debt 54–56

as democracy 20, 64, 194–199, 202–207, 224
    and economic freedom *197*
    and elites 17, 18, 19
    and European Union 35, 62
    and fragmentation 199
    as garrison state 196–198
    and Human Development Index 2, *3*, 38, 202
    and Human Poverty Index *7*
    independence 10
    and inflation 69, 71, 203, 206
    and information flows 75, *82*, 195
    and the Internet 61, 81, 195
    and military expenditure 103, *104*, 206
    and peace process 12–13, 33, 201
    and political capacity 75, 76–78, *77*, *80*, *82*, 83, *84*, 195, 203, 218
    and private sector 204–207
    and privatization 204
    and public sector 72–74, 204–206
    and stock market *86*, 89, 196, 204
    and structural adjustment 26, 62, 67–69, *70*, 71, 72–74, 203, 206
    and trade 41, 42–43, *43*, 67, *68*, 203, 204, 208
    and US aid 33, 69, 74
Istanbul Stock Exchange (ISE) 85
Italy, and colonialism 9, 18, 124

Jabar, Faleh A. 99
Japan
    and capital markets 23, 85
    and Iraq 30–31
    and trade 41
Jeune Afrique 112
Jewish National Fund 89
joint ventures
    in bully states 151–152, 156–158
    in bunker states 117, 177
    in monarchies 168, 169, 180
Jordan
    and Arab–Israeli peace process 12–13, 191–192
    and banking system *86*, *88*, 92, 93, 189, 192
    and capital flows *50*, 182, 190–1
    and civil and political rights *65*
    and debt *53*, 54–56, *57*
    and economic freedom *197*
    and European Union 35, 41, 62
    and guest workers 36
    Higher National Economic Consultative Council 191
    and Human Development Index *3*, 38
    and Human Poverty Index *7*

Jordan (*cont.*)
  and inflation 54, 69, 71, 203
  and information flows 81, *82*, 193
  and Islamist opposition 20, 187–188,
    191–193
  and militarization 10, 103, *104*, 175, 192
  as monarchy 20–21, 64, 168, 170–171,
    175, 188–193
  and political capacity 76–78, *77*, *80*, 81,
    82, 83, *84*
  and private sector 189, 191
  and privatization 72, 191–192
  and public sector *73*
  and stock market *86*, 92, 189
  and structural adjustment 19, 26, 28–29,
    52, 62, 67–71, *70*, 118, 191–192
  and trade 41, 42, *43*, 66–67, *68*, 208
Juan Carlos of Spain 175
Justice Party (Turkey) 209

Karl, Terry Lynn 61, 132
Kemal, Mustafa (Atatürk) 23–24, 212
Khamani'i, Ayatollah 215
Khatami, Muhammad 201, 214–216
Khodja, Abdallah 107, 108, 116
Khomeini, Ayatollah Ruhollah 202, 214,
    215
Kingdom Holding 183
Kostiner, Joseph 193
Kostiner, Joseph 193
Krimly, Rayed 179
Kurds
  in Iran 201
  in Syria 126, 130
  in Turkey 200, 202, 209–210
Kuwait
  and banking system *86*, *88*, 91–92, 93,
    95, 184, 188–189, 190
  and British colonialism 9
  and civil and political rights *65*
  and concession loans 54
  and economic freedom *197*
  and foreign aid 187
  and guest workers in 36
  and Human Development Index 2, *3*
  and Human Poverty Index *7*
  and information flows *82*, 193, 195
  and the Internet 81, 195
  and Iraqi invasion 20, 33, 39
  and Islamist opposition 187–188, 190,
    192, 193
  and labor force 190
  and military expenditure *104*
  as monarchy 20, 64, 168, 170, 187–190,
    192–193
  and oil revenues 8, 39, *40*, 170, 190

  and political capacity 76, *77*, *80*, 81, *82*,
    84, 195
  and public sector 72, 170, 190
  and stock market *86*, 92, 188, 190, 193
  and structural adjustment 67, *70*, 190
  and trade 43, *43*, 67, *68*, 189

labor
  competitiveness 38, 59–60, 144
  international division 30
  migration 35–36, 95–96, 118, 124, 181,
    211
Labor Party (Israel) 25, 198, 206
Lamari, Mohammed 120–121, 123, 131
landownership, urban 17–18, 19
Latin America, and debt 53, *53*
law, economic, in Egypt 148
Lawrence, T. E. 168
Lawson, Fred 122
Lebanon
  amd Arab–Israeli peace process 33, 198,
    201
  and banking system 78–79, *86*, *88*, 94,
    196, 218–220
  and budget deficits 51, 69, 185, 219
  and business class 25
  and capital flows *50*, 51, 218, 220
  and capitalism 25, 96
  and civil and political rights *65*
  and civil war 25, 26, 200–201, 202,
    217–218
  and coalitions 198, 200–201
  and de-globalization 201
  and debt 26, 53–54, *53*, 56, 185, 218
  as democracy 20, 64, 194, 200–201,
    217–221, 224
  and economic freedom *197*
  and European Union 35, 41, 43, 67
  and French colonialism 9, 18, 96
  and Human Development Index *3*, 38,
    218
  and Human Poverty Index *7*, 69
  and inflation 54, 69
  and information flows *82*, 195, 218
  and the Internet 195
  military expenditure *104*
  and political capacity 76, *77*, *80*, *82*, 83,
    84, 195, 200, 218, 220
  postwar economy 1, *3*
  and private sector 219–220
  and public sector 202
  and sectarianism 10, 200–201
  stock market *86*, 196
  and structural adjustment *70*, 71
  and Syria 41, 128–219, 201, 219–220
  and trade 41–43, 67, *68*

L'Economiste 174
legitimacy 8
  in bully states 63, 134, 136, 139, 153
  in bunker states 99, 102, 103, 111–112,
    122
  deficits 11
  Islamist 20, 182, 192–193
  in monarchies 168, 170, 172, 182, 183,
    192–193
  and social fundamentalism 75
Leveau, Rémy 18, 121, 172, 178
Leys 98
Libya
  and banking system *88*, 89
  as bunker state 20, 63, 99–100,
    122–123, 124, 133
  and capitalism 95
  and civil and political rights *65*
  and economic freedom *197*
  and economic integration 132–133
  and elites 131
  and European Union 35
  and Human Development Index 2, *3*
  and Human Poverty Index *7*
  and information flows *82*, 165, 193
  and interest rates 71
  and the Internet 81
  and Italian colonialism 9, 124
  and militarization 19, *104*, 122–123
  and monarchy 18
  and oil revenues 36, *40*, 124
  and political capacity *80*, 81, *82*, 83, *84*
  and private sector 124
  and structural adjustment *70*, 71, 132
  and "Third Way" 19
  and US sanctions 35, 132
Likud Party (Israel) 205–206
literacy 2, 38, 127, 218
loans
  concession 54, 93
  interest-free 71
  non-performing 114, 157, 165, 173
Lustick, Ian S. 15

Mack, Arien 222
Madani, Abbas 115–117
Maghreb Weekly Monitor 123, 178
Mahdavy, Hussein 132
Mahroug, Moncef 166
makhzan (royal household; Morocco)
    171–172, 175–177, 178
Malta, and European Union 35
manufacture
  in bully states 136–137, 141, 142–145,
    151–152, 164, 166
  in bunker states 127–128, 132

  in democracies 203, 204–205, 208, 214
  and economic reform 74
  and exports 67, *68*
  and free trade 42
  and globalization 60
  investment in 49
  and labor 59
  see also industry
markets, financial
  and capital flows 44–52
  and capitalist varieties 22–23
  liberalization 62, 97–98
  and public sector 72, 76
  see also stock markets
Mauritania, and public sector *73*
Maxfield, Sylvia 49, 61
media, in bunker states 123
MENA
  definition 8
  effects of colonialism on 8–15, 223–228
middle classes *see* elites
Middle East Development Bank 33
The Middle East Economic Digest (MEED)
    51, 58, 93, 179, 182, 183–184, 185,
    188, 191
Middle East International 75, 123
Middle East Times 143
Mittelman, James H. 61
Mohammed V of Morocco 170
Mohammed VI of Morocco 175, 178, 193
Mohammed Al-Faisal of Saudi Arabia 183
Mohieldin, Mahmoud 157
monarchies 168–193
  and accountability 79–80, 83
  and banking systems 91, 93, 95
  and capitalism 25, 26, 27–29, 63–64, 66,
    96, 226
  and civil and political rights *65*, 66
  and civil society 66, 93, 169, 170–171,
    177, 224, 229
  and colonialism 168–169, 170–171, 192,
    224
  and dialectic of colonialism 18, 20–21,
    63
  and information flows 26, *82*, 165,
    174–175, 193
  and nationalism 169
  and opposition 169, 175, 177–178,
    187–188, 191–192, 193
  and private sector 168–169, 172–173,
    178, 179–181, 186, 189–191
  and privatization 72, 173–174, 176,
    190–191
  and public sector 72, 170, 171–174, 176,
    186, 190
  and traditional elites 20

monarchies (*cont.*)
    and transparency 81, *82*, 83
    see also Bahrain; Jordan; Kuwait;
        Morocco; Oman; Qatar; Saudi
        Arabia; United Arab Emirates
money, contract-intensive *see* CIM ratios
monopolies
    abolition 113, 114, 116, 130–131
    of imports 100, 109, 116, 117, 119, 124,
        155, 163, 204
    of services 149
Monroe, Elizabeth 30
Montety, Henri de 17
moralists and globalizers 15, 19–20, 75, 84,
        223, 225–227
    in bully states 163
    in bunker states 115–116
    in democracies 210–213
    in monarchies 178, 187–188
Morocco
    and banking system *86*, *88*, 91–92, 93,
        96, 172–178
    and budget deficits 176
    and business class 24–25, 173
    and capital flows *50*, 51, 176, 180
    and capitalism 23, 24–25, 28, 97, 136,
        172–174, 182
    and civil and political rights *65*
    constitutional, legal and regulatory
        structure 149
    and debt 53, *53*, 58, 208
    and economic freedom *197*
    and economic integration 133
    and effects of Cold War 2
    and elites 135
    and European Union 35, 62, 176
    and French colonialism 9, 17–18, 24–25,
        170, 171–172, 178
    and Human Development Index *3*
    and Human Poverty Index *7*, 176
    and inflation 69, 71, 203
    and information flows *82*, 174–175, 193
    and labor migration 36, 95–96
    and the military 103, *104*, 174–175
    as monarchy 18, 20–21, 24, 28, 64,
        168–178
    and opposition 175, 177–178
    and political capacity 76, *77*, *80*, *82*, 83,
        84, 165
    postwar economy 1
    and private sector 172–173, 178
    and privatization 72, 173–174, 176
    and public sector *73*, 172–174, 176
    and stock market *86*, 91, 174, 176
    and structural adjustment 19, 26, 28, 52,
        62, 67–71, *70*, 118, 172

    and trade 41–43, *43*, 67, *68*, 119, 172
Mostafa, Hadia 159, 160
Mubarak, Ala' 154
Mubarak, Hosni 81, 140–141, 150,
        153–155, 177
Multifibre Agreement 143
Multinationals
    foreign direct investment by 12, 25, 46,
        49
    and joint ventures 151–152
    oil companies 38–39
Murphy, Emma C. 167
Muslim Brotherhood
    Egypt 146
    Jordan 191–192, 193
    Syria 121–122, 125–126
Myntti, Cynthia 138

Naim, Moises 14
Nasser, Gamal Abdel 115, 122, 166, 192,
        212
    and Arab socialism 88–89, 137, 138–140
    and crony capitalism 138–140, 152–153
    and executive 149–150
    and Free Officers 18, 24
    and industrialization 105, 109
    and justice system 148
    and militarization 103
National Democratic Party (Egypt) 141,
        146, 160
National Islamic Front (Jordan) 192
National Islamic Front (Sudan) 99
National Religious Party (Israel) 198
nationalism
    and business elites 24, 63, 138, 156
    and dialectic of globalization 15–20, 166,
        224
    and monarchies 169, 170–171, 187, 191,
        192
    and traditional elites 99
negation, and dialectic of globalization
        15–16
Neo-Destour Party (Tunisia) 16
Netanyahu, Benjamin 136
Newspapers *see* press
Numeiri, Jaafar Muhammed 122

October War (1973) 69
oil
    and colonialism 8–9, 11
    and development 1, 11
    and external intervention 30–31
    and foreign investment 51
    and militarization 11
    restricted production 179
    and welfare states 8

oil revenues 8, 9
  in bully states 140
  in bunker states 102, 105–111, 117, 120,
    124, 126, 132
  in democracies 213, 215
  increase in 56, 69, 190
    in monarchies 39, *40*, 71, 75–76,
      169–170, 178–180, 185–187
  and political capacities 75–76
  reduction 12, 30–33, *32*, 36, 38–40, *40*,
    44, 52, 54, 59, 172
Okruhlik, Gwenn 186
Oman
  and banking system *86*, *88*
  and civil and political rights *65*
  and economic freedom *197*
  and Human Development Index 2, *3*
  and Human Poverty Index *7*
  and information flows *82*
  and monarchy 20, 64, 168
  and oil revenues *40*
  and political capacity 76, *77*, *80*, *82*, *84*
  and public sector *73*
  and stock exchange *86*
  and structural adjustment *70*
  and trade 42, *43*, 208
Öniş, Ziya 222
Organization of Petroleum Exporting
    Countries (OPEC) 38–39, 178
Oslo Accords (1993) 26, 58, 136
Osman, Osman Ahmad 139–140,
    153–155
Ouyahia, Ahmed 118–119
Owen, Roger 29
Özal, Turgut 211
Ozbudun, Ergun 222

Palestine
  and banking system *88*, 189
  as bully state 20, 28, 63, 134–137, 166
  and capitalism 28, 96, 136–137, 154,
    156, 166
  and colonization 17
  and European Union 35–36
  and guest workers 36
  and private sector 136–137
  and public sector 135
  and stock exchange 58
Palestine Liberation Organization 58
parties, political 83
  in bully states 146, 160, 163, 165
  in bunker states 16, 99, 114–117, 123,
    129
  in democracies 198–199, 204–206, 209
  in monarchies 170, 172, 175–177,
    182–183

patronage networks
  and banking 49, 90–91, 93, 95, 97–98,
    173–174
  in bully states 134–136, 139–140,
    149–150, 152, 153–155, 166
  in bunker states 108, 111, 120, 126
  in democracies 200, 216, 220
  and economic reform 11, 27–28, 52
  in monarchies 171–174, 180, 188
  and privatization 72
Patton, Marcie J. 173
Peres, Shimon 69
Perthes, Volker 99, 131, 133
Picard, Elizabeth 222
Piro, Timothy J. 189
Plessner, Yakir 204–205, 222
politics
  and accountability and transparency
    74–75, 78–83
  in bully states 138, 139, 146–149,
    153–155, 156, 160, 161–163, 166
  in bunker states 112–117, 119–120, 121,
    122
  and capitalist legacies 62–98
  and coalition-building 134–135,
    198–201, 206, 209
  in democracies 194–195, 198–202,
    205–207, 209–211, 214–217, 221
  and economic reform 14, 15, 28–29, 52,
    61, 119–120, 121, 227–229
  and extractive capability 74, 75–78,
    81–83
  and information flows 27, 46–48, 66,
    74–75, 76, 81–83
  in monarchies 168, 170–171, 172,
    174–175, 178, 187–188, 190–192
  and state reforms 74–75, 112–117,
    119–120, 122
  see also capacity, political
Popular National Congress (Sudan) 99
poverty, levels 6, *7*, 69, 176
press 81, *82*, 83, *84*
  in bully states 81, 142, 146
  in bunker states 81, 123, 127
  in democracies 81, 195, 220
  in monarchies 81–83, 170, 175, 191, 193
private sector
  in bully states 135–136, 139, 141–145,
    148, 151, 155, 158, 158n., 165
  in bunker states 114, 118–119, 121,
    123–125, 131–132
  and capitalist varieties 21–22, 27
  in democracies 23–24, 185, 204–207,
    208–209, 213, 219–220
  in monarchies 168–169, 172–173, 178,
    179–181, 189–191

privatization 59, 71–72
  of banks 89, 90, 91, 95, 97, 140, 141,
    204
  in bully states 140, 141–142, 144,
    148–149, 152, 157, 162, 165
  in bunker states 113, 121, 131, 133
  in democracies 72, 204, 208, 212,
    214
  in monarchies 72, 173–174, 176, 178,
    186, 190–191
productivity 128, 132, 144, 162
property rights 11, 74, 185, 187
  in bully states 143
  in bunker states 63, 79, 102, 116, 124,
    127, 130
  in democracies 79
  in monarchies 79
protectionism, in Lebanon 218
Przeworski, Adam 98, 116
public sector
  in bully states 62, 72–74, 73, 135, 138,
    140–141, 143–145, 149–152,
    157–158, 164–165
  in bunker states 62, 113–115, 118–119,
    124
  decentralization 113
  in democracies 72–74, 73, 199, 200,
    202, 205–206, 209–209, 213–215
  marketization 72, 113–115, 118
  in monarchies 72, 170, 172–174, 176,
    186, 190
  size 6, 71–74, 73, 118–119, 124

Qaddafi, Muammar 19, 99, 122–123, 124,
    133
Qatar
  and banking system 86, 88, 189
  and British colonialism 9
  and civil and political rights 65
  and economic freedom 197
  and Human Development Index 2, 3
  and Human Poverty Index 7
  and information flows 82, 165, 193
  and the Internet 81
  and military expenditure 104
  as monarchy 20, 64, 168, 170
  and oil revenues 40
  and political capacity 80, 81, 82, 84, 195
  and public sector 72
  and stock exchange 86
  and structural adjustment 70
  and trade 43
Quandt, William B. 133

Radwan, Samir 141
Rawabdeh, Abdel Raouf 191

rejectionism, and dialectics of colonialism
    17
rents
  oil 8, 11–12, 38–40, 75–76, 124, 129,
    132, 223
  remittance 36–38, 46, 124, 131, 159,
    208
  rent-seeking 8, 38, 111, 116, 124, 126,
    134–136, 161, 163
  strategic 11–12, 30–36, 56, 123–124,
    128–129, 140, 161–162, 188, 223
  from trade 40–44, 119, 124, 135
representation, and taxation 75–76, 78
Republican People's Party (Turkey) 209
republics, Islamic 64
republics, praetorian 20–21, 187, 224
  and accountability 79–81, 83
  and banking systems 95
  and business class 24
  and capitalism 25–26, 27–29, 63, 66,
    95
  and civil society 226, 228
  and transparency 81, 82
  see also Algeria; bully states; bunker
    states; Egypt; Iraq; Libya; Palestine;
    Sudan; Syria; Tunisia; Yemen
revivalism, Islamic 19
Richards, Alan 29, 140
rights, civil and political 64–65, 65, 123,
    165, 181–182
Rivlin, Paul 43
Roberts, Hugh 115
Rocard, Michel 167
Rodrik, Dani 61
Rogowski, Ronald 38, 61
Ross, Michael L. 132
Roy, Sara 135–137
Russia
  and Iraq 30–31
  and Kuwait 187
Ryan, Curtis R. 192

Sachs, Jeffery 1, 2, 12, 61
Sadat, Anwar 138–140, 152–154
Sadowski, Yahia M. 167
Saïdi, Fodhil 120
Salamé, Ghassan 131
Saleh, Ali Abdullah 99, 122, 131–132
Salehi-Isfahani, Djavid 214, 216
Salem, Eli 1
Saudi Arabia
  and banking system 86, 88, 91, 92–93,
    95–96, 180, 182–183, 186, 225
  and budget deficits 179, 185
  and capital flows 44, 51, 180, 187
  and capitalism 28, 96, 182–185

and civil and political rights 65, 181–182
and concession loans 54
and debt 56, 179–180
and economic freedom 197
and extractive capacity 75–76
guest workers in 36–38, 124
Higher Economic Council 179–180
and Human Development Index 2, 3
and Human Poverty Index 7
and information flows 76, 82
and Islamist opposition 20, 181–182,
    186
and Israel 26
and labor force 180–181
and military expenditure 33, 104, 179
as monarchy 18, 20, 28, 64, 75,
    168–171, 178–187
and oil revenues 8, 9, 39, 40, 71, 75–76,
    169, 178–180, 185–187
and political capacity 76, 80, 82, 84
and private sector 179–181, 186
and privatization 178, 186
and public sector 72, 73, 186
and stock market 86, 93, 180, 186
and structural adjustment 67, 69–71, 70,
    180
and trade 41, 43, 67, 68
and US influence 9, 39, 169, 181
Saudi Arabian Monetary Agency (SAMA)
    39, 56, 71, 93, 180
Saul, Samir 22
sectarianism, and effects of colonialism 10
seignorage, and economic reform 67–69,
    70, 71, 214
services, trade in 43–44
Seznek, Jean-François 186
Shafik, Nemat 61
Shalev, Michal 206
Shishakli, Adib 122
Snider, Lewis W. 71, 79, 98
socialism
    Arab 137, 138–139, 143, 147, 166
    state 21, 24
Sorsa, Piritta 119
Souaïdia, Habib 120
Spanish Sahara 133, 172
Stallings, Barbara 61
state
    bully 20, 63, 66, 79–81, 134–167
    bunker 20, 27, 51, 63, 65–66, 71, 79–81,
        83, 99–133
    legitimacy deficits 11
    military 10–11, 13, 18–19, 20, 25, 103,
        104, 105–106, 122, 129
    "national security" 6–8, 10–11, 129,
        131, 152

"of concern" 33
    police 20, 165
    reforms 74–75
    typology of see democracies; monarchies;
        republics, praetorian
    welfare 8
    see also politics
stock markets 60, 86, 89, 90
    and Anglo-American capitalism 21–22,
        85, 91, 93, 158, 174
    in bully states 86, 90, 141, 158–159, 165
    in democracies 196, 204, 208
    and foreign investment 12, 48, 49, 51,
        58, 97–98
    and information flows 49
    and insider trading 22, 159
    in monarchies 86, 91, 174, 176, 180,
        185–186, 188–190, 193
Stockholm International Peace Research
    Institute (SIPRI) 33
Stone, Martin 122
Subramanian, Arvind 142, 157
succession
    in bunker states 123, 131
    in monarchies 185
Sudan
    and banking system 86, 88, 90
    and budget deficits 132
    as bunker state 20, 63 90, 99–100, 124
    and capital flows 50, 51
    and capitalism 19, 25–26, 90, 95
    and civil and political rights 65
    and civil war 132
    and colonialism 10, 17
    and debt 53, 56, 57
    and economic freedom 197
    and Human Development Index 2, 3
    and Human Poverty Index 7, 176
    and inflation 214
    and information flows 82
    and interest rates 71
    and the Internet 81
    and middle class 124
    and militarization 19, 104, 122, 124
    and oil revenues 132
    and opposition 131, 132
    and political capacity 80, 81, 82, 83, 84
    and private sector 209
    and public sector 72, 73, 124
    and stock market 86
    and structural adjustment 70, 71
    and trade 41, 68
Syria
    and Arab–Israeli peace process 12–13,
        33, 129, 132, 201
    and banking system 79, 86, 88, 89, 127

Syria (*cont.*)
  as bunker state 20, 63, 99–100,
      121–122, 124, 125–130, 133, 226
  and business class 24, 126, 129–130
  and capital flows *50*, 51, 128
  and capitalism 25, 26, 95–96, 126–130
  and civil and political rights *65*
  and debt *53*, 54, 56, *57*
  and economic freedom *197*
  and effects of Cold War 2
  and elites 99, 125–126, 129–131
  and European Union 35, 41
  and factor productivity 128
  and French colonialism 9, 10, 18, 21, 96,
      125
  and Human Development Index *3*, 128
  and Human Poverty Index *7*
  infitah 125
  and inflation 69
  and information flows *82*, 127
  and interest rates 71
  and the Internet 81, 127
  and Iraq 128, 133
  and Islamist opposition 121–122,
      125–126, 210
  and Lebanon 41, 128–129, 201,
      219–220
  and middle class 125, 130
  and militarization 10, 19, *104*, 111, 122,
      125–126, 129
  and oil revenues 40, *40*, 69, 126
  and political capacity 76, *77*, *80*, 81, *82*,
      83, *84*, 126, 129, 226
  postwar economy 1
  and private sector 121–122, 125, 209
  and public sector 62
  and stock market *86*
  and structural adjustment 67, 69, *70*, 71,
      132
  and trade 41, *43*, 67, *68*, 127–128, 129,
      137
  and transaction costs 127

Tantawi, Muhammad Sayid 160
tariff barriers 41–42, 44, 46, 67, *68*, 74
  in bully states 42, 137, 142, 163, 166
  in bunker states 127
  in democracies 203, 205, 214, 219
  in monarchies 172
taxation
  corporate 190
  and development 11, 124
  direct 8, 76–78, 155
  indirect 78
  Islamic 76, 116
  and political capacity 74, 75–78, 83, 100

  and representation 75–76, 78
  see also customs duties; tariff barriers
terrorism 33, 146, 154, 192
Terterov, Marat 72
textile industry
  in bully states 42, 143–145, 157
  in bunker states 119, 128
  in democracies 214
  and labor 59, 103
tourism 43, 44, 146, 150
Tozy, Mohamed 175
trabendo commerce (Algeria) 79, 111, 114,
    122
trade 40–44
  and competitive advantage 42
  with European Union 12, 41, 43–44, *43*,
      67, 142, 143, 164, 165–166
  intra-industry (IIT) 42–44, *43*, 46, 49,
      62, 128, 203, 208
  liberalization 42–44, 62, 66–67, 119,
      121, 132, 172
  non-tariff barriers 143
  in services 43
  volatility 40
  see also exports; imports; tariff barriers
trade unions 83
  in bunker states 113, 123, 130
  in democracies 212
  in monarchies 176
transaction costs 127, 221
transparency 14, 74–75, 78–83, 225
  and banking 22, 28, 48–49, 52, 56,
      92–98, 113–114, 185
  in bully states 56, 150, 151, 159, 162,
      164–165
  in bunker states 113–114, 116, 126
  in democracies 203, 208, 215, 216, 218,
      220
  and information flows 11, 81–83, 85
  in monarchies 165, 178, 185, 190, 191,
      192, 193
  and taxation 76
Triangle Index 195
Trucial States *see* United Arab Emirates
Tunisia
  and banking system *86*, *88*, 90, 165, 225
  as bully state 20, 63, 134–137, 164–166,
      226
  and business class 24, 165
  and capitalism 23, 24, 28, 90, 96,
      136–137, 154, 156, 164
  and civil and political rights *65*, 165
  constitutional, legal and regulatory
      structure 149
  and debt 53–54, *53*, 58
  and economic freedom *197*

and elites 16–17, 18, 19
and European Union 35, 41, 62, 137,
    164, 165–166
and French colonialism 9, 16–17, 21, 24,
    170
and Human Development Index *3*
and Human Poverty Index *7*, 176
and inflation 69, 71, 203
and information flows 81, *82*, 165, 174,
    193
and the Internet 81, 165
and Islamist opposition 17, 20
and labor migration 95–96
military expenditure 103, *104*, 137
oil revenues *40*, 164
and political capacity *77*, *80*, 81, *82*, 83,
    84, 226
and private sector 136, 165, 166
and privatization 72, 165
and public sector 72–74, *73*, 135
and stock market *86*, 90, 165
and structural adjustment 26, 51–52, 62,
    67–69, *70*, 71, 74, 97, 118
and trade 41–43, *43*, 66–67, *68*, 119,
    137, 208
in World War II 9
Turabi, Hassan 99, 122, 124
Turkey
    and banking system 23–24, *86*, *88*, 95,
        196, 211
    and budget deficits 69, 200, 208
    and business class 24, 25
    and capital flows 46, 49–51, *50*, 97,
        208
    and capitalism 22, 23–25, 85, 93, 96,
        210–211
    and civil and political rights 65
    and coalitions 198, 209
    and constitutional legal and regulatory
        structure 149
    and debt 53, *53*, 58
    as democracy 20, 64, 194, 199–200,
        207–212, 224
    and dialectics of colonialism 17
    and economic freedom *197*
    and effects of Cold War 2
    and elites 17–18, 19
    and European Union 35, 62, 210
    and fragmentation 199–200, 202, 209
    and guest workers 35, 36, 211
    and Human Development Index *3*
    and Human Poverty Index *7*
    and inflation 51, 69, 200, 208, 214
    and information flows 75, *82*, 195
    and the Internet 61, 81, 195
    and Islamism 20, 71, 209–212, 225–226

and militarization 10, *104*, 194, 198,
    199–200, 209–211
and political capacity 75, 76–78, *77*, *80*,
    82, 83, *84*, 195, 208, 218
postwar economy 1
and private sector 23–24, 208, 209
and privatization 72, 208, 212
and public sector 72–74, *73*, 200,
    208–209
stock market 49, 85, *86*, 93–94, 196,
    208
and structural adjustment 26, 51–52,
    62, 67–71, *70*, 93, 207, 211
and trade 41–43, *43*, 66–67, *68*, 155,
    203, 208

Unemployment
    control 74, 98
    increase in 117, 118–119, 179, 185–186,
        214
    levels 59, 176, 178
Union du Maghreb Arabe 132–133
Union Socialiste des Forces Populaires
    (USFP; Morocco) 175–176
United Arab Emirates
    and banking system *86*, *88*
    and British colonialism 9
    and civil and political rights 65
    and concession loans 54
    and economic freedom *197*
    and Human Development Index 2, *3*
    and Human Poverty Index *7*
    and information flows *82*
    and the Internet 81, 195
    and militiary expenditure *104*
    as monarchy 20, 64, 169
    and oil revenues *40*
    and political capacity 76, *77*, *80*, 81, *82*,
        84, 195
    and privatization 72
    and public sector 72, *73*
    and stock market *86*
    and structural adjustment *70*
    and trade *43*
United Nations
    and Algeria 121
    and arms transfers 33
    and colonialism 9–10
    and Egypt 33, 90, 139–140, 143
    and foreign aid 36
    and Iraq 20, 30–31, 33
    and Iran 31, 33, 53, 213, 217
    and Israel 56, 69, 74
    and Jordan 56, 192
    and Kuwait 20, 187
    and MENA 30, 33–35

United Nations (*cont.*)
  and Saudi Arabia 9, 39, 169, 181
  and trade 41
unrest, social 74
USAID 14, 144–145, 148–149, 195

Vandewalle, Dirk 133
violence
  in bully states 63
  in bunker states 99–100, 102, 111,
    120–121, 125, 126, 131, 133
  and colonialism 16–17
  in democracies 200, 201–202, 209, 217,
    221
  in monarchies 181
Virtue Party (Turkey) 210
Vitalis, Robert 76

wage levels 118, 144–145
Waldner, David 127, 128, 133
Walid al-Talal, Prince 183, 186
Warde, Ibrahim 51
Washington Consensus 19, 21, 30, 223,
    225
  and bully states 147, 161, 163
  and bunker states 121, 130
  and democracies 196, 207, 212
  and financial markets 52, 59, 90
  and Islamism 121, 193, 225–226
  and monarichies 168, 176, 185, 193
  national responses to 26–29
  and public sectors 71
  Ten Commandments 12, *13*, 14, 15, 69,
    121, 228
  and trade 44
Waterbury, John 29, 71, 78, 167, 193
Weber, Max 134
Welfare Party (Turkey) 209–210, 212
Westley, John 158
Wiktorowicz, Quintan 192
Williamson, John 14, 21
Willis, Michael 133
Winters, Jeffrey A. 21
World Bank
  and aid 14, 26, 137, 212
  and Anglo-American capitalism 225
  and banking systems 92, 140
  and capital flight 97, 155
  and economic adjustment 48, 51, 61,
    88, 114, 172, 176, 207, 209–210
  and Egyptian military 152
  and free trade 42, 44

  and political capacities 98
  and public sectors 135, 144
  and transparency 74
World Economic Forum 191
World Trade Organization 41, 62,
    186–187, 191
World War I, and European interests 8–9
World War II, and European interests 9

Yassine, Sheikh Abdeslam 178
Yemen
  and banking system *86*
  as bunker state 20, 63, 99–100, 124
  and business class 124
  and capital flows *50*, 127
  and capitlaism 19, 95
  and civil and political rights 65
  and civil war 131, 132
  and colonialism 10
  and debt *53*
  and economic freedom *197*
  and guest workers 36–38
  and Human Development Index 2, *3*,
    38
  and Human Poverty Index *7*
  and information flows *82*, 83, 127
  and interest rates 71
  and the Internet 81
  and militarization 19, *104*, 122
  and oil revenues *40*, 69, 132
  and opposition groups 131
  and political capacity 76, *77*, *80*, 81, *82*,
    83, *84*, 124
  and private sector 124, 209
  and public sector *73*
  and stock market *86*
  and structural adjustment 69, *70*, 71,
    132
  and trade 41, *68*
Yemen Arab Republic 124
Yemen, People's Democratic Republic 124
Yeşilada, Birol 35
Youssef, Tarik M. 156
Youssoufi, Abderahman 175–176

Zangeneh, 213
Zartman, W. 167
Zeroual, Liamine 112, 118, 119–120,
    122–123
Zghal, Abdelkader 17
Zionism 25, 204, 205, 207
Zysman, John 21, 98